■SCHOLASTIC

Grades 3–8

Integrating Test Prep
into Reading & Writing Workshops

Nancy Jennison

New York • Toronto • London • Auckland • Sydney
Mexico City • New Delhi • Hong Kong • Buenos Aires

Teaching *Resources*

Dedication

I'd like to dedicate this book to my husband Chris
who helped me to remember "one page at a time,"
and to my loving family and friends who cheered
me on during the most challenging times.

Credits:

pages 30–33: From Texas Assessment of Knowledge and Skills Information Booklet, Grade 4, 2004 Revised. Copyright © 2004 Texas Education Agency.

page 40: From New Jersey Assessment of Skills and Knowledge 2007. Copyright © 2006 by The Riverside Publishing Company.

pages 76–77, 110: From HATCHET by Gary Paulsen. Copyright © 1987 by Gary Paulsen. Published by Simon and Schuster.

page 81: "America the Beautiful" by Natalie Smith is reprinted from *Scholastic News*, January 25, 2010. Copyright © 2010 by Scholastic Inc.

page 82: "Marine Invaders" by Jennifer M. Walters, is reprinted from *Scholastic News*, March 22, 2010. Copyright © 2010 by Scholastic Inc.

pages 89–90: "Fueling the Future" by Paul Coco is reprinted from *Scholastic News*. Copyright © 2005 by Scholastic Inc.

page 97: "The Cruelest Show on Earth" by Paul Janeczko, is reprinted from WRITING WINNING REPORTS AND ESSAYS by Paul Janeczko. Copyright © 2003 by Paul Janeczko. By permission of Scholastic Inc.

page 162: From COME ON, RAIN! by Karen Hesse. Copyright © 1999 by Karen Hesse. Reprinted by permission of Scholastic Inc.

Acquisition Editor: Joanna Davis-Swing
Editor: Sarah Glasscock
Cover designer: Brian LaRossa
Cover photograph: © Corbis
Interior designer: Kelli Thompson
Interior photos: Melissa Erickson (page 56), Christie Mortara (page 72)

ISBN: 978-0-545-14711-8

Text copyright © 2011 by Nancy Jennison
All rights reserved. Published by Scholastic Inc.
Printed in the U.S.A.

1 2 3 4 5 6 7 8 9 10   40   17 16 15 14 13 12 11

Contents

Introduction

Why Integrate Test Prep into Reading and Writing Workshops?

Teachers often show me skill-and-drill test-prep workbooks, shake their heads, and say, "I don't like to use these, but I don't know what else to do." Unfortunately, such materials convey unconnected facts to students in unrelated contexts, foster their lack of interest, and rob them of the essence of literacy (Calkins, Montgomery, & Santman, 1998). If students are uninterested, how can we expect them to do well on state tests?

A reality that we face as educators is that most of us feel pressured to make sure that our students do perform well on state tests. It seems as if our districts' test scores appear everywhere, from the front pages of local and state newspapers to the briefcases of well-meaning real estate agents. Testing is always in the headlines, because testing is big business.

We all share the obvious goal of wanting our students to score well. As a reading specialist and a language arts staff developer, I have worked with teachers to prepare students for state tests for the past 18 years. As a national language arts consultant, I have been hired to work with teachers and schools to help them raise their test scores. I know what works in raising students' test scores, and I know what doesn't. That is why I wrote this book: to help classroom teachers and administrators more effectively prepare students for state tests. It will show you a different way of preparing your students for state tests without sacrificing your best teaching practices and without teaching to the test.

When you integrate test prep into reading and writing workshops, you use solid teaching practices to prepare your students for state tests. Reading and writing skills taught in authentic contexts promote success. Research shows that students with strong language arts skills perform better on state tests. As literacy expert Janet Angelillo states, "I believe that good teaching all year long prepares students for test-taking" (2005b, p. 5).

WHAT CAN YOU LEARN FROM READING THIS BOOK?

This book is unique, since it will show you in very concrete ways how to plan and teach units and mini-lessons during reading and writing workshops that are authentic and mirror what students need to know to do well on state tests. You will learn how to look closely at your state tests to become familiar with their formats, language, time demands, skills tested, and the strategies that your students will need to score well on them. You will see how to easily adapt your content and language arts instruction to integrate the skills that your state will test later in the school year. You will learn how to develop differentiation plans to improve students' scores on reading and writing tests. Finally, you will find out how to plan and customize your test-prep unit to match your state test and to match your students' needs.

HOW CAN YOU USE THIS BOOK AS A RESOURCE?

I designed this book with consistent text features that will help you organize and adapt instruction. The following special sections appear in each chapter:

■ **Highlights:** Opens each chapter and summarizes the major topics in it.

■ **Try It:** Offers ways for you to apply ideas from the book in your own class. You can also discuss the Try It section with colleagues, and as a group plan how and when you might use these activities with your students.

■ **Read How It Worked:** Describes how real teachers with whom I have worked have designed their best classroom lessons and/or activities related to integrating test prep into reading and writing workshops. You may want to adapt their strategies and lessons on your own or discuss them with colleagues.

■ **Food for Thought:** Ends each chapter and offers you and/or your colleagues opportunities for further thinking and possible discussion topics that relate to it. Food for Thought provides ideas that you can incorporate and use with grade-level colleagues or with mixed-grade study groups. For example, you can use the discussion ideas in Food for Thought as a springboard in your school or in your school district or college course for conversations about how to improve your students' test scores. Or you and other teachers in your school can form your own study group for professional development and use Food for Thought as a guide for discussions about each chapter.

WHAT DO THE CHAPTERS INCLUDE?

Chapter 1 shows 14 categories of common reading skills that appear in multiple-choice questions on state tests and helps you analyze what your state's reading test asks your students to do. It also examines states' open-response questions and offers strategies for insightful thinking connected to read-alouds that will raise scores in open-response questions. Finally, this chapter offers you links to Web sites that show the released samples of reading tests from several states.

Chapter 2 examines common writing skills that states test in multiple-choice writing questions and gives you assessment ideas and tips to help you evaluate what your students need to know to score well. You will discover routine procedures and lesson ideas for how to teach writing skills authentically within writing units and how to hold students accountable for what you teach. You will also read about common writing genres that often appear on state tests and how to determine where your students need help in these areas.

Chapter 3 explores authentic activities that teachers have used to help their students comprehend texts more deeply and perform better in open-response questions. You will learn how to create open-response questions that link to what you teach and how to use time-saving, small-group coaching strategies to help your students. You will also see how one teacher has used best practices in conferring and content integration to improve her students' open-ended responses, and you will read about two games that have helped students score higher on their open-ended responses.

Chapter 4 investigates strategies for studying fiction texts that strengthen students' comprehension. You will find practical strategies to help students figure out unfamiliar vocabulary by using context clues. This chapter also includes lesson ideas to explicitly teach students important nonfiction comprehension skills that often appear on state tests. You will read suggestions for how to create your own test-prep materials to match your content and study a sample nonfiction science test that I created for test prep to match my district's curriculum.

Chapter 5 offers sample mini-lessons and planning ideas for two writing units that often appear on state tests: persuasive writing and fiction. It shows amazing results from a fifth-grade teacher whose students' fiction writing improved dramatically when she linked reading fiction to writing fiction and used strategic conferring in writing workshop. In addition, you will read about a middle school creative writing teacher's very unusual ideas that improved students' written vocabulary and word usage.

Chapter 6 examines specific suggestions for how to differentiate instruction and improve scores on the state reading test. It addresses actual reading problems that students have had and shows solutions that teachers and I have used with our students. Chapter 6 also tackles the following reading issues: fluency, lack of reading stamina, loss of focus and meaning, lack of motivation to read, the inability to recall information from one part of a text to another, difficulty with reading and following directions, and trouble locating the main ideas in a text.

Chapter 7 explores proven ideas for how to differentiate instruction and raise scores on the state writing test. It also addresses actual writing problems that my students have had that interfered with their performance on writing tests and shows the solutions that their teachers and I have used. You will see how I addressed the following writing topics: how to include and get to the problem in stories, effective elaboration in stories, editing errors, literary devices, clear paragraphs, appropriate leads and endings, transition words, sentence structures and voice, and word choices. In addition, you can examine the framework of an all-purpose writing lesson and read about a revision activity that my students loved.

Chapter 8 shows the nuts and bolts of how to design a test-prep unit in reading workshop that matches your state test. It examines proven strategies for raising students' scores on multiple-choice and open-ended response questions. You will also see how to use practice tests to assess your students, create study packets that match your state reading test and help raise students' confidence, design time-management test tips, and discover how to develop a series of test-prep lessons that match exactly what your students need to know to do well on the reading test.

In **Chapter 9** you will learn how to plan a writing test-prep unit that reflects the format of your writing test so that your students will feel ready to take the test. You will study how test prep for narrative, explanatory/descriptive, and persuasive writing differs, and examine proven lessons, games, and activities that energize students while they are in the middle of test prep. Chapter 9 also includes time-management tips and examples of daily lessons, and a revision activity my students loved that you can use with all types of writing.

My hope is that this book will take the worry out of the state test by helping you use best teaching practices so your students will feel confident and be able to easily show what they know.

CHAPTER 1

What State Reading Tests Expect Students to be Able to Do

Highlights

- Analyze what your state reading test asks your students to do.

- Examine 14 categories of common reading skills that appear in multiple-choice questions on state tests.

- Note the reading strategies students need to be successful with each type of multiple-choice question.

- Administer a multiple-choice practice reading test to determine where your students need help.

- Understand the skills that readers need to answer open-ended response questions.

- Use read-alouds to teach insightful thinking strategies that will raise scores on open-response questions.

Integrating Test Prep into Reading & Writing Workshops © 2011 by Nancy Jennison • Scholastic Teaching Resources

Do you feel overwhelmed when you think about your state reading test? We are in the midst of a testing hysteria. More pressure is on our students, and on us as teachers, every year, as states expand the grade levels that will be tested and continue to alter their tests' components. Does your administrator wait anxiously for your school's test results? Is there a climate of worry in your building? How can your students perform better on state tests? Has your district adopted inappropriate practice materials with drill-and-kill exercises that are harmful for students? Are you interested in learning new ideas for authentic test preparation for your students?

How can we integrate excellent teaching with test preparation without sacrificing the benefits of either? There is an *authentic* way to prepare students for state tests. This book will show you the nuts and bolts of how to prepare your students to show what they know on state tests without compromising the best teaching practices that you believe in.

Author Mike Schmoker concluded that when improved test scores occurred as a result of best teaching practices and strong curriculum, teachers and administrators achieved true gains (2006, 2009). I have included numerous suggestions in this book to help you to strengthen your language arts curriculum, as well as your test-preparation unit, and I think you'll be very pleased with your students' results.

What Is Your State Reading Test Asking Your Students to Do?

This chapter will help you analyze your state's reading test to determine what it is really asking students to do. It highlights common state tests' reading components and examines 14 types of common reading multiple-choice questions. It links those test questions back to actual classrooms by addressing the following for every category of reading question:

- First: Students who can do this can _____.
- Second: In a formal assessment context, students would be able to _____.

A COMMON TYPE OF STATE READING TEST

The State of New Jersey has developed the New Jersey Assessment of Skills and Knowledge (NJ ASK), a test similar to those used in many other states. The reading test components in grades 3 through 8 include multiple-choice and open-ended, or open-response, reading questions. In NJ ASK, students read narrative and informational passages that are approximately 950–1,000 words. They write their responses for open-ended questions that are text-based, and these responses are worth up to 4 points each.

However, the traditional multiple-choice questions are each worth 1 point. NJ ASK limits the amount of time students have to complete each test. Numerous other states include timed tests, and it is vital that our students practice how to complete tasks within the time criteria that each state sets.

COMMON READING SKILLS IN MULTIPLE-CHOICE QUESTIONS

Charles Fuhrken, reading test expert and author, tells teachers that from state to state "reading tests are mostly the same." Even if states write curriculum standards and test objectives somewhat differently, students in all states meet similar categories of reading questions for similar reading standards (2009, p. 23).

When I analyzed multiple-choice reading questions that were released on the Internet by numerous states, I found overlapping clusters of common reading skills. I grouped a number of sample questions into 14 categories to help you evaluate what your state's questions are asking your students to do. Once I studied my state test and other state resources on the Internet and knew the main reading skills that my students were expected to know, I planned how to address those skills throughout the year in reading workshop and in reading in the content areas. The chapters in this book offer ideas that will help you to do the same. For example, you will see concrete examples of how I did this, such as content materials I created that strengthened my students' understanding of my district's requirements for content knowledge, and at the same time helped them become familiar with the format of my state test.

Confusing Language in Multiple-Choice Questions

Researchers who studied the language of multiple-choice questions in state tests urge us to study our own state test's language, since so often the language is different from that of the typical classroom. Charles Fuhrken (2009), an expert in designing reading tests, points out that often test terms differ from classroom language. That difference can get in the way of students' showing what they know. Consequently, it is crucial to use specific test language during the test-prep unit of study, and to integrate some of that language into your teaching throughout the year. For example, suppose the main idea test question includes different vocabulary from what you taught in your classroom. Even if your class's best reader is an expert at locating the main idea within classroom texts, your state won't recognize that skill if the student doesn't answer main idea questions correctly within the test (Greene & Melton, 2007).

In other words, if you use the term *main idea* in your classroom, but your state test uses the term *theme* in a multiple-choice question, some of your students may not know the meaning of the question. (The Try It section on page 21 addresses confusing test language.)

Categories of Common Reading Skills in Multiple-Choice Tests

The following 14 categories of common reading skills appear on many multiple-choice state reading tests. As you read through them, note which types also appear on your state test. Examine the ideas listed under *Students who can do this can . . .* and *In a formal assessment context, students would be able to . . .* for your state's multiple-choice categories. These ideas clarify and explain each category in more depth.

▶ Category 1:
Recognition of Central Idea or Theme

Examples of central idea or theme questions on actual state tests:

- "Which of the following statements BEST expresses the article's main idea?" (NJ ASK)

- "*Pirates in Tuxedos* is specifically about a struggle between . . ." (NJ ASK)

- "What are paragraphs 2 and 3 mostly about?" (Texas Assessment of Knowledge and Skills Released Items)

- "Which statement is a theme of this story?" (California Standards Test)

✔ **Students who can do this can** use clues from the reading passage and their own ideas to state what the reading passage is mostly about. They can determine the most important point that the author made in the text. They can also identify the theme, which is an idea that is broad enough to fit the entire text. The theme is the big idea (Greene & Melton, 2007).

✔ **In a formal assessment context, students would be able to** notice main idea words or phrases in the question, such as *mostly about*, *main idea* or *theme* or *central idea*.

- Students substantiate their choice of a central idea or theme when they locate key words and supporting details from the text and state their implied meaning.

- Another way that students determine the theme is to look for a pattern of the author's repetition of the same thought in different ways throughout the text.

- An additional strategy students use is to notice what the author tried to convey and wants the reader to know through the characters and events in the story, such as observing the characters' feelings, what the main character learned, and the characters' actions as possible clues to the theme.

- You can tell your students that the main idea is the gist of the story, or what the story is mostly about. It is important that students look for and study the key words in the multiple-choice answers that best match evidence they observed that aligns with the central or main idea (Fuhrken, 2009).

▶ Category 2:
Identifying Supporting Details

Examples of identifying supporting detail questions on actual state tests:

■ "Which detail supports the author's main idea?" (NJ ASK)

■ "Hudson and the crew did not continue sailing up the river because . . ." (Texas Assessment of Knowledge and Skills Released Items)

■ "According to the selection, how does Joanna Cole prepare to write a new book?" (MCAS English Language Arts Reading Comprehension Test, Grade 3, Massachusetts Department of Education)

✓ **Students who can do this can** point out the specific information in the text that describes the main idea and makes it stronger. In this type of question, they find the answer stated directly in the text. Inference is not needed. So students realize that they need to return to the passage to locate the answer (Fuhrken, 2009). In a fiction text, this information often relates to the development of the character or the plot. In a nonfiction text, this information often links to statements in the text that support and develop key concepts and ideas.

✓ **In a formal assessment context, students would be able to** notice if supporting detail words or phrases appear in the question, such as *according to the selection*, *stated in the text*, or *detail*.

● Students name the supporting details and locate them in the text.

● In addition, students explain why the supporting details define, describe, provide more information, help clarify, or illustrate the main idea and make it stronger. All of these strategies help students select the correct supporting details.

▶ Category 3:
Vocabulary Word Meanings and Origins

Examples of vocabulary word meanings and origin questions on actual state tests:

■ "Read the meanings for the word, <u>raise</u>. Which meaning best fits the way raised is used in paragraph 20?" (Texas Assessment of Knowledge and Skills Released Items)

■ "What word in paragraph 3 helps you understand what <u>hibernate</u> means?" (Delaware Department of Education Test Sampler)

■ "The origin of the word astronomer is the Greek word *astro* meaning . . ." (California Standards Test)

✓ **Students who can do this can** determine the meaning of the vocabulary word by using the meaning of the text, the context around the unfamiliar word, and syntax as clues. Also, they can notice definitions, synonyms, or paraphrases of the word in the text as additional signals of the word's meaning. Finally, some state tests expect students to identify any Latin or Greek roots, prefixes,

Integrating Test Prep into Reading & Writing Workshops © 2011 by Nancy Jennison • Scholastic Teaching Resources

or suffixes in order to use them as clues to the meaning of vocabulary words built on these elements.

✓ **In a formal assessment context, students would be able to** understand the meaning of common terms that appear in the question. For example, students need to know the differences between *synonyms* and *antonyms*, *prefixes* and *suffixes*, *root* or *base words*, and a *dictionary* and *thesaurus* (Fuhrken, 2009).

- Students correctly choose the meaning of the word that is most appropriate and fits best in the context of the text.

- A key strategy for students to use is to return to the passage and reread the paragraph that the word is in. This creates a context for the word that helps them determine its correct meaning.

- After analyzing the vocabulary sections of reading tests, Lucy Calkins and her colleagues began to encourage students to ask themselves three questions about unknown vocabulary words (Calkins et al., 1998): Did students recognize the unfamiliar vocabulary word from a book that they read? Where had they heard the unknown word? What other words usually accompanied it? These strategies help students figure out the meaning of the difficult vocabulary word.

▶ **Category 4:**
Inferential Thinking

Examples of inferential thinking questions on actual state tests:

■ "Where are you most likely to find a centipede?" (Oregon Department of Education Sample Test, Grade 5)

■ "Why did Frank move quietly while he dumped the bees into the hive?" (Oregon Department of Education Sample Test, Grade 5)

✓ **Students who can do this can** infer a personal meaning from the text by thinking about information in the text and linking it to their own relevant prior knowledge. They go far beyond simply restating a section in the text. Inferential thinkers can create a new meaning of the text that was not explicitly stated (Keene & Zimmerman, 2007).

✓ **In a formal assessment context, students would be able to** recognize the inferential words or phrases that appear in the question. Often, readers need to infer if the question includes the phrases *most likely*, "*the reader can infer*," or "*the author probably thinks*" (Fuhrken, 2009, p. 99).

- Students think inferentially about their prior knowledge and experiences and locate specific text references that support their thinking.

- They realize why their inference helps them understand the text more deeply. Students connect what they know with information from the text and then they use these text references to gather evidence that their response choice is clearly correct.

▶ Category 5:
Recognition of Text Organization

Examples of recognition of text organization questions on actual state tests:

- "Why does the author use the introduction in *Sailing for Home*?" (Texas Assessment of Knowledge and Skills Released Items, Grade 5)
- "What makes the structure of this story most effective?" (Oregon Department of Education Sample Test, Grade 7)

✓ **Students who can do this can** notice how the author organized ideas in fiction and nonfiction texts. For example, they understand that fiction includes the characters, plot, setting, problem, and solution, as well as how authors sometimes use symbols and repetition as patterns in the story.

In addition, students are familiar with the way that a nonfiction text is structured, such as sequential, problem and solution, cause and effect, descriptive, comparison and contrast, persuasive, and question and answer. Also, students can think about the strategic reasons why the author organized the text in a specific way, such as to connect ideas logically, subordinate some ideas to others, or emphasize specific ideas.

✓ **In a formal assessment context, students would be able to** observe the *text organization words or phrases* that might appear in the question, such as *structure of the story or article*, *"best describes how the passage is organized,"* and *information is "mainly organized"* (Fuhrken, 2009, p. 113).

- Students understand different text structures, recognize the way that the author organized the text, and can describe the article's structure.
- They also notice and reflect on why the author arranged and included different ideas and parts of the text, such as the introduction, summary, and so on. They can use this knowledge as a tool to help them locate the correct answer.

▶ Category 6:
Recognition of a Purpose for Reading

Examples of recognition of a purpose for reading questions on actual state tests:

- "By the end of the story, readers understand _____." (NJ ASK)
- "The author tells the story from Lekani's point of view to help the reader understand . . ." (Texas Assessment of Knowledge and Skills Released Items)
- "The author's purpose in writing this selection was probably to . . ." (Tennessee Comprehensive Assessment Program)
- "What lesson does the author *most* want the reader to learn from this passage?" (California Standards Test)
- "How does the author's attitude about bees change in this selection?" (Oregon Department of Education Sample Test, Grade 5)

Integrating Test Prep into Reading & Writing Workshops © 2011 by Nancy Jennison • Scholastic Teaching Resources

✓ **Students who can do this can** reflect on the reason why they think an author wrote a text. Some common authors' purposes include writing to inform, describe, entertain, persuade the reader, or teach the reader a lesson. Students also can recognize and infer the reader's purpose for reading and can state what lesson they think readers learned from the passage.

✓ **In a formal assessment context, students would be able to** notice author's purpose words or phrases that appear in test questions: *The author's purpose in writing the passage was _____, readers understand _____ after reading the passage, The author wants the reader to learn _____*, and so on (Fuhrken, 2009).

- Also, students notice the details in the text that caused them to interpret the author's purpose, such as the topic sentence, the progression of ideas in the article, as well as the concluding thoughts in the text.

- In addition, when they observe and note the author's style of writing and the organization of the text, students think about why the author wrote it.

- Students link the current selection to familiar texts that entertain, inform, describe, persuade, or teach the reader a lesson.

- Finally, they can also state what they feel is the reader's purpose, such as reading the text for pleasure, gaining new knowledge, locating answers to questions, or confirming and strengthening understandings.

▶ **Category 7:**
Prediction Based on Text Information

Examples of prediction based on text information questions on actual state tests:

- ■ "Based on the article that you read, what prediction would you make about _____?" (NJ ASK)

- ■ "According to the information in the story, what is <u>most likely</u> to happen next?" (Tennessee Comprehensive Assessment Program)

- ■ "Read the following chart which shows the differences between the two selections. Which of the following information could be added to the two charts?" (Texas Assessment of Knowledge and Skills Released Items)

✓ **Students who can do this can** preview and use information from the text as clues that help them infer outcomes, events, or actions that will happen. They activate relevant background knowledge related to what they are reading and check their predictions with text evidence to make sure that they make sense. When they read on, students continue to make more logical predictions and revise them as they continue to read (Keene & Zimmerman, 2007).

✓ **In a formal assessment context, students would be able to** notice key prediction words in the question. Often, test writers use the phrases *make a prediction, most likely happen, occur next*, or *occur after the end of the story* (Fuhrken, 2009).

- Students determine their prediction and prove it by locating the specific text features or structures of the text that caused them to make the predictions.

For example, nonfiction readers use text structure characteristics, such as thinking about the setup of comparison and contrast texts. Or, they use text features, such as subheadings, as prediction tools.

- Fiction readers can think about what they know so far about the story that they are reading, how stories work in general, and what has happened so far regarding the characters and events in the story and use them as clues to select the correct answer.

▶ Category 8:
Differences Between Facts and Opinions

Examples of differences between facts and opinions questions on actual state tests:

- "Which statement from the article is an opinion?" (New York State Testing Program, English Language Arts Book 1, Sample Test Grade 5)

- "Which sentence from the story is an opinion?" (Tennessee Comprehensive Assessment Program)

- "Which of the following statements from this article is a fact rather than an opinion?" (Oregon Department of Education Sample Test, Grade 7)

✓ **Students who can do this can** distinguish the differences between statements in the text that are facts and those that are opinions.

✓ **In a formal assessment context, students would be able to** immediately notice the word *fact* or *opinion* in the question.

- Students recognize the differences between facts and opinions and can locate facts and/or opinions in a text.

- They realize that an opinion is someone's view or feeling about an issue, based on personal judgment.

- In contrast, a fact is something that is concrete and can be verified or shown to be true, that really exists, or that really happened. By thinking about these differences, students will be able to select a fact or an opinion as the appropriate response.

▶ Category 9:
Asking Questions

Examples of asking questions test items on actual state tests:

- "Which question does this passage answer?" (Tennessee Comprehensive Assessment Program)

- "Which of the following questions could you ask to help you decide on _____ about the article?" (NJ ASK)

✓ **Students who can do this can** generate questions before, during, and after reading, depending on their purpose in reading (Keene & Zimmerman, 2007). They are familiar with how asking questions and looking for answers to their own questions

Integrating Test Prep into Reading & Writing Workshops © 2011 by Nancy Jennison • Scholastic Teaching Resources

improve their comprehension of the text, and they know how they can ask questions to improve their understanding (Keene, 2008).

✓ **In a formal assessment context, students would be able to** do the following:

- Immediately notice that the word *question* is part of the multiple-choice item.

- In addition, students realize that they can ask questions about what they are reading before, during, and after reading and read with a purpose in mind, such as clarifying meaning or deepening their comprehension (Keene, 2008).

- They also know how to locate answers to their explicit questions and clues to answer their implicit questions.

- Students also recognize that they can ask a question during and after reading to reveal their understanding of the text's main idea, important details, and textual inferences. They can select a correct question response in a multiple-choice question that is similar to their own question.

▶ Category 10:
Forming Opinions

Examples of forming opinion questions on actual state tests:

- ■ "Which of the following contributes MOST to the suspense of the story?" (NJ ASK)

- ■ "What does paragraph 7 suggest about Rico?" (Massachusetts Comprehensive Assessment System English Language Arts Reading Comprehension)

- ■ "Two of the characters in the story, _____ and _____, differ in what ways?" (NJ ASK)

✓ **Students who can do this can** read and think about a text so deeply that they develop views and ideas about a particular issue in the text. Students do this by activating their prior knowledge and experiences and linking them to information from the text as they are forming the opinion.

✓ **In a formal assessment context, students would be able to** notice key words or phrases in the question that ask them to give an *opinion*. For example, testers ask students to do a task that causes them to form an opinion: *compare or contrast*, *tell what contributes most or least*, *tell why*, and so on.

- Students develop an opinion or view about the text, think about why it makes sense, and locate the proof in the text that substantiates it. Proof includes nonfiction or fiction supports, such as information about the characters and events in the story.

- In nonfiction texts, students form opinions as they notice what is important and think about nonfiction features, such as bold words and topic and concluding sentences.

- They also use nonfiction text structures to help them, such as noting how the comparison/contrast structure helps them develop an opinion about how something differs.

- Students select the best multiple-choice answer that matches their opinion.

▶ Category 11:
Drawing Conclusions

Examples of drawing conclusions questions on actual state tests:

- "What are the two main problems in the story that are solved?" (NJ ASK)

- This passage would <u>most likely</u> be in a book called . . ." (Delaware Department of Education Item Sampler)

- "Read the following diagram about Lekani. Which of the following ideas best completes the diagram?" (Texas Assessment of Knowledge and Skills Released Items)

- "From information about the Masai people provided in this story, the reader can conclude that . . . " (Texas Assessment of Knowledge and Skills Released Items)

✓ **Students who can do this can** assimilate information from the text and consider it in relation to their own beliefs, knowledge, and experiences. Then they use it to draw a logical conclusion that was implied in the text. These students are proficient at reading between the lines in a text to draw a reasonable conclusion.

✓ **In a formal assessment context, students would be able to** notice drawing conclusion words or phrases that might appear in the question. For example, in the questions that appear above, the reader must *conclude*, tell *what idea best completes* a diagram, and *draw a conclusion* about a title of a book, based on information in a story.

- Students locate specific pieces of information in the text that they feel helped them come to a particular conclusion.

- They can think about why their conclusion makes sense and fits with the expository information or character details, events, or patterns in the text.

- They can also notice how their conclusion links with relevant prior knowledge from their life, beliefs, knowledge, and what they know about other stories and expository passages that they have read.

- They discuss why and how their conclusions helped them understand the text better (Keene, 2008). By practicing these strategies throughout the year, students will be better able to use all of the above to select the correct multiple-choice response on the day of the test.

▶ Category 12:
Interpreting Literary Devices and Literacy Techniques

Examples of interpreting literary devices and literacy techniques questions on actual state tests:

- "The author uses a flashback in paragraphs 2 to 4 in the selection to . . ." (Texas Assessment of Knowledge and Skills Released Items, Grade 6)

- "When the music box plays again, it is a symbol of . . ." (California Standards Test)

- "The phrase 'people who marched through her young life' means that Yoshiko . . ." (California Standards Test)

- "What is the effect of the figurative language in lines 23–23?" (Massachusetts Comprehensive Assessment System English Language Arts Reading Comprehension)

- "In this selection, the author makes the pig seem almost human. This is a technique called . . ." (Oregon Department of Education Sample Test, Grade 5)

✓ **Students who can do this can** recognize and name different types of literary devices that appear in texts. They understand and interpret the reasons why the author of a particular text chose to use that particular literary device, as well as realize the implied meaning and effects of the use of the device in the text.

✓ **In a formal assessment context, students would be able to** notice literary device words that are part of the question. So they not only need to immediately recognize the literary device term or the text example, but also understand why an author used it.

  - Students distinguish these common types of figurative language that appear in many state tests: simile, metaphor, alliteration, onomatopoeia, and personification.

  - Depending on the grade level, students recognize the following: symbolism, hyperbole, irony, pun, oxymoron, and use of flashbacks.

  - Students also realize what effect and significance the literary device or technique that the author used had in the passage, and they use this as an aid to select the correct answer.

▶ Category 13:
Analyzing and Interpreting Story Elements, Including Character Inference

Examples of story element questions on actual state tests:

- "The setting of *Sailing for Home* is important because it helps the reader understand . . ." (Texas Assessment of Knowledge and Skills Released Items)

- "Which sentence from the passage <u>best</u> describes the setting?" (Tennessee Comprehensive Assessment Program)

- "The tone of paragraph five can be best described as . . ." (Texas Assessment of Knowledge and Skills Released Items)

- "Based on the events described in this passage, Mr. Edison can *best* be described as . . ." (Delaware Department of Education Item Sampler)

✓ **Students who can do this can** understand, interpret, and realize why the following story elements are important in a text: characters, plot, setting, conflicts, problems, climax, solution, mood, tone, lesson, and theme. They also think of the importance of the story elements as they read the text. Some states also include character inferences in this type of question.

✓ **In a formal assessment context, students would be able to** recognize story element words that testers place in the questions: *characters*, *plot*, *setting*, *problem*, *solution*, and so on.

- Students locate the story element in the text and answer specific questions related to its use.

- In addition, they infer why the author developed the story element in the text and interpret its effect in the story.

- Students use their prior knowledge of story elements, how narrative text works, text evidence, and their own personal opinions to draw conclusions about the uses of story elements.

▶ Category 14:
Understanding Features of Informational Texts and Text Types

Examples of features of informational texts and text type questions on actual state tests:

- ■ "The timeline helps the reader to . . ." (California Standards Test)

- ■ "Why are the words 'potsherds' and 'temper' written in quotation marks in paragraphs 2 and 4?" (California Standards Test)

- ■ "Why did the author most likely use the subheading 'The Science of Popcorn' in the article?" (New York State Testing Program, English Language Arts Book 1, Sample Test Grade 5)

- ■ "(*Title of the reading passage*) is an example of what type of genre?" (NJ ASK)

✓ **Students who can do this can** identify and reflect on the characteristics of the text type or genre of the text, such as mystery, biography, persuasive essay, and so on. Students also know the types of nonfiction features that the author has used to enhance their comprehension, such as the use of timelines, captions, maps, drawings, headings, subheadings, labels, bold words, and so on. In addition, students explain the importance of text features to help them more deeply comprehend the text.

✓ **In a formal assessment context, students would be able to** recognize nonfiction text feature words that appear in the question, such as *heading*, *diagram*, *label*, *caption*, and so on. Also, students need to recognize the genre or think about the structure of the passage and why the author used it.

- Students not only recognize the nonfiction text features that the author used, but can also evaluate how effectively they were used and think about why the author used them.

- Possible reasons students might cite for the author's use of text features include: to clarify the text, to tell more information about the text, to work with another feature in the text to extend its meaning (for example, how an

Integrating Test Prep into Reading & Writing Workshops © 2011 by Nancy Jennison • Scholastic Teaching Resources

arrow works with a diagram), and to provide a visual illustration that more easily shows what the words in the text mean.

● Students also can think about what they know about how nonfiction texts work to closely examine nonfiction features and answer multiple-choice test questions based on them.

● In addition, by thinking of what they know about genre and the characteristics of texts, they can answer text type questions.

Try It

What reading skills do your state's multiple-choice questions measure?

Ask your administrator for common planning time for you and your grade-level colleagues to analyze sample multiple-choice questions from your state's reading test.

✓ Examine your state education Web site, locate lists of the tested reading skills in your state test, and make your own list of your state's tested categories.

✓ Compare your list to the list of skills that appears in this chapter and consider my ideas of what students need to know to be successful in answering the reading questions on the state test.

✓ Note the language your state uses in each released test question to assess each reading skill. Is this the same language that you use in the classroom? How can you integrate the test language into your classroom this year so that your students will understand it more easily?

✓ Examine state standards to see if there are other terms that you may want to integrate into your teaching; for example, use of the term *antonym*, instead of *word that means the opposite*.

✓ What are some areas that need more focus in your classrooms?

Administer a Multiple-Choice Reading Test to Determine Where Your Students Need Reading Help

Consider administering a state-released sample reading test if you are unsure of where your students need help. This is a demand test that is used for practice. (I am borrowing the term "demand" from work done at the Teachers College Reading and Writing Project.) Visit your state education Web site and use a state-released sample of a multiple-choice reading test. If you give this type of test during your test-prep unit right before the state test, keep the time limits, format, and number of questions consistent with what students will encounter on your actual state test. If it is not used immediately before the state test, the time limit need not be enforced. You can use the test to inform your planning for reading lessons that you will need to teach within subsequent reading units during the school year.

HOW TO DEVELOP YOUR OWN MULTIPLE-CHOICE DEMAND READING TEST

If your state includes a multiple-choice reading test for your students but does not offer released samples on your state education's Web site, one option is to use another state's released test if it matches what students receive in your state. If you have students who read one or more levels below your grade, consider using a lower-grade demand test without the grade level attached. You want to get an accurate measure of where your students need help, rather than wondering if a too-hard text got in the way of showing you how they really performed.

If the released samples from other states do not match what you want, consider developing a reading test with colleagues that reflects your curriculum. In other words, if your grade level studies pollution in science, take a pollution text that contains the same approximate number of words that appear on your state's reading test. (See Chapter 4, pages 89–94 for an example of a demand test that I created.) Then use the sample questions in released state samples from your state or questions from this chapter to create similar types of multiple-choice questions for the text that you selected.

ASSESS YOUR STUDENTS' PERFORMANCE ON A MULTIPLE-CHOICE DEMAND READING TEST

Before you evaluate your students' performance on the practice test, make a list of the reading skills that are reflected in the multiple-choice questions on the test. Jot the names of your students who need help under each skill. For example, if one of the reading skills tested was locating the central idea, jot down the names of the students who need help in this area.

Based on the assessments from this demand test, plan read-aloud work, reading units, and mini-lessons that will address students' needed reading skills. Small-group, one-on-one, and partner coaching and conferring will all help address individual students' needs. More specific and detailed information on how to do this appears in Chapters 3, 4, 6, and 8.

State Reading Tests and Open-Ended Questions

Open-ended questions are a common feature on state reading tests. New Jersey is an example of a state that includes reading comprehension tests in grades 3 to 8 using open-ended questions, in addition to multiple-choice questions. Often, open-ended questions require students to draw conclusions or form opinions. They generate their responses in sentences on test sheets that the state provides. Open-ended responses are usually worth much more than multiple-choice answers. States often score them by using a rubric that highly values text evidence and thoughtful, reflective answers. For example, to earn the highest score of 4 on New Jersey's Open-Ended Scoring Rubric for Reading, Listening, and Viewing, students in grades 5 and 6 must show evidence of the following: "A 4-point response clearly demonstrates understanding of the task, completes all requirements, and provides an insightful explanation/opinion that links to or extends aspects of the text."

Other states, such as Delaware and California, include open-ended reading questions scored on a rubric as part of the writing section of the test.

Examples of typical open-ended questions:

- "In paragraph 12, the author decides not to say a word to the receptionist about his true feelings. Suppose he were to speak to her.

  - What might he say?
  - Explain why he might say this.

  Use information from the article to support your response." (NJ ASK)

- "Explain how the health habits of the 18th century are alike and how they are different from the health habits of today. Use information from the article in your answer." (Delaware Department of Education Item Sampler)

- "Based on the selection, describe **three** eating habits of the Pilgrims **and** give a reason for each one. Look at the samples in the boxes below, but use **different** examples in your answer." (Massachusetts Comprehensive Assessment System English Language Arts Reading Comprehension)

Note: If a link below does not work, please go directly to that state education department's home page. Sometimes states change their links and offer the same information in a different location on their Web site.

You can visit these Web sites for examples from other states:

Arizona: www.azed.gov/standards/AIMS/AIMSSupport.asp

California: www.cde.ca.gov/ta/tg/sr/css05rtq.asp

Connecticut: www.csde.state.ct.us/public/cedar/assessment/cmt/cmt_handbooks.htm

Delaware: www.doe.k12.de.us/aab/sample_items/default.shtml

Massachusetts: www.doe.mass.edu/mcas/testitems.html

New Jersey: www.nj.gov/education/assessment/es/sample/

New York: www.nysedregents.org

Ohio: www.ode.state.oh.us/GD/Templates/Pages/ODE/ODEPrimary.aspx?Page=2&TopicID=9&TopicRelationID=1070

Oregon: www.ode.state.or.us/search/page/?=443

Tennessee: www.state.tn.us/education/assessment/tsachsamp.shtml

www.state.tn.us/education/assessment/ach_samplers.shtml

Texas: ritter.tea.state.tx.us/student.assessment/resources/release/index.html

Washington: www.k12.wa.us/assessment/WASL/Testquestions.aspx

West Virginia: wvde.state.wv.us/oaa/pdf/westest-reading.pdf

IMPROVING STUDENTS' OPEN-RESPONSE ANSWERS

I have developed numerous strategies for strengthening students' responses to open-ended questions. Through teaching comprehension strategies in authentic ways in mini-lessons and in activities connected to the read-aloud, as well as through oral and written partnership activities and games, you can improve students' comprehension, elaboration, and insightful thinking. An in-depth analysis of how to do this appears in Chapters 3, 4, and 8.

Read How It Worked

Use the Read-Aloud to Help Students Think More Deeply and Insightfully

This section highlights the work of Donna Klein, a talented special education/regular education teacher from Mackay School in Tenafly, New Jersey. Donna demonstrates how to develop deeper thinking from your read-aloud. This work prepares students to write more insightful answers to open-ended questions on state tests. You can use her ideas to help strengthen your read-aloud and increase your students' comprehension. Donna has seen very positive changes in her students, and she feels that the strategies that she delineated in her write-up dramatically improved her students' ideas and understanding of texts. Donna based some ideas on Lucy Calkins' work.

The state tests all expect that our students can infer, draw conclusions, and think deeply. As students think more insightfully, their test scores go up. This past school year, Donna Klein's fifth-grade students thought more insightfully in their discussions about the read-aloud. In fact, Donna said that in all of her years of teaching, these were the best thinkers she has had. Why? This year Donna did more modeling of her ideas. She modeled more concretely and wrote her oral reaction to an exciting event in the read-aloud, and the result was that her students had more confidence! That was the difference this year.

Donna stated: "As the teacher, it is the quality of my modeling. I was in the moment with the students, acting as if I were reading the book for the first time, and I responded as a passionate reader as I elaborated on my ideas. For example, this is how I used *The Tiger Rising* by Kate DiCamillo: I paused after reading an unforgettable scene and simultaneously wrote and said this to the students: 'I am so angry that Rob's father slapped him on the day of Rob's mother's funeral. The father only thought of his own feelings, and he didn't think of Rob's great sadness and loss. I cannot imagine a father treating his son so cruelly.'

"One of my students, Jon, had a different response to the scene. I think that this occurred because I encouraged all students to push their thinking. [See Figure 1.1 on page 26.]

"I also modeled how my thinking changed while I was reading. Often, I might say, 'I never thought of it that way before . . .'

"In addition, I asked students to share their ideas in partnerships. They were eager to respond, because I invited them to. I said, 'Does anyone have something to piggyback off of what I just said?'"

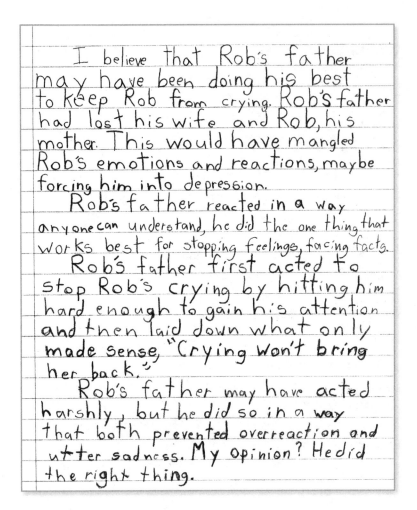

I believe that Rob's father may have been doing his best to keep Rob from crying. Rob's father had lost his wife and Rob, his mother. This would have mangled Rob's emotions and reactions, maybe forcing him into depression.

Rob's father reacted in a way anyone can understand, he did the one thing that works best for stopping feelings, facing facts.

Rob's father first acted to stop Rob's crying by hitting him hard enough to gain his attention and then laid down what only made sense, "Crying won't bring her back."

Rob's father may have acted harshly, but he did so in a way that both prevented overreaction and utter sadness. My opinion? He did the right thing.

Figure 1.1

Jon, a fifth-grader, thought more deeply about a scene in *The Tiger Rising*.

Use Sticky Notes to Help Students to Think and Talk More Insightfully

"Later in the month as I read aloud, I asked students to jot down their thinking on sticky notes when I paused while reading aloud. I wrote my ideas on the whiteboard while they wrote their own individual ideas on sticky notes. I shared what I wrote. Then I invited them into the conversation again by asking, 'Does anyone have something to piggyback off of what I just said?'

"I began making the students feel comfortable with sharing their sticky notes by asking them to read what they wrote aloud. Students all listened carefully to see if that particular reader's sticky note linked to someone else's idea. I scaffolded their sharing by allowing them to read what they wrote or just say aloud their new ideas. I did this whole-class and then in partnerships. I found that because of this activity, hesitant students recognized that they were thinking the very same things that others had jotted. This helped them recognize that their ideas had merit.

Integrating Test Prep into Reading & Writing Workshops © 2011 by Nancy Jennison • Scholastic Teaching Resources

"We used students' sticky notes in a number of ways related to the *teaching points* I made:

- Often, they reread their sticky notes and noticed character changes, character traits, or character relationships.

- Daily conversations about the read-aloud after writing sticky notes is the key to developing more insightful thinking.

- The sequence of the activity was pausing while reading aloud, jotting, talking, and then continuing to read aloud. Perhaps this occurred twice during the read-aloud.

"Periodically, I collected students' sticky notes and kept track of the reading skills that they used: inferring, predicting, synthesizing, and so on. I found *Stone Fox* to be another excellent text to use for this read-aloud activity.

"After reading over students' sticky notes, I would often collect several and display them on the whiteboard to launch a new teaching point, such as how to predict by thinking of what you already know happened in the book.

"Sometimes during class discussions, we talked about a particular question that related to the read-aloud, and then I also asked students to write a response in their readers' notebooks to that question or a different question. Over time, their responses were more detailed and reflected deeper thinking."

Food for Thought

▼

DEVELOP A PLAN USING YOUR READ-ALOUD TO HELP YOUR STUDENTS THINK MORE DEEPLY, BASED ON DONNA KLEIN'S WORK. WHY NOT CONSIDER DISCUSSING DONNA KLEIN'S IDEAS FOR HOW TO HELP YOUR STUDENTS THINK MORE INSIGHTFULLY?

- Think of how you model comprehension ideas in your read-aloud, and consider if you can use some of Donna's ideas to enrich your modeling.
- Discuss why her students felt comfortable to share their ideas and expand their thinking. What did she do to create that climate?
- List ways that you will modify your modeling and your students' responses to it during your read-aloud, based on Donna's work and ideas of your own.

For more extensive ideas on using read-alouds to improve students' comprehension and prepare them for state reading tests, please see Chapter 3.

CHAPTER 2

What State Writing Tests Expect Students to be Able to Do

s students' interest in writing in the United States in decline, or is it experiencing a resurgence? Kathleen Blake Yancey, past president of the National Council of Teachers of English, speaks about the unique time period that we live in, the 21st century, where "writing occurs everywhere." Excitement about writing is in the air, because writers of all ages choose to communicate with each other outside of school. Dr. Yancey explains that audiences are everywhere, from MySpace to Facebook to the blogosphere, and that the 21st century marks a writing breakthrough that she calls the "Age of Composition." She urges educators to change their thinking, to consider writing as a subject, to plan curriculum accordingly, and to capitalize on students' enjoyment of composing for real audiences (2009, pp. 4–5, p. 7).

Part of this book's focus is on how to weave writing test prep into instruction in authentic ways. You can plan rich writing units that will provide a strong foundation for the writing test, but also include units where students strengthen their skills as 21st-century writers who can write inside of school for real audiences. Later chapters in this book will show you how to blend writing test prep and writing instruction in a way that results in writers who love to write (see Chapters 5, 7, and 9).

Examples of Common Writing Skills in Multiple-Choice Questions on State Tests

Not all states include multiple-choice questions in their writing tests. However, here are a few examples of some common writing skills tested on these tests. Students select the correct multiple-choice answers for tasks such as the following:

- combine two sentences
- create a complete sentence
- distinguish correctly formed sentences from sentence fragments or run-on sentences
- recognize and eliminate irrelevant sentences in a passage or story
- select the correct sentence based on the appropriate organization and clarity of ideas in a text
- use a more effective word to strengthen the meaning of a sentence or passage
- locate errors in spelling, punctuation, capitalization, and editing
- choose the correct way to revise ideas within a sentence
- understand aspects of letter writing
- select an appropriate topic sentence for a passage
- use homonyms correctly, such as *principal* or *principle*
- select a clarifying sentence to follow another that is already in the text
- choose a correct part of speech
- understand standard grammar and usage issues

A Few Typical Samples of Multiple-Choice Writing Questions

Multiple-choice writing questions often present students with a brief passage that contains various types of errors based on some of the criteria on the list on page 29. The test questions usually refer back to numbered sentences in that passage. Here are a few examples of the most recently revised multiple-choice test from *TAKS Texas Assessment of Knowledge and Skills Information Booklet, Writing, Grade 4, Revised.*

▶ Writing Skill:
Combining Two Sentences

Example of a Test Question:

"What is the **BEST** way to combine sentences 16 and 17?

Ⓐ The quarters for Massachusetts and Virginia have pictures, the pictures show important parts of their history.

Ⓑ The quarters for Massachusetts and Virginia have pictures, and the pictures are for showing important parts of their history.

Ⓒ The quarters for Massachusetts and Virginia have pictures, but they show important parts of their history.

* Ⓓ The quarters for Massachusetts and Virginia have pictures that show important parts of their history."

(TAKS, 2004, p. 27)

Explanation of the Writing Skill: Combining Sentences

"When students are asked to combine two sentences, they should keep in mind that the right answer must be a grammatically correct sentence, must be the most effective sentence (not wordy or awkward), and must not change the original meaning." (TAKS, 2004, p. 27)

▶ Writing Skill:
Coherence

Example of a Test Question:

"Which sentence does **NOT** belong in this paper?

Ⓐ Sentence 2   * Ⓒ Sentence 15

Ⓑ Sentence 9   Ⓓ Sentence 18"

(TAKS, 2004, p. 28)

Explanation of the Writing Skill: Revising Sentences for Coherence With a Logical Progression of Ideas

"This item requires students to recognize an extraneous, or unnecessary, sentence in the passage. When students revise their own writing, they may often discover that they have included a sentence that does not move their composition forward; in other words, the sentence may have some link to the overall topic but is not directly related to the other sentences. An extraneous sentence can stall the progression of ideas and cause the reader to wonder why it has been included." (TAKS, 2004, p. 28)

▶ Writing Skill:
Replacing an Ambiguous Pronoun With a Specific Noun

Example of a Test Question:

"The meaning of sentence 4 can be improved by changing *it* to —

Ⓐ the cardboard holder

Ⓑ my collection

Ⓒ the book

* Ⓓ the state quarters program"

(TAKS, 2004, p. 27)

Explanation of the Writing Skill: Using Pronouns and Clear Antecedents

"This item asks students to replace an ambiguous pronoun (a pronoun whose antecedent is unclear) with a specific noun to clarify the meaning of the sentence." (TAKS, 2004, p. 27)

▶ **Writing Skill:**

Editing Spelling Errors

Example of a Test Question:

"What change, if any, should be made in sentence 11?

(A) Change *noticed* to **notice**

* (B) Change *worryed* to **worried**

(C) Change *Dad's* to **Dads**

(D) Make no change"

(TAKS, 2004, p. 31)

Explanation of the Writing Skill: Editing Spelling

"Effective writers examine their work for correct capitalization, punctuation, and spelling. . . . Correct spelling also helps the writer communicate clearly." (TAKS, p. 23)

▶ **Writing Skill:**

Identifying a Sentence Fragment

Example of a Test Question:

"Which of the following is **NOT** a complete sentence?

(A) Sentence 1

(B) Sentence 5

* (C) Sentence 8

(D) Sentence 12"

(TAKS, 2004, p. 32)

Explanation of the Writing Skill: Identifying Sentence Fragments

Students need to "recognize fragments and run-on sentences and determine the best way to correct them . . ." (TAKS, 2004, p. 21)

▶ Writing Skill:
Capitalization

Example of a Test Question:

"What change, if any, should be made in sentence 19?

(A) Change *interesting* to **intresting**

(B) Add a comma after **states**

* (C) Change *american* to **American**

(D) Make no change"

(TAKS, 2004, p. 28)

Explanation of the Writing Skill: Using Proper Capitalization

"Effective writers examine their work for correct capitalization, punctuation, and spelling. Capitalization and punctuation marks take the place of the pauses, stops, and intonations used to convey meaning in oral communication. Accuracy in language mechanics helps the reader 'hear' those nuances and better understand what the writer is trying to communicate." This question "tests the student's ability to recognize and correct errors in capitalization, punctuation, and spelling in the context of peer-editing passages." (TAKS, 2004, p. 23)

▶ Writing Skill:
Subject/Verb Agreement

Example of a Test Question:

"What change, if any, should be made in sentence 2?

(A) Change *flowers* to **Flowers**

* (B) Change *was digging* to **were digging**

(C) Change *fence* to **fense**

(D) Make no change"

(TAKS, 2004, p. 31)

Explanation of the Writing Skill: Using Standard Grammar and Proper Usage

"To communicate clearly, the writer must also know how to apply the rules of standard grammar and usage. Incorrect use of tense, lack of agreement between subjects and verbs, and unclear pronoun referents can cause the reader to misunderstand the writer's meaning . . ." (TAKS, 2004, p. 22)

Try It

What writing skills do your state's multiple-choice questions measure? Work with colleagues to analyze the writing skills that your students need, so that you can more effectively plan your writing units.

✓ Visit your state Web site to locate documents that explain expected writing skills for your grade level. (States often post the list of skills on their education department Web sites.)

✓ Use the list of writing skills in this chapter as a tool to help you categorize your state's sample questions according to key writing skills.

✓ What areas in which students need more work can you link into your writing workshop units and mini-lessons throughout the year? (To help you determine your focus, look at the skills that the state expects your students to be able to demonstrate, and analyze their writing with those expectations in mind.)

✓ How can you integrate some of your state's confusing or unfamiliar writing terms into your writing workshop and possible content study this year? (For example, words such as *combine* or *identify* sometimes confuse students.)

Determine Where Your Students Need Writing Help—Administer a Demand Test

If you are unsure about how your students will perform on your state's multiple-choice writing test, administer a demand multiple-choice writing test. (I am borrowing the term "demand" from work done at the Teachers College Reading and Writing Project.) When students are familiar with the format of the test, time limit, and number of questions, they feel more comfortable and confident. (See Chapter 8, pages 183–186 for strategies for helping students to become successful in answering multiple-choice questions.)

■ The demand test is a practice multiple-choice writing test.

■ Use the released sample of your state multiple-choice writing test for your demand test.

■ If you distribute the demand test to students at the beginning of your test-prep unit before the state test, keep the time limits, format, and number of questions consistent with what students will see on your actual state test.

Integrating Test Prep into Reading & Writing Workshops © 2011 by Nancy Jennison • Scholastic Teaching Resources

If your state includes a multiple-choice writing test for your students but does not offer released samples on the education department's Web site, one option is to administer another state's released test, if it matches what you know about your state's multiple-choice writing test. (For links to released samples and information about multiple-choice tests on state education department's Web sites, see page 42.)

DEVELOP YOUR OWN DEMAND MULTIPLE-CHOICE WRITING TEST

Another suggestion is to work with colleagues to develop your own multiple-choice writing test. I have created steps to help you develop your own multiple-choice demand writing test. Adapt them to fit the way your state test works.

For example, if your state asks students to fix the errors in a writing sample, you can do something similar. Locate a student's draft from a previous year that contains errors. If the draft contains spelling errors, and your state assesses spelling skills in multiple-choice questions, create a question about one or more of the spelling errors similar to the Editing Spelling Errors multiple-choice sample question that appears on page 32. Here are general directions that you can use and adapt to create your own multiple-choice test:

■ Obtain a sample of a state-released multiple-choice writing test.

■ Use a former student's unedited draft for the passage on your demand test. Retype it and insert a consecutive number inside parentheses before each sentence.

■ Use the multiple-choice writing questions in the released state samples from your state or another state as a guide.

■ Consider the writing skills that your state tests. Decide which skills you want to include in your multiple-choice questions.

■ Use the same type of test language as your state does and create multiple-choice questions about the elements that need to be fixed in the student's unedited draft, by referring to the numbers of the specific sentences in it.

■ Administer the multiple-choice writing test, assess your students, and then note their strengths and areas where they need more support.

TEACHING WRITING SKILLS BASED ON YOUR ASSESSMENT OF STUDENTS' NEEDS

Based on the assessments from the demand multiple-choice writing test, jot down the areas in which your students need help. For example, list all the skills that your state tested and write the names of your students under each area where they had difficulty. If, for example, a quarter of your students had difficulty with understanding how to correctly capitalize words, and a majority of your students were unable to correctly answer the question about how to write a paragraph, that tells you that you need to address capitalization and paragraph writing. You may want to plan a series of whole-class lessons on how to write paragraphs, but only meet with *one or two small groups* to do coaching on capitalization.

MAKE PLANS FOR TOPICS FOR FUTURE WRITING UNITS

- Locate information on your state's education department Web site about the additional writing skills that did not appear on the test you administered, but which your state expects students to know.

- Brainstorm future topics for writing units with colleagues, based on what your students need to know and what units you plan to teach.

  For example, suppose that you have already taught a unit on personal narrative, and you planned for realistic fiction to be your next writing unit. Since you observed that your students had difficulty with writing a paragraph, you would include a series of lessons designed to strengthen this skill. These paragraph lessons will be part of *revision* in your upcoming realistic fiction unit. Realistic fiction is a reasonable unit for you to teach since it flows nicely after personal narrative, and also because your state expects students to write a story on the state test.

- Plan tentative lessons on revision, editing, grammar, sentence formation, and punctuation in future writing units. Based on your continual assessment of students during writing workshop, this list may change once each unit gets under way. (See an example in the Read How It Worked section below.)

 Read How It Worked

Fifth-Grade Teacher Kathy Doyle Demonstrates the Authentic Teaching of Grammar Skills Within Her Writing Units

At the beginning of the school year, Kathy Doyle, an exemplary fifth-grade teacher from Smith School in Tenafly, New Jersey, noted as she studied her students' writing that her students needed help in sentence construction. They wrote some complete sentences but also wrote incomplete and run-on sentences. In addition, they did not

Integrating Test Prep into Reading & Writing Workshops © 2011 by Nancy Jennison • Scholastic Teaching Resources

vary their sentence structures. (Sentence construction often appears on state multiple-choice writing tests, and students must know proper sentence construction for writing genre tests, too.)

Teach the skill of sentence construction for the first time during revision. Kathy planned to interweave teaching sentence construction in her first writing unit during the revision section. When she planned her first unit, small-moment personal narrative (stories about small moments in a writer's life), Kathy taught several mini-lessons on sentence construction when students *revised* their personal narratives.

First Revision Lesson: In one revision lesson, Kathy helped her students see how a sentence differs from a fragment. She showed them some incomplete sentences— "Under the bed . . . When I say, under the bed, do you understand what I am talking about?"— then shared complete sentences and other phrases or fragments. As she did, she asked her students questions such as, "Is this a full thought or is this a puzzle?" and "Does this sound clear or confusing?" After this mini-lesson, students revised their own writing and made sure to write complete sentences. (Another option is to use sentences and phrases from your current read-aloud as your examples.)

Second Revision Lesson: Kathy planned another revision lesson because she found that when her students read aloud their writing pieces to each other, some students were still writing fragments or writing sentences that were too long. In the second revision lesson, she showed students the first two pages of Patricia MacLachlan's *Journey* as an example of an author whose sentences are alive and interesting. Kathy and her students studied how this mentor author used an economy of words to show so much in her writing.

As she and her students studied *Journey*, Kathy also pointed out what writing teacher William Zinsser (1998) said about good writing being a balance of long and short sentences by saying: "When Patricia MacLachlan was a little girl and she was reading, she thought that the books had too many words. So, now as an author, the last thing that she does is to reread her draft and take out every unnecessary word. Patricia believes that you only put in an adjective if it really makes a difference. The key is to use strong nouns and verbs." After students studied the sentences in *Journey* with Kathy, they went back to their own sentences, revised them to make them complete and/or stronger, and read them aloud to their writing partners.

Reinforce sentence construction in the second writing unit during *drafting*. When students wrote drafts during the second writing unit, Kathy expected them to recall how to write complete sentences and incorporate what they learned from the first writing unit. In other words, she required that students show what they knew about sentences when they *drafted* their story, not just when they *revised* their stories. So Kathy held students accountable for showing what they learned about sentence construction from her mini-lessons and revision work in the previous unit.

Example:

In Kathy's second writing unit, realistic fiction, she taught her students a strategy that she always uses to check her sentences when she writes. She demonstrated for the class how she writes three sentences in her draft, pauses, and then rereads what she has written aloud to make sure that the sentences are complete, clear, and make sense. After Kathy showed students how she strengthened her sentences by pausing and reading them aloud every three sentences or so, she asked students to do the same thing when they began their drafts. (If your students have trouble doing this, you could construct a checklist to help them.)

As students worked on sentence construction during drafting within their realistic fiction unit of study, Kathy noted that they wrote clear and complete sentences more often. She felt that her lessons had started to pay off! Her students were showing signs of becoming stronger writers.

Hold students accountable for using complete sentences during *all* types of writing.
In the third writing unit, personal essay, Kathy expected her students to use complete sentences whenever they were writing during that unit of study and in all written work. She also required students to make the style of their sentences more and more interesting, no matter what genre or subject area. Kathy's students realized that they were continually being held accountable for all writing skills that she modeled.

Create yearlong activities to help students write sentences with beautiful words.
All year long, Kathy's students collected breathtaking sentences that they loved and admired. They located them in Kathy's read-alouds, their own independent reading, and classmates' writing. Her students wrote these sentences in their writers' notebooks or in word pool notebooks. In addition, they collected lines from poems that they loved. So Kathy did much more than just teach students about sentence construction; she turned her students into lovers of words and beautiful language (Scott, Skobel, & Wells, 2008). (For more information on incorporating grammar and usage lessons in a similar framework, consult *The Power of Grammar* by writing experts Mary Ehrenworth and Vicki Vinton [2005.] I use this book as a handy resource for my mini-lessons.)

Innovative Resource Book for Teaching Punctuation

Janet Angelillo has written an outstanding book, *A Fresh Approach to Teaching Punctuation: Helping Young Writers Use Conventions With Precision and Purpose* (2002), that shows teachers how to guide students to excel at using punctuation as a tool for making meaning in their writing. Students discover how real authors use punctuation as a craft to make their writing stronger, and they try using some of those same techniques in their own writing in different genres. I often use this book for mini-lesson ideas, too.

An Example of Common Genre Writing Components in State Writing Tests

NEW JERSEY ASSESSMENT OF SKILLS AND KNOWLEDGE (NJ ASK)

On its writing test, NJ ASK, the State of New Jersey requires students to write in different genres, as do many other states. NJ ASK requires students to write two different types of genre responses based on written prompts—writing topics that are usually phrased in the form of questions or ideas. Students think about the testers' questions and ideas and respond by writing for the test (Angelillo, 2005b).

Students in New Jersey must write their responses within a limited time. All students in grades 3 to 5 write a story based on a speculative prompt and a composition that answers questions from an explanatory prompt related to their own experiences or ideas. In contrast, students in grades 6 to 8 write a persuasive essay or letter and also respond to an explanatory prompt. So, in prompt writing, students must carefully understand and keep in mind everything that the prompt states and write their best work that is generally graded with a rubric. It is a complex process, especially if students have to demonstrate their very best writing in a short amount of time (Angelillo, 2005b).

An Example of a State Holistic Scoring Rubric

New Jersey's writing test is scored according to a 5-point or 6-point holistic scoring rubric, depending on students' grade levels. This rubric is consistent with what other states require for qualities of good writing, so it is a good example to study. Categories include content and organization, usage, sentence construction, and mechanics. The highest score indicates that the student has a "Strong Command" of each area in each specific genre that NJ ASK tests. See Figure 2.1 for the state-released *Grade Five New Jersey Holistic Scoring Rubric*.

DIFFERENT NAMES FOR THE SAME COMPONENTS ON STATE WRITING TESTS

Some states call their writing test by certain names, yet the tests are tremendously similar. Delaware's test, for example, includes a persuasive letter-writing component, called a Stand-Alone Writing Prompt, which is also scored on a five-point rubric. This rubric expects the most advanced writers to show an "exceptional awareness of the writing purpose and the concerns and needs of the audience; insightful and/or reflective analysis of ideas; distinctive style, voice, tone and compositional risk; exceptional use of literary devices, and language conventions to enhance meaning and support style and voice" (2008, Delaware Rubric for Stand-Alone Writing).

Language Arts Literacy • Writing
New Jersey Holistic Scoring Rubric—Grade 5

In scoring consider the grid of written language	Inadequate Command	Limited Command	Partial Command	Adequate Command	Strong Command
Score	**1**	**2**	**3**	**4**	**5**
Content & Organization	• May lack opening and/or closing	• May lack opening and/or closing	• May lack opening and/or closing	• Generally has opening and/or closing	• Opening and closing
	• Minimal response to topic; uncertain focus	• Attempts to focus • May drift or shift focus	• Usually has single focus	• Single focus	• Single focus • Sense of unity and coherence • Key ideas developed
	• No planning evident; disorganized	• Attempts organization • Few if any, transitions between ideas	• Some lapses or flaws in organization • May lack some transitions between ideas	• Ideas loosely connected • Transition evident	• Logical progression of ideas • Moderately fluent • Attempts compositional risks
	• Details random, inappropriate, or barely apparent	• Details lack elaboration that could highlight paper	• Repetitious details • Several unelaborated details	• Uneven development of details	• Details appropriate and varied
Usage	• No apparent control • Severe/ numerous errors	• Numerous errors	• Errors/patterns of errors may be evident	• Some errors that do not interfere with meaning	• Few errors
Sentence Construction	• Assortment of incomplete and/ or incorrect sentences	• Excessive monotony/same structure • Numerous errors	• Little variety in syntax • Some errors	• Some variety • Generally correct	• Variety in syntax appropriate and effective
Mechanics	• Errors so severe they detract from meaning	• Numerous serious errors	• Patterns of errors evident	• No consistent pattern of errors • Some errors that do not interfere with meaning	• Few errors

Figure 2.1

Note the qualities of good writing that appear in the New Jersey Holistic Scoring Rubric for Grade 5. These categories appear on many other states' rubrics.

In contrast, other states administer a performance-based, genre-writing test only in certain grades. For example, some states ask one grade level to write a story and require other grade levels to write an expository essay. (For examples and links, see the list at the end of this chapter on pages 42–43.) Many similar terms are repeated from state to state in rubrics and other writing assessments, but regardless of how a state structures its assessment, the goal is simply to ascertain the quality of each student's writing.

Develop a Practice Test to Assess Where Your Students Need More Support for the Genre Writing Tests

If you are unsure of where your students need help with the genre writing that will appear on your state writing test, administer a demand test using a prompt similar to your state prompt. When I wanted to create a narrative prompt similar to a prompt from my New Jersey state test, I visited the New Jersey Department of Education Web site and read over a couple of examples of released narrative prompts. Then I constructed the following prompt: *It was the first day of school for twins Melissa and Ryan. They had been excited for the school year to begin. As they walked and neared the entrance to their school, they had an unexpected problem. Write a story about what happened to the twins and how they solved their problem.*

STEPS FOR CREATING A DEMAND WRITING TEST IN A PARTICULAR GENRE

1. Create a prompt based on a state writing test prompt.

2. Score your students' responses to the prompt by using your state rubric and jot down areas of focus.

3. As you plan your writing units this year, insert lessons on areas in need of more support that you observed in the demand test. Writing researchers have found that teachers who use best practices teach writing units throughout the year that meet students' needs and prepare them for state tests while teaching effective writing strategies (Allan, McMackin, Dawes, & Spadorcia, 2009). For example, if your students wrote leads that need more work, plan strategy lessons that teach them how to write strong leads in several of your writing units.

Writing skills are cumulative and transfer from one writing unit to another. In other words, if you have taught your students how to write effective leads in a personal narrative unit of study, they can use similar strategies for writing leads in a fiction study.

(For more information on writing units, mini-lessons that you can teach, and demand writing tests, please see Chapters 5, 7, and 9.)

Links to Web Sites for Multiple-Choice Writing Questions

Note: If a link below does not work, please go directly to that state education department's home page. Sometimes states change their links and offer the same information in a different location on their Web site.

Texas: ritter.tea.state.tx.us/student.assessment/resources/release/index.html

Wisconsin: dpi.wi.gov/oea/lasamples.html

California: www.cde.ca.gov/ta/tg/sr/css05rtq.asp

Connecticut: www.csde.state.ct.us/public/cedar/assessment/cmt/cmt_handbooks.htm

New Hampshire, Vermont, Rhode Island:
www.ride.ri.gov/Assessment/necap.aspx

Links to Web Sites for Released Writing Samples of Writing Genres

Although states' writing tests may change from year to year, at the time that I wrote this book, examples from some of the states that had writing genre tests were available online. A number of them have rubrics and anchor papers with scoring that you could analyze. (*Note:* States tested these genres at the time that this book was written.)

Alabama: www.alsde.edu. (Click on *Sections* along the left-hand side of the screen, select *Student Assessment*, then select *Publications*. The documents can be found under *Publications*.)
• Grade 5: descriptive, narrative, and expository
• Grade 7: descriptive, narrative, expository, and persuasive

Arizona: www.azed.gov/standards/AIMS/AIMSSupport.asp
• Grades 3, 4, 5: narrative • Grade 6, 7, 9: persuasive

Connecticut: www.csde.state.ct.us/public/cedar/assessment/cmt/cmt_handbooks.htm
• Grades 3 and 4: narrative • Grades 5 and 6: expository
• Grades 7 and 8: persuasive

Integrating Test Prep into Reading & Writing Workshops © 2011 by Nancy Jennison • Scholastic Teaching Resources

Delaware: www.doe.k12.de.us/aab/sample_items/default.shtml
• Grades reported on Web site for Stand-Alone writing assessment: persuasive

Massachusetts: www.doe.mass.edu/mcas/testitems.html
• Grade 4: narrative • Grade 7: explanatory and/or persuasive

New Hampshire: www.ed.state.nh.gov/instruction/assessment/necap/prephtm
• Grade 3: narrative •Grade 8: persuasive

New Jersey: www.nj.gov/education/assessment/es/sample
• Grade 3–5: speculative (narrative) and expository (explanatory)
• Grades 6–8: persuasive, narrative, and/or expository

New York: www.nysedregents.org
• Grades 4–8: explanatory writing related to the reading passage

Oregon: www.ode.state.or.us/search/page/?id=523
• Grades 4 and 7: narrative, expository, imaginative, and persuasive; students receive a choice of three prompts, each in a different mode.

Tennessee: www.state.tn.us/education/assessment (Click on TCAP Writing Assessment on left column.)
• Grade 5: narrative • Grade 8: expository essay

Washington: www.k12.wa.us/assessment/StateTesting/TestQuestions/Testquestions.aspx
• Grade 4: narrative and expository prompt
• Grade 7: narrative and persuasive prompt

West Virginia:
• Grades 3–8: narrative, descriptive, informative, or persuasive
• Grade 3: descriptive: wvde.state.wv.us/oaa/pdf/WESTEST2 OnlineWriting-ReleasedField-TestedGrade3DescriptiveSample.pdf
• Grade 6: Persuasive: wvde.state.wv.us/oaa/pdf/WESTEST2 OnlineWriting-ReleasedField-TestedGrade6PersuasiveSample.pdf

Wyoming: www.k12.wy.us/SA/Paws/index.asp
• Grade 3: expository letter • Grade 4: personal narrative
• Grade 5: response to literature • Grade 6: fictional narrative
• Grade 7: problem/solution essay • Grade 8: expository essay

Food for Thought

YOUR STATE EXPECTS THAT YOUR STUDENTS HAVE LEARNED CERTAIN WRITING SKILLS. WHY NOT PLAN TO MEET WITH COLLEAGUES TO DISCUSS YOUR STATE WRITING RUBRIC, STATE WRITING STANDARDS, PREVIOUS STATE GENRE TESTS, AND WHAT GENRES MAY APPEAR ON FUTURE STATE TESTS?

This activity will inform your teaching and raise your awareness of what the state expects from your students. Perhaps you and your colleagues could meet at the beginning of the school year.

- Visit your state education Web site, examine your state writing rubric, and list the main writing skills and genres that your students need to know for the state test.

- Based on those genres, think about what writing units of study and mini-lessons you will need to teach. See Chapter 5 for suggestions on how to develop writing units that help prepare your students for state writing tests.

- Study your state test prompts and state standards for writing terms that your state expects your students to know that may appear on the test and may confuse them. List those terms and think of ways to incorporate them in your teaching.

- Based on your students' writing work, what genres, formats, and time demands on the state test will be a challenge for them? See Chapters 5, 7, and 9 for specific writing suggestions.

- Consider when you will conduct your test-prep writing unit. Ideas that you can modify for that unit appear in Chapter 9.

Integrating Test Prep into Reading & Writing Workshops © 2011 by Nancy Jennison • Scholastic Teaching Resources

CHAPTER 3

Authentic Activities That Offer a Strong Foundation for Deeper Thinking and Higher Scores

on't let state tests rob you of your joy of teaching language arts. Authentic reading and writing activities are the heart and soul of teaching. As we continue to maintain "thinking-centered classrooms," we expand our professional knowledge, teaching expertise, and high expectations for all students (Conrad, Matthews, Zimmerman, & Allen, 2008, p. 3).

In contrast, researchers determined that asking students to complete workbook page after workbook page to prepare for state tests resulted in too little time left for real reading and writing activities (Darling-Hammond, 1997; Kohn, 2000). Instead, when we establish meaningful language arts routines at the beginning of the year and build on them throughout the year, we offer students sound language arts practices that help them develop a lifelong love of reading and writing, give them confidence in what they know, and help them show what they know on state tests.

 ## Read How It Worked

Two Teachers Use Their Read-Aloud to Improve Students' Comprehension and Performance on Answering Open-Response Questions

While working on my book, I had the pleasure of conducting research and teaching several lessons in two separate classrooms, one belonging to Melissa Erickson and the other belonging to Stephanie Tesorero, two talented third-grade teachers from Richer Elementary School in Marlborough, Massachusetts. As we worked together, they conducted their read-alouds differently and noticed dramatic improvements in their students' comprehension and attitudes about reading. Melissa and Stephanie implemented strategies and routines suggested by literacy expert Lucy Calkins (2001) that helped their students think, talk, and later write responses that connected to the read-aloud. When teachers think aloud as they read aloud, they clearly demonstrate for students how an expert reader comprehends the text (Tovani, 2000).

Melissa and Stephanie chose *The Hundred Dresses* by Eleanor Estes and *Lavender* by Karen Hesse as strong characterization read-alouds.

- First, they <u>each</u> modeled their own reactions as they paused at strategic points while reading *The Hundred Dresses*. For example, Melissa thought aloud: "Wow, no one even notices when Wanda is absent from school. Why not? Maybe Wanda is really quiet."

- Then, after Melissa continued to model how she thought aloud, she asked her students to speak with their partners about another prompt connected to *The Hundred Dresses*: "It's time to talk to your partner. Why do you think Peggy is treating Wanda like that? Tell your partner what you think and why you think that."

- Once students were very comfortable speaking to partners, on another day, Melissa modeled how to stop and write her ideas on a very large model of a sticky note. After several repetitions of this, she told her students: "Now it is time to stop and write your ideas. How do you think Maddie is feeling right now? Write your ideas in your little memo pad."

- Once students knew how to stop and write down their ideas, both teachers continued to model more challenging characterization prompts. They also asked students to talk to partners, while at other times, they asked students to stop and write their responses.

Melissa and Stephanie explained, "By recalling and discussing parts of the story with peers, children were able to gain a better understanding of the text. We gave the students opportunities to engage in dialogue, and it held them accountable for their responses. Frequent stop-and-write entries on their small memo pads made it easier for them to recall or remember information. The students were really able to explain their thinking not only to one another but also in their writing. With each new entry on their memo pads students showed us they could use the following skills: recall details, sequence events, compare and contrast characters, make inferences, and draw conclusions.

What's so great about this is we can actually see students' progression with each entry in their notebooks. We can go back to the very first stop-and-write entry and see what they were having difficulty with and look at the growth they have made by reading the last entry. We can also help students to improve by matching our teacher modeling to what our students need that was evident on their stop-and write responses. It is very enlightening and also shows the hard work that was put into each entry both by the students and ourselves. The best accomplishment was watching the children transfer these skills to other content areas."

When Melissa and Stephanie asked each student to respond briefly on a little memo pad, "I learned" was an appropriate prompt for the beginning of the text to see if students noticed important details about the story. They expected students to tell information about the characters, plot, and/or setting. In Figure 3.1 notice how Tim told many details about the characters and plot in this very early stop-and-write response.

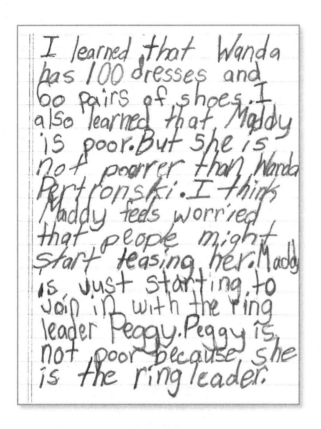

I learned that Wanda has 100 dresses and 60 pairs of shoes. I also learned that Maddy is poor. But she is not poorrer than Wanda Pertronski. I think Maddy feels worried that people might start teasing her. Maddy is just starting to join in with the ring leader Peggy. Peggy is not poor because she is the ring leader.

Figure 3.1

Tim noticed important details and began to make inferences about *The Hundred Dresses* in a beginning-of-the-book entry.

Melissa and Stephanie noted the students' reading skills that appeared in the stop-and-write responses. Note the inferential thinking apparent in Jamie's response (see Figure 3.2), and how Jill drew a conclusion, made a prediction, and asked a question (see Figure 3.3). The teachers' modeling of how to write responses always pushed the students to deeper thinking.

Comprehension improved when Melissa modeled "talking the text talk" with questions such as the following: "How do you think Maddie is feeling now? Be sure to explain your ideas by using evidence from the text to prove that you are right." Students stated their opinions about the text, but needed to ground their opinions in text talk or text evidence. That is, students learned how to support and prove their ideas by referring to the text. Ramon talked the text talk as he gave his opinion, referred to the text, predicted, and showed deeper, insightful thinking about Maddie possibly losing Peggy's friendship and defending others from bullies (see Figure 3.4).

Melissa and Stephanie developed routines during their study of fiction and characterization that strengthened students' comprehension: "When we worked on the characterization and fiction study, we asked students important questions to activate their prior knowledge: 'I am going to read you a new story, so what important parts of a story will you listen for first?' By doing this, we strengthened students' understanding of story schema and helped their comprehension as well."

Integrating Test Prep into Reading & Writing Workshops © 2011 by Nancy Jennison • Scholastic Teaching Resources

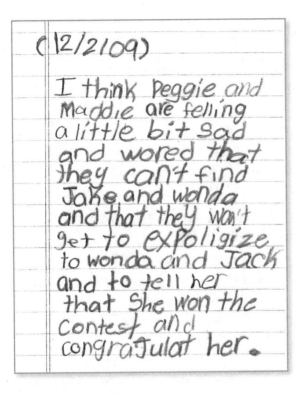

(12/2/09)

I think Peggie and Maddie are felling a little bit sad and wored that they can't find Jake and wonda and that they won't get to expoligize to wonda and Jack and to tell her that she won the contest and congrajulat her.

Figure 3.2

Jamie gave her opinion and referred back to the text to explain her thinking.

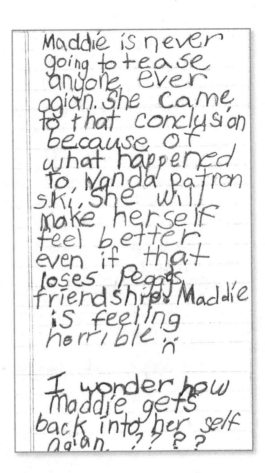

Maddie is never going to tease anyone ever agian. She came to that conclusion because of what happened to Wanda patron ski. She will make herself feel better even if that loses Peggs friendship. Maddie is feeling horrible n

I wonder how Maddie gets back into her self agian ??? ?

Figure 3.3

Jill revealed deeper thinking as she drew a conclusion, made a prediction, and asked a question.

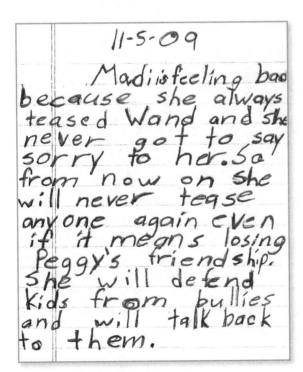

11-5-09

Madi is feeling bad because she always teased Wand and she never got to say sorry to her. So from now on she will never tease any one again even if it means losing Peggy's friendship. She will defend kids from bullies and will talk back to them.

Figure 3.4

Ramon "talked the text talk" in *The Hundred Dresses.*

Weekly Open-Ended Questions Related to the Read-Aloud Strengthen Students' Responses on State Tests

It is vital that we integrate deeper thinking routinely into regular instruction throughout the year. Reading experts Dr. Douglas Fisher and Dr. Nancy Frey advocate that we embed aspects of the state test into best practice instruction. When teachers know what their state test expects students to know, and they use authentic teaching activities to strengthen those skills, students develop the skills and stamina that they need to score well on state tests (2009). One way to integrate test prep is by asking students to do a weekly response related to your read-aloud to strengthen their comprehension, elaboration, and deeper thinking. (This response does not always have to be written, and suggestions follow that show other ways of responding.)

When Melissa and Stephanie began to embed questions into their read-aloud, they modeled each type of response for students. First they showed students how to respond orally to questions from the read-aloud. Students turned and spoke to read-aloud partners. Once students were comfortable with this, the teachers modeled how to write a response, then asked students to pause and write a response in a tiny memo book. Later, students wrote longer responses in their readers' notebooks. Each week, the teachers made their questions match their teaching points and gradually included more state-test-like open-ended questions.

> *Example of an easier question:* How did Maddie change in the story? Prove your ideas by telling about things that happened to her in the story.

> *Example of a harder question:* How does Maddie change in the story? What influenced those changes? Some readers may feel that characters have influenced the changes, but others may feel that events changed Maddie. What is your opinion?

Melissa and Stephanie linked students' understanding of fiction to authentic test prep for the open-response questions on the state test. They asked students to answer a demand open-response question from the read-aloud *Lavender,* by Karen Hesse. (I am borrowing the term "demand" from work done at the Teachers College Reading and Writing Project.) The teachers and I asked students to respond to an open-response question, but we did not coach them while they wrote the answer. We wanted to use this as a baseline assessment, so all students answered the question independently.

Integrating Test Prep into Reading & Writing Workshops © 2011 by Nancy Jennison • Scholastic Teaching Resources

Teachers' Knowledge of Typical State Reading Test Questions is an Asset

The state of Massachusetts often integrates characterization work into open-response questions on its state reading test. Previously released third-grade samples included numerous questions on characters, such as how characters' actions revealed what they were like and how to compare two characters. Consequently, Melissa and Stephanie worked on character development connected to the read-aloud.

Their question for the baseline assessment on character relationships, based on the read-aloud *Lavender*, was very appropriate for their third-graders and prepared students for questions on the state reading test: *Describe the relationship between Aunt Alix and Codie. Use details from the text to support your answer.* (Later, during read-aloud work, they gradually created more difficult open-response questions.)

DIFFERENTIATION ACTIVITIES THAT IMPROVE STUDENTS' COMPREHENSION

I assessed student responses for both classes and grouped students according to areas of difficulty (see Figure 3.5 below). This grouping makes it easy to see how to differentiate instruction to help students through follow-up strategy lessons and read-aloud teacher modeling, small-group coaching, and individual conferring.

Follow-Up Needed For Baseline Open-Response Assessment

Cannot answer the question or give an opinion	Confuses the characters	Needs proof	Needs to explain	Needs closing sentence
Jim **José** **Erik** **Billy**	**José** Ida **Billy**	Ana Peter Jill **Jim** Sean **José** **Erik** Gina **Billy**	Peter Celia Jill Ramon **Jim** Sean **José** **Erik** Gina Ida Tim **Billy**	Joanna

Figure 3.5

This follow-up from our baseline assessment of one class shows which skills students need and helped us plan follow-up mini-lessons. I typed the names of students who needed small-group coaching in bold. (All names are pseudonyms.)

The strategy lesson I designed for Stephanie and Melissa's classes introduced two tools—the I ROPE Hamburger, and My Answer Checklist—that turned out to be tremendously helpful to students. Melissa and Stephanie commented, "When practicing with the I ROPE Hamburger model, we could see how it provided the students with more structure when answering any kind of open-response question."

How to Improve Students' Open-Ended Responses to the Read-Aloud

Follow-Up Comprehension Lesson for Grade 3

Materials:

■ My Answer Checklist chart (page 53)

■ The I ROPE Hamburger (Figure 3.6)

■ Students' responses to open-response question

■ Teachers' response to open-response question

■ Follow-Up Needed for Baseline Open-Response Assessment Chart (Figure 3.5)

(I credit Lucy Calkins and the Teachers College Reading and Writing Project for the following terms used in the lesson: CONNECTION, TEACHING, ACTIVE ENGAGEMENT, and LINK.)

▶ Connection:
Link to past work, name the teaching point, and tell how it will help students.

"I was excited to read your answers to your open-response question about *Lavender.* I think that you had some important things to say about the story. One thing that I noticed, though, is that sometimes it was hard for me to understand your ideas. So today I am going to show you two charts that will help you: My Answer Checklist chart and the I ROPE Hamburger. You can use these charts whenever you write an answer to an open-response question. You will be amazed at how much easier it will be to show your wonderful thinking when you use the charts."

▶ Teaching:
Demonstrate for students.

"So watch me as I reread the question that you answered: *Describe the relationship between Aunt Alix and Codie. Use details from the text to support your answer.* First, I will show you how I wrote my answer. Watch closely, because soon you will be revising what you wrote, and this will help you. So I will read My Answer Checklist chart. This is my checklist of what to do:

Integrating Test Prep into Reading & Writing Workshops © 2011 by Nancy Jennison • Scholastic Teaching Resources

> **My Answer Checklist**
>
> ☑ **Opinion:** Tell what I think.
>
> ☑ **Proof:** Quote from the text or talk about the text in my own words.
>
> ☑ **Explain:** Explain how my proof fits my opinion.

So when I write my answer, it is easy.

First, I give my opinion when I tell what I think.

Second, I give proof with a quote from the text or by talking about the text in my own words.

Third, I explain how my proof fits my opinion.

Look at how the I ROPE Hamburger helps me to do that. We call it I ROPE, because each letter in ROPE stands for something that you do:

R = **R**ead the Question

O = Give your **O**pinion.

P = Give your **P**roof.

E = **E**xplain how your proof fits your opinion."

(I ROPE is a chart that I developed and refined with many colleagues, while I was a literacy staff developer in Tenafly, New Jersey. I ROPE signifies that students can **rope the answer** and use the chart to help them write a powerful answer. This chart contains choices of words that they will use to organize parts of their answer. After students compose their answer, they use the I ROPE Hamburger as a check to make sure that they have answered the question completely.)

"Now, let's study how I wrote my answer:

I *think* that Aunt Alix and Codie have a loving relationship *because* they spend time together hugging each other. <u>I read,</u> "Aunt Alix holds me close against her big, hard belly where the baby is growing." Then, Codie tried to hug Aunt Alix back. <u>So, that shows</u> their relationship is loving, because they are happy to be very near each other. I <u>learned</u> how much they care."

I then showed students how I used the I ROPE Hamburger to write each sentence. I demonstrated how I quoted the exact text from pages 6 and 8 of *Lavender*. I underlined key words that I used from the I ROPE Hamburger to make the different sections of the answer clear to students. Finally, I showed how the answer included the three sections in the My Answer Checklist chart.

Figure 3.6

The I ROPE Hamburger helps students organize their thinking and answer an open-response question completely.

The I ROPE Hamburger

OPINION

I think _____.

(character's name) is _____.

In my opinion, _____.

PROOF

Because _____.

In the text it says _____.

The story says _____.

I read _____.

EXPLAIN

So, that shows _____.

Therefore, _____.

In other words, _____.

ADD INSIGHT!

I learned _____.

Now I realize _____.

I used to think _____, but now I think _____.

 Remember to add your BRILLIANT INSIGHTS!

✓ Sum Up Teaching Points:

"Remember that when we look at the My Answer Checklist chart, first we tell the opinion, then we give proof, and then we explain. Now let's review how we use the I ROPE Hamburger, because it helps us to know what to say . . ."

▶ Active Engagement:
Have students turn and talk to practice what you modeled.

✓ ROPE the teacher's answer:

"Now it is your turn to help me. I will ROPE my answer. That means I'll label each part of it. As I do this, I want you to tell me one of four things about each sentence: that the sentence is an opinion, that it is proof that is a quote from the text, that it is proof from the text that is given in my own words, or that it is an explanation." I did not mention insight since I was working with third graders, and they were just learning this strategy. "You will work with your group to decide." I divided the students into four groups: <u>O</u>pinion, <u>P</u>roof that is a quote, <u>P</u>roof that is in my own words, and <u>E</u>xplanation. "Raise your hand if the sentence matches what your group is looking for." (Remember that the <u>R</u> in Rope stands for <u>R</u>ead the question.)

Based on the group's responses, I labeled each part of my answer as shown below:

O (Opinion)	<u>I think</u> that Aunt Alix and Codie have a loving relationship,
P (Proof/own words)	<u>because</u> they spend time together hugging each other.
P (Proof/quote)	<u>I read</u>, "Aunt Alix holds me close against her big, hard belly where the baby is growing."
P (Proof/own words)	Then, Codie tried to hug Aunt Alix back.
E (Explain)	<u>So, that shows</u> their relationship is loving, because they are happy to be very near each other.
E (Explain)	<u>I learned</u> how much they care.

✓ Write an answer as a class:

"Now it is your turn again to help me write another answer to the question. I want you and your partner to have an opinion that you can give me when I ask you the same question. Your opinion has to be different from what you just saw me write about. Here is the question again: *Describe the relationship between Aunt Alix and Codie. Use details from the text to support your answer.*

"Remember, when you start your answer by stating your opinion, use some of the words from the question to help you state it. You might say, 'I think that Aunt Alix and Codie . . .' and then you tell what you think about their relationship, because that was what was mentioned in the question. Turn and speak to your partner."

I began to write the class response: First, I wrote an opinion statement about Aunt Alix and Codie's relationship that one partnership shared, and then I continued to compose the rest of the response with the class. We used the I ROPE Hamburger for prompts of what to say and asked students to turn and speak to a partner to continue to tell me how to write the answer.

✓ ROPE the class answer:

After we wrote a complete answer as a class, students ROPEd that answer. Once again, they quickly labeled it in their same ROPE groups, as I read aloud each sentence and then wrote their labels on the class response.

✓ Sum up teaching points:

"So, students, we have used My Answer Checklist chart to help you know what should go into an answer. First, the opinion: I tell what I think; second, the proof: a quote from the text, or proof: talk about the text in my own words; and third, explain: explain how my proof fits my opinion.

"Then we used the words in the question to help us start our answer. Next we used the I ROPE Hamburger so we knew which words to use to give an opinion, proof, and an explanation."

▶ Link:
Link the lesson to students' work of the day.

"Now it is your turn. Your job is to read over the answer you wrote to the open-response question about Codie and Aunt Alix's relationship and then think about how you can make your answer better. Rewrite your first answer so that it is much stronger. You can use the My Answer Checklist chart and the I ROPE Hamburger chart to help you. Does anyone have any questions? I will be meeting with some of you in a group while you are working on rewriting your answer. If you finish early, answer the same question with a different opinion."

Students in Melissa Erickson's third-grade class worked in groups to ROPE my answer. I coached the four groups: opinion, proof that is a quote, proof that is in your own words, and explanation.

Integrating Test Prep into Reading & Writing Workshops © 2011 by Nancy Jennison • Scholastic Teaching Resources

Successful Time-Saving Strategies for Small-Group Coaching Sessions

Key Question: What were the other students in Stephanie's class doing while I met with a small group? They were working at their seats and revising their answers to the open-response question that they answered on the demand test.

After I modeled the above lesson, I asked four students to join me for a small-group coaching session. I selected those four students because their names appeared most often on the follow-up chart (see Figure 3.5), which indicated they needed the most support.

The students brought their response notebooks and a pencil when they met with me (the fourth student was meeting with a specialist). I used a coaching format designed by Teachers College Staff Developer Melanie Brown. This is a great format for small-group coaching, especially when time is limited.

■ **Begin the session with a specific compliment for each student about something he or she did well, or almost did well.**

I began the coaching with specific compliments for each student on their written responses. For example, I told Billy, "You know a lot about the story, Billy. You know that Codie made a quilt for her Aunt Alix." (I emphasized the word *her*, since Billy thought that the character Codie was a boy.) While I complimented each student, I asked others in the group to reread the beginning of their answers with an eye toward how the I ROPE Hamburger could help them, and then start to revise their answers.

Tips for Getting Started With Small-Group Coaching

■ While you are meeting with your coaching group, give the rest of your class important work related to your teaching point.

■ Begin by asking your students who need similar learning support to meet you in a small group.

■ Work with a small number (perhaps two students), until you can speed up as you move from one student to another.

■ Once your speed improves, try to limit your group size to no more than five students.

■ Try to limit your coaching to no more than ten minutes with each group.

- **Demonstrate your teaching point with the group. Then coach each student, and expect that students will work on the teaching point while you quickly move to the next student.**

After I gave a quick, specific compliment, I began my first teaching point. It was how to reread the open-ended question and use the I ROPE Hamburger to help each student form an opinion about the answer and organize a response. I asked each student to reread the question, use the prompts on the I ROPE Hamburger chart with me, and decide how each would begin. Everyone wanted to use "I think." I showed them how to use part of the question in their answer, along with "I think." (Melissa Erickson told her students to be a "question thief" and use some of the words in the question in their answer. I thought that was an excellent idea.) While other students reread their answer and tried to figure out how the I ROPE Hamburger could help them, I continued to coach one student at a time in this manner: "Billy, what do you think about the relationship between Codie and Aunt Alix? Tell me." Then, to help Billy as he repeated some of the words from the question in his answer, I pointed to the I ROPE Hamburger chart and prompted, "I think . . . I think that Aunt Alix and Codie . . ." Next, Billy told me his thought, "I think that Aunt Alix and Codie have a good relationship." I was thrilled and said to him, "Wonderful! Write that in your reading notebook, and I will be right back to you."

- **Other students benefit as they hear your quick coaching while they are working on their own revision since they all have similar issues.**

I then coached the next student in the group in a similar fashion and moved to the next student. By the time all the students had worked with me just saying an opinion aloud and then writing it on their own, I was back to Billy again, and now we were on the next part of the answer—the proof. Once again, I moved from student to student while the other two students finished writing the beginning of their response and worked on the proof. Then, after students finished proving their opinions, I coached them about how to use the I ROPE Hamburger to write the explain section until the lunch bell rang.

- **Compliment the students again on their work in the conference and summarize the teaching points at the end of the coaching session.**

Stephanie and I were amazed at the students' brilliant responses. I gave quick compliments to each and summarized the teaching point: "Use part of the question in your answer and look at the prompts in the I ROPE Hamburger to help you with writing your answer." The entire coaching session lasted only eight minutes, and that was deliberate. By coaching quickly while I move from one student to another, I ensure that all students keep working while I work one-on-one with individuals.

Integrating Test Prep into Reading & Writing Workshops © 2011 by Nancy Jennison • Scholastic Teaching Resources

Billy's answers appear in Figures 3.7 and 3.8. Figure 3.7 shows Billy's Demand Baseline Response, which indicates that his response to the question was off topic and that he was confused about whether the character Codie is a boy or a girl. In the answer in Figure 3.8, Billy used the I ROPE Hamburger to organize his thoughts, and he also showed insightful thinking by predicting at the end of his answer.

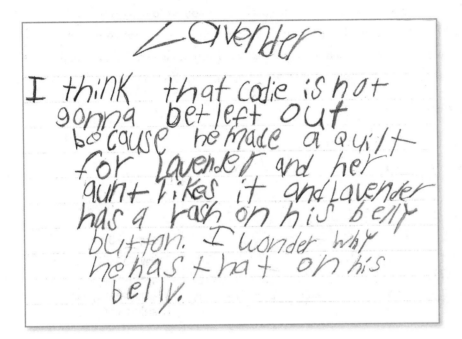

Figure 3.7

Billy showed confusion about the main character and was off topic in his response.

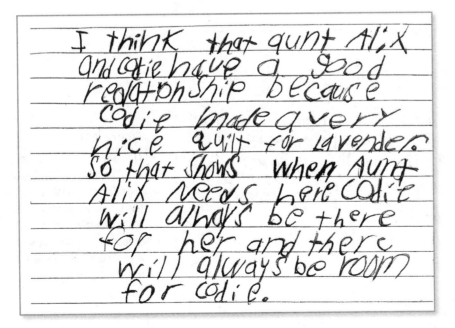

Figure 3.8

After an eight-minute small-group coaching session, Billy wrote a much clearer response that also was on topic. In addition, he made a relevant prediction that showed insightful thinking.

■ **Keep a record of each student's progress.**

In our small-group coaching sessions with third-graders, we recorded each student's progress in two ways: our specific compliments that began the conference and comments about our work with each student.

I also taught a similar lesson to Melissa's class and then met with a group of four students who needed extra support. After a six-minute coaching session, note what Ray did. In the Demand Baseline Response, he did not answer the question and just referred to events in the text. However, in the after-coaching response, Ray clearly answered the question by using the I ROPE Hamburger as a guide for how to structure his response. See Figures 3.9 and 3.10.

> 1/28/09
>
> The relationship between Aunt Alex and codie is they are both making quilts for Lavender. When Aunt Alex knows the words on the radio they make words up.

Figure 3.9

Ray did not answer the question and gave details about the story that did not make sense.

> I think Aunt Alex and codie have a good relationship because they like to make quilts and sing together. So, that shows they have a good relationship. I learned they feel happy happy together.

Figure 3.10

After a coaching session, Ray answered the question clearly and referred to events in the text to support his opinions. In his last sentence, he showed deeper thinking when he said more about how the characters feel about being together.

Integrating Test Prep into Reading & Writing Workshops © 2011 by Nancy Jennison • Scholastic Teaching Resources

A Rubric to Improve Students' Comprehension and Their Answers to Open-Response Questions in Science, Social Studies, and Reading

Year after year in my test-prep work, I have found that when I take the time to ask students to revise their open-ended responses, that is when their responses show dramatic improvements, and that is when their scores go higher and higher. Donna Klein, a fifth-grade teacher from Mackay School in Tenafly, New Jersey, showed her students how to use the I ROPE Hamburger (Figure 3.6) as a tool to revise their responses. The next step was to help Donna create a tool her students could use to score their routine responses throughout the year. Donna and I developed the Levels of Responses Rubric (see Figure 3.13). We designed it to match the New Jersey scoring guide for open-response questions, but we made our levels more difficult. This is how we created our own fifth-grade rubric that students used to score their open-ended responses throughout the year in science, social studies, and reading.

Step 1: Examine your state test's rubric for open-response questions.

In this case, we examined the State of New Jersey's rubric.

Step 2: Create a rubric including language that students understand that is similar to the components of the state rubric.

We needed to use terms to describe each level that the fifth-grade students understood. First, we thought of where the fifth-grade students were in terms of their comprehension.

Donna decided to make the rubric more challenging than the State of New Jersey's open-response rubric, since her students had already done extensive comprehension work with the read-aloud and in independent reading. You may want to make your class's rubric more challenging than your state rubric, too.

Donna used this rubric to score open-ended questions related to read-alouds and to content articles for reading, science, and social studies. The Levels of Responses Rubric applied to the three subject areas and helped Donna confer with students about their open-ended answers. She expected students to dramatically improve when they revised their answers. Revising answers is the important link that helps students transfer what they learn from regular curriculum open-ended questions to those used in state tests.

 ## Read How It Worked

Use Conferring to Improve Students' Open-Ended Response Scores and Improve Their Deep Thinking

Donna Klein has mastered the art of conferring with fifth-grade students to increase scores on their open-ended questions. Students' responses to one weekly open-ended question related to the curriculum improved dramatically when Donna took just a few minutes to confer with them. It was just the right scaffolding that they needed. In this case, Donna's question linked to her science curriculum, since her students had studied the environment.

Her students read "Warming Up" by Paul Coco, an article about global warming from Scholastic's *Teaching Text Structures: A Key to Nonfiction Reading Success*. Then Donna posed the following question: *Do you think global warming is responsible for causing the ice in the Arctic and Antarctic to melt? Be sure to use information from the article to support your opinions.*

Donna's work with one of her fifth-grade students, Rachel, appears on pages 64–65 in Figure 3.11 and Figure 3.12. She began the conference with a compliment.

Teacher (T): Rachel, it looks like you wrote a lot about the topic. You must care about global warming.

Student (S): Yes, Mrs. Klein, I want to stop it.

T: That is wonderful! Rachel, what do you think about the way you wrote your response? Why don't you read over what you wrote and tell me your thoughts about your response.

S: My examples didn't seem to fit with the text. And then, what I said about my own life doesn't seem to go with the question.

T: Wow, Rachel, you really thought about your answer and what you need to do to fix it. If you look at the I ROPE Hamburger, the first thing to do, after you read the question, is to state your opinion. What is your opinion? Do you think that global warming is responsible for causing the ice in the Arctic and Antarctic to melt?

S: I think that global warming is the main reason why the ice is melting.

T: You are off to a great start. Now let's look at the I ROPE Hamburger again. Can you see that you need proof? So now you will find something in the article that supports your thinking and also defines what global warming is.

S: The text said, "Global Warming is a gradual rise in the Earth's temperatures."

T: Can you explain your thinking? Tell why it backs you up. Explain it by telling what it means to you.

S: When temperatures rise, things start to melt. Ice has already started to melt. As humans, we use so much gas and electricity! We have been adding to global warming.

T: Rachel, this sounds much better! Sometimes it is not enough just to use only one quote from the text. You will need to keep going back to the article "Warming Up" to make sure that you are including all of the right information to support your opinion. Why don't you take a minute, read the article again, and mark anything else that supports your opinion.

(Rachel found two more sections to add to make her response stronger.)

T: Go back to your original and see if there are any other parts that do not fit in your answer.

S: Well, I should get rid of that section about going to the zoo.

T: That makes a lot of sense, Rachel. What else would you change?

S: I want to add my new thinking about how I could make a difference with global warming.

T: What could you do to revise your answer on your own?

S: I will read my old answer, use ROPE, go back to the text for evidence, explain it, and add my own thoughts.

T: So you are doing a great job! I know that you can revise your answer on your own now.

Figure 3.11

Rachel gave an opinion, but did not support it with evidence from the text. Her connections caused confusion. Her answer lacked clarity and organization.

Do you think that Global Warming is responsible for causing the ice in the Arctic and Antarctic to melt? Be sure to use information from the article to support your opinions.

I think that Global Warming is responsible for causing the ice in the Artic Antartic to melt. *It reminds me of the time when I went to the zoo. I saw the Polar bears in captivte, and I felt discourged and wanted to help recycle a little more. I started bringing a reusable snack container instead of plastic bags.

In the text it says "Global Warming has melted and area the size of Texas and Arizona combined!" I learned that Global Warming has caused so much damage that their is so much Ice melting.*Also when I was little their was this heat wave that was like 99° hot and I had to stay inside for the whole day I would pass out if went out side. Global Warming has affected humans as well and for instance "Polar Bears get food and fish, seals, from the ice. Seals come on Ice to give birth." That tells me that the Animals whole life is on Ice and in the Arctic or Antartic. And I thinks Gibbal warming is causing this.

After reading this article I decided that instead of using another sheet of paper I would just use the back. Also the article influenced me to start recycling a little more, so in my classroom we have paper recycling and plastic recycling. I hope the recycling helps stop Global Warming.

* in animals habitat

Integrating Test Prep into Reading & Writing Workshops © 2011 by Nancy Jennison • Scholastic Teaching Resources

> I think that Global Warming is the main reason why the ice in the Arctic and Antarctic is melting, "Since Global Warming is a gradual rise in the Earth's temperature's." I also read in the text "Acording to a new report called the Arctic Climate Impact Assement (ACIA), Arctic tempatures have risen up to seven degrees over the past 50 years!" When temperatures rise things start to melt, ice has already started to melt and "Scientists believe that the Arctic which has ice year round, could be ice-free during the summers in about 100 years." I feel responsible because as humans we use so much gas and electricity, that we don't know how much we actually have been contributing to the earth's atmosphere. We have been adding to Global Warming, and as a result of that, ice is melting, polar bears and seals etc. are losing their habitat. After I read this article I will be more cautious about my contribution to global warming, for instance in my classroom we recycle plastic and paper, And I know I can do more to prevent Global Warming.

Figure 3.12

Rachel rewrote her answer after conferring with her teacher. Her second answer was much more organized, it used proof from the text, explained her thinking, and showed insight.

Then we recapped what we talked about:

- Use evidence from the article to support your opinion.
- Explain your thinking about why the evidence fits.
- Elaborate to make sure that you are making your readers understand your thinking.

Rachel revised part of her response during our conference and the rest of it on her own. Figure 3.11 shows her original response, and Figure 3.12 shows her revised answer.

I feel Rachel improved from a Level Two to a beginning Level Four in the rubric (see Figure 3.13 on page 66). In her revised answer, Rachel showed that she understood the question, used quotes that strengthened her opinion, gave clear explanations, and added insight. She talked about how humans do not even know about how they contribute to global warming, which is sophisticated thinking. Overall, her response was organized, cohesive, fluid, and on topic. It made more sense and was a stronger answer.

Figure 3.13

Grade 5 Levels of Responses Rubric

to Score Open-Response Questions in Reading, Science, or Social Studies

Level One:

The student <u>did not understand</u> how to answer the question. The student either totally forgot about text evidence or just mentioned the text with no specific evidence. The student also did not explain his/her thinking.

Level Two:

The student only understood <u>part</u> of what the question asked. The student struggled with using text quotes and referrals to support ideas. For example, the student may have used the wrong quote. Consequently, the student's explanation wasn't quite right.

Level Three:

The student <u>understood</u> what the question asked and answered all parts of the question. In addition, the student included appropriate text quotes and referrals that supported his or her ideas. However, the student included only part of the explanation about why the quotes and referrals fit. Level Three answers do not have enough explanations and specific details.

Level Four:

The student <u>understood everything</u> that the question asked and answered all parts of the question. In addition, the student included appropriate text quotes and referrals as text evidence to support ideas. The student used very specific information and very clear explanations to support all opinions and ideas and also included unusual insightful thinking. Level Four answers are complete in every way.

Integrating Test Prep into Reading & Writing Workshops © 2011 by Nancy Jennison • Scholastic Teaching Resources

Strengthening Students' Comprehension in the Content Area

Create open-ended questions that link to your social studies or science curriculum and consider doing this weekly.

Examples of Actual Open-Ended Questions for Science

Topic	Open-Response Question Example
The Solar System	As we look at the shape of the moon, its shape appears to change from day to day. Explain if the moon's shape is really changing. Then describe the phases of the moon. Use information from the article to help you.
Batteries	Suppose you had to give a report to your class on this passage. In your report be sure to include the following: • Directions on how to make either a lemon battery or a vinegar battery • How this homemade "wet" battery compares to a "dry" battery (Thanks to Joan Shayne from Smith School for her help with this question.)
Chemical Reactions	Think like a scientist. Design an experiment to show why the colored comic book pages near the window changed color. Be sure to use information from the text to support your ideas.
Food Chains	Explain how a meadow food chain works. Use information from the article to support your ideas.
The Environment	Southern California, an area long plagued by droughts, made major changes in saving water in the 1990s. Write about how Southern Californians fought the drought and give your opinion on which water conservation measures you think would work the best in our state. Use information from the text to support your opinions.
Native Americans	Do you think that the Cherokee tribe has been a resourceful nation? Use information from the text to support your opinions.
Women's Suffrage	If you were a historian, would you agree that Wyoming was a leader in the United States in supporting women's rights? Cite at least two reasons to support your opinion. Use evidence from the text to support your ideas.
The Explorers	Do you think that Matthew Henson and Robert Perry are heroes? Be sure to give at least three reasons in your response. Use information from the text to support your opinion.
Forefathers	Explain details and events that prove that Abraham Lincoln was really honest. Refer back to the text to support your ideas.

How Games Increase Students' Comprehension and Insightful Thinking

Even though we routinely constructed open-response questions related to our read-alouds and also used them in science and social studies, we found we still needed to do more to help students think insightfully. Thinking insightfully gives students higher scores on open-ended and constructed responses on the state test. These questions usually involve inferential thinking. However, Chris Tovani, an adolescent-comprehension specialist and author, states that readers who need more support have difficulty with answering inferential questions, since they think that answers to all questions are directly located in the text. In addition, all students need to learn that inferential thinking demands that they use an appropriate amount of prior knowledge in conjunction with textual evidence (Tovani, 2000). One can see why all of this is confusing for students.

State tests expect students to think of the meaning of the reading passage in innovative ways that extend their thinking. Brain research points to the effectiveness of students' discussing ideas to expand their understanding and consider other viewpoints.

Tips on How to Help Students Who Have Limited Prior Knowledge About a Topic

When encountering a topic that is almost completely unfamiliar, students often lose confidence, but there are a few things that they can ask themselves whenever they feel they have no prior knowledge of a topic. If asked to write a story about sailing on the ocean, students could ask themselves the following questions:

■ Have I ever been to the ocean? What was it like?

■ Have I noticed sailboats or other boats on the ocean?

■ Have I seen a movie or TV show or pictures about boats and the ocean?

■ Have I ever heard or read a book that mentioned the ocean or sailing on the ocean?

■ Have I ever heard people talking about their experiences on a boat on the ocean? How about sailing on the ocean?

■ If the answer is no to all these questions: What do I think of when I imagine sailing on the ocean?

However, experts report that although students need guided practice, the brain pays more attention to novel stimuli (Fisher, Frey, & Lapp, 2009). I developed an activity called Minds on Fire Thinking that provides students with the novel stimuli that motivates them, improves their insightful thinking with read-alouds and independent reading, and prepares them to think more deeply when they encounter open-ended questions on state reading tests. (I am borrowing the term "Minds on Fire" from work done at the Teachers College Reading and Writing Project.)

MINDS ON FIRE: HOW TO HELP YOUR STUDENTS DEVELOP INSIGHTFUL THINKING

In New Jersey, the key to earning the highest score on open-ended questions is to demonstrate deep thinking. How do you make insightful thinking concrete for students?

Step 1: Ask an open-ended question connected to your read-aloud.

As fifth-grade teacher, Donna Klein, read *The Hundred Dresses*, she asked, "Why was Maddie bothered when Peggy asked Wanda how many dresses and shoes she owned?"

Step 2: Write two student-like responses to share: one that is insightful and one that isn't.

Write your own responses to match your own grade level. Here is an example for *The Hundred Dresses* question.

Answer 1 (lacking insight):

Maddie was upset because she felt embarrassed. She wished that Peggy would stop teasing Wanda. Peggy should have stopped teasing Wanda, because Wanda didn't like it. I don't like to be teased either. I wish that Peggy would stop teasing Wanda. Teasing is mean and should be stopped. At my school, we have a bullying program, but it doesn't always work. Once I was bullied by a kid in my class, and I didn't want to go to school. I don't like bullies.

Answer 2 (containing insight):

Maddie was bothered because she felt embarrassed and scared. She knew that Wanda was poor and didn't have many clothes. Maddie didn't have a lot of clothes either. She wished she had better clothes. She was afraid that Peggy and the group that teased Wanda might also tease her. I think she was scared that Peggy would make fun of her because of her clothes. If that happened, Maddie knew Peggy would not be her friend anymore, and Peggy was popular. So, then the other girls probably wouldn't like Maddie either. Maddie wanted Peggy to stop picking on Wanda, because Peggy knew she might get picked on next, and she didn't want that to happen.

Step 3: Share both responses with students and demonstrate why one shows Minds on Fire Thinking.

For several days, use the well-written, insightful response to demonstrate the qualities of Minds on Fire Thinking. Each day, demonstrate another characteristic of Minds on Fire Thinking that appears in this version. Add that new characteristic to a Minds on Fire Thinking chart, so that students see a cumulative list of strategies for adding insight to their responses. Then ask students to copy the list into their Readers' Notebooks to use as a reference that helps them write more insightful responses.

Here is an example of what Donna Klein's fifth-grade class and I developed:

Minds On Fire Thinking

✔ Say what you have figured out about the text on your own.

✔ Push yourself to think differently about details and information from the text.

✔ Compare two things or people to explain your thinking.

✔ Put your feelings into the answer to show how your insight affected you.

✔ Say more to have a complete explanation, but don't repeat yourself.

✔ Think about what you already know in your own life to help you with making the insight.

✔ Vary your sentence lengths as you are adding your smart thinking. This is one way to make the insight more noticeable.

✔ Sum up your thinking at the end of your response or at the end of each part of the response.
   Examples: Say, "I learned; This makes me think; I realize; In conclusion; or However."

✔ Use a "Fireworks Ending" that really packs a powerful punch at the end of your response because of your insight.

Step 4: Once students know what Minds on Fire Thinking is, play Go for the Gold.

After students understand how to play Go for the Gold, play the Minds on Fire game on page 72.

Directions for Playing the Go for the Gold Game

Materials:

- Signs: Gold—Level 4; Silver—Level 3; Bronze—Level 2; Copper—Level 1
- Open-ended question on a whiteboard or chalkboard
- sheet of paper for each cooperative group of students
- Your class Levels of Responses Rubric (See Figure 3.13 for a sample.)
- The I ROPE Hamburger (See Figure 3.6.)
- sticky notes

Procedure:

- Divide your class into four teams.
- Make sure that your class is familiar with the Levels of Responses Rubric and the I ROPE Hamburger.
- Ask an open-ended question from the read-aloud or from a text that your students have read. (Each team receives the same question.)

Round 1

- Ask each team of students to work together to answer the question. One person from each team writes its answer on a sheet of paper.
- Each of the teams selects what points they want to achieve: gold, silver, bronze, or copper; for example: "Team One is going for the Gold—Level 4."
- Move from team to team helping with management as students work together to answer the question.
- Each team tells the class what points it wants to achieve: "We're going for a Silver— 3 points." Next, team members share their answer to the open-ended question.
- The rest of the students and the teacher score each response on sticky notes, holding up a note that shows the rating 4, 3, 2, or 1. Classmates must give specific reasons for their scores, and they also must jot notes on another sticky note for how team members can increase their score. Classmates share their feedback.

Round 2

- Each team reads the suggestions from classmates for how to raise its score. The team members revise their response, present it again, and classmates rescore it.

Directions for Playing the Minds on Fire Thinking Game

Materials:

- A question connected to the read-aloud that will stretch students' thinking

- A chart showing Minds on Fire Thinking Strategies

- 4 beanbags, or another type of bag, labeled as follows:
  - O for **O**pinion
  - P for **P**roof
  - E for **E**xplain
  - *flames* for Minds on Fire

Procedure:

- Ask another question related to the read-aloud, and toss the O beanbag. The student who catches it gives an opinion that answers the question.

- Then throw the P beanbag. The catcher—the P student—refers to the text for proof to support the other student's opinion and, using his or her own words, recounts some language from the text to support that opinion. Of course, the student could quote directly from the text if he or she recalls a quote.

Alan, a fifth-grade student, gave an insightful answer in the Minds on Fire game to the delight of his classmate Megan. Teachers Christie Mortara and Arnold Almaguer from Mackay School in Tenafly, New Jersey, planned the activity and used plastic bottles instead of beanbags and red ribbons that signified Minds on Fire flames.

- Next, throw the E beanbag. The E student explains what the quote or referral means and how it fits the opinion.

- Finally, throw the beanbag representing Minds on Fire. The student who catches it has to respond to the question, using one of the strategies on the Minds on Fire strategies chart. Each time the students hear thinking that qualifies for Minds on Fire, they all call out "That's HOT!" Then they jump up and down and turn around.

Take a picture of the student who made a Minds on Fire answer, and post the photo and his or her response on a Minds on Fire bulletin board.

Food for Thought

▼

CUSTOM-DESIGN OPEN-RESPONSE QUESTIONS THAT LINK TO YOUR CURRICULUM AND HELP IMPROVE YOUR READING TEST SCORES. WHY NOT CONSIDER INTEGRATING OPEN-ENDED QUESTIONS ACROSS YOUR CURRICULUM?

- Study the open-ended questions that appear in released samples of your state test.

- Follow the suggestions in this chapter to develop a Levels of Responses Rubric (page 66) for open-ended questions.

- Create your own questions for fiction, social studies, and science. Begin with fiction read-alouds, since these are usually easier for students. Start with an easier question and gradually build up to harder questions.

- Do the same for social studies and science. Alternate your weekly assessment questions among social studies, science, and reading.

CHAPTER 4

Mini-Lessons and Teaching Strategies That Strengthen Students' Reading Skills for State Tests

Highlights

- Examine strategies for studying fiction texts that increase students' comprehension.

- Discover the significance of Golden Lines, character study, and comprehension.

- Learn how to help your students tackle unfamiliar vocabulary.

- Consider how explicitly teaching strategies for reading science and social studies texts links to stronger comprehension and higher reading scores.

- Create test-prep materials that strengthen students' content knowledge and test-taking skills.

Integrating Test Prep into Reading & Writing Workshops © 2011 by Nancy Jennison • Scholastic Teaching Resources

et's make reading easier for our students! The more we link reading to writing in our lessons, the easier it is for our students to understand how to read well and how to write well. Authors often say that the best way to become an author is to be a reader. That's why we ask students who write fiction to first carefully read fiction in reading workshop: because the work becomes more authentic. Reading researchers Nell K. Duke and Nicole M. Martin would agree. They found that when students understand that there is a larger purpose for the work—such as, that studying fiction will help them write stronger fiction stories—students become more motivated to use comprehension strategies, and their comprehension definitely improves (2008).

Strategies for Studying Fiction Texts That Increase Students' Comprehension

Becoming a careful reader helps you notice much more information about how authors reveal characters, and that helps you understand the fiction story better. Writing teacher and author Ralph Fletcher speaks of Golden Lines, his term for incredible writing that you want to reread and that instills immediate life into the writing and jolts your reader to pay attention (1999). The renowned author and writing teacher Donald Graves advised asking students to locate and study these lines in fiction texts to deepen their comprehension as they learn about what the characters are like and develop new thinking about them. In other words, closely studying how characters are revealed strengthens students' comprehension as they draw conclusions, predict, infer, and gather information about what characters are like (Graves, 2000).

Jennifer Angerson, an innovative fifth-grade teacher at Mackay School in Tenafly, New Jersey, and I brainstormed ways to help Jen's fifth-grade students improve their comprehension through closely studying how authors revealed characters. Inspired by the research of reading authority Nell Duke on how students who read and write texts in authentic contexts increase their reading comprehension, Jen and I decided to link her reading study of author Gary Paulsen to a fiction unit of study in writing workshop. (Chapter 5, pages 108–113, describes how this study improved fiction writing.)

 **Read How It Worked**

Students Studied Golden Lines to Enrich Their Comprehension of Characters

Jen Angerson stated, "I wanted to link reading workshop to my writing workshop to improve my students' comprehension and my students' writing. So I began by asking my students to study Golden Lines or exquisite writing in Gary Paulsen's books to learn more about how he revealed characters.

"During our reading workshop, the students were reading fiction stories written by their mentor author, Gary Paulsen. As a class, we noticed Paulsen's use of beautiful language threaded throughout all of his books. For example, as I read aloud from the first chapter of his book *Hatchet*, the students acted as 'Golden Lines Detectives' and listened with keen ears. When I stopped reading, I asked, 'Did anyone hear a Golden Line?' Many hands shot up in the air. First we did this work as a class. The next day I asked students to identify Golden Lines in their independent reading books. They also pushed their thinking to learn more about their characters, just as they had done as a class."

Figure 4.1

Studying Golden Lines in Gary Paulsen's books helped Jen Angerson's students dramatically improve their comprehension.

Short Sentences: Golden Lines

WOW: Write down the Paulsen example you found.

"The thinking started. Always it started with a single word.

Divorce. It was an ugly word, he thought. A tearing, ugly word that meant fights and yelling . . . and the breaking and shattering of all the solid things . . . Divorce. A breaking word, an ugly, breaking word." *Hatchet*, pp. 2 & 3

Push your thinking and REACT to this part. What does it make you think and feel?

It seems like Brian can't accept his parents' divorce. He was so negatively affected by their break up. And although he has memories of his parents fighting and yelling, it still seems like he would do anything to keep them together. He seems desperate to get "his family" back. It must be so hard for him to ever have a clear head. His parents' divorce is the only thing that he thinks about. I can't imagine what that must be like for him. I'm about his age, and I think about school and sports and stuff. Poor Brian can't even think about those things. He is so focused on his family falling apart and the fact that he desperately wants his family back.

Integrating Test Prep into Reading & Writing Workshops © 2011 by Nancy Jennison • Scholastic Teaching Resources

Figure 4.1 (continued)

Repetitive Words: Golden Lines

WOW: Write down the Paulsen example you found.

"He was stopped. Inside he was stopped. He could not think past what he saw, what he felt. All was stopped. The very core of him, the very center of Brian Robeson was stopped and stricken with a white-flash horror, a terror so intense that his breathing, his thinking, and nearly his heart had stopped. Stopped." *Hatchet*, p. 12

Push your thinking and REACT to this part. What does it make you think and feel?

I feel like everything just froze for Brian. There was no sound, no thoughts, no movement. He must have been so frightened by the pilot's sudden collapse that he couldn't move. What was he going to do now? He is flying in a plane with no pilot! Maybe if he's brave enough, he'll jump into the pilot seat and try to fly himself. Brian must have felt like he was in an old silent movie in this part.

Intense Description: Golden Lines

WOW: Write down the Paulsen example you found.

"His hands began trembling again. He did not want to touch the pilot, did not want to reach for him. But he had to. Had to get the radio. He lifted his hands from the wheel, just slightly, and held them waiting to see what would happen." *Hatchet*, p. 17

Push your thinking and REACT to this part. What does it make you think and feel?

Brian feels like the only one who can save himself. He's feeling desperate again, desperate to save his own life. He is terrified of touching the "dead pilot" but has no choice. How else will he be able to radio for help without reaching out to grab the pilot's headset? Here, he is faced with a tough situation and he has to face it alone. His mom is not there. His dad is not there. So the only one he can depend on is himself. He has a decision to make. It's a matter of life or death. I don't think he should be afraid because the truth is he's got nothing to lose, and I think Brian knows that. I feel so scared for him. He is trying to remain calm in a panic situation. Poor Brian. One minute, he was struggling with his parents' divorce and now he is struggling with staying alive!

Golden Lines Appeared in Short Sentences

Figure 4.1 gives examples of Golden Lines from Gary Paulsen's *Hatchet* that students identified as a class. Jen continues: "They observed that Paulsen wrote three different types of Golden Lines: short sentences, repetitive words, and intense description. In the section on short sentences, students noticed the way the character referred to the word *divorce* and called it 'ugly.' Then the character Brian continued to define what divorce meant. He said it meant 'breaking' and 'shattering of all solid things.' The students empathized with this character and his powerful thoughts and feelings as they focused on those Golden Lines. I said, 'Push your thinking and react to this part. What does it make you think and feel?' As their responses in Figure 4.1 demonstrate, they understood the text at a deeper level when they used comprehension skills. The key question throughout this study was, *How did Gary Paulsen use Golden Lines to reveal what Brian is like?*"

Golden Lines Contained Repetitive Words

Page 12 of *Hatchet*, which is shown in the Repetitive Word section of Figure 4.1, describes a revealing scene in which Brian feels frozen in terror when a pilot suffers a heart attack. Jen continues: "That section contains many repetitive words as Golden Lines. The students put themselves in the characters' shoes, envisioned how the word *stopped* developed a mood of silence, asked a question out of concern for the character, and made a prediction."

Golden Lines Included Intense Description

"In the scene from page 17 of *Hatchet*, where the author used Intense Description as Golden Lines, students used more comprehension strategies in their responses. They accumulated information, as shown in their statement that he felt 'desperate again.' The students also connected more deeply with the character; they truly felt sorry for Brian and recognized the threatening situation he was in. In addition, they summarized what Brian must do to save himself, asked another question, gave opinions and made inferences. This shows a deep comprehension of many elements of the story."

Studying How Authors First Introduce Their Characters Improves Comprehension

Donald Graves suggested that students pay attention to how the author first shows readers the characters in a book. He said these introductions are purposeful and offered the following ways to find out what a character is like (2000):

■ Did the author name the character to hint at the character's personality?

■ Does the main character say something, have a thought, or display an action?

■ Did the author, or another character, describe the main character?

■ Do you learn about the main character by what he sees, or how he responds in a particular situation?

■ Does the author tell you what the main character wants, especially through making the character experience tension? Often, some kind of tension surrounds the way the author introduces the reader to the main character.

Integrating Test Prep into Reading & Writing Workshops © 2011 by Nancy Jennison • Scholastic Teaching Resources

For instance, in *The Tiger Rising*, by Kate DiCamillo, the author immediately uses tension to stir up questions in the reader's mind. The main character, Rob, only has a weak notion that a sign hanging over his head will bring him good luck. A few lines later, Rob wishes that a bear would eat him, so he would never have to attend school again. The reader immediately worries what happened to make this young man so down-trodden. As we hook our students to study the main character, it motivates them to read on. Then they read more carefully as they continue to study what happens to the main character.

How to Help Your Students Deal With Unfamiliar Vocabulary Words

In addition to using strategies for reading more closely to learn how authors first introduce their characters, students also need strategies for determining difficult vocabulary. Do you have students in your class who freeze when they encounter unfamiliar vocabulary words in test questions? If that is the case, Charles Fuhrken, an author and a writer of reading tests, wants us to tell students that test writers purposely place difficult vocabulary in reading tests to see how well students can discover the meaning by using their own strategies. He suggests that if there is a question about an unfamiliar vocabulary word that the student must define, a key strategy is always to reread at least the entire paragraph where the targeted word appears. If that is not helpful in determining the meaning, students need to expand their detective work. The next step is to reread the paragraphs before or after the section where the unfamiliar vocabulary word appears. (Fuhrken, 2009). By doing so, students can then apply their reading strategies for unfamiliar words and more easily determine the correct meaning.

In my work with students, I use the six different types of context clues that Charles Fuhrken recommends for determining a word's meaning: synonyms, antonyms, examples, descriptions, definitions, and cause and effect clues (2009). I plan my strategy lesson as authentically as I can, often in conjunction with difficult words in context from my read-aloud, or in conjunction with difficult words in our science or social studies reading. These examples are usually easy to locate, but if I cannot locate all of the context examples from our texts, I create examples and use the same content theme. Here is one example of a synonym clue from Kathi Appelt's award-winning *The Underneath*. A synonym clue makes the definition clear. "She should have been *concerned* about the lightning, slicing the drops of rain in two and electrifying the air. She should have been *worried* in the falling dark" [italics added] (2008, p. 1).

Figure Out Unfamiliar Vocabulary by Using Clues From Context

Synonym

The angry teacher was so **incensed**, she kept the entire class inside for recess.

- What word is the synonym for *incensed*?
- What does *incensed* mean?

Antonym

Jonathan wanted to be **punctual** for a change. He was tired of getting pink slips for being late to school.

- Find the word that is the antonym for *punctual*.
- What does *punctual* mean?

Example

While the musician loved playing several wind instruments, the **piccolo** was his favorite.

- Find the example for *piccolo*.
- What does *piccolo* mean?

Description

José was **ravenous**! His stomach was growling, since he forgot to eat breakfast and lunch.

- Find the description for *ravenous*.
- What does *ravenous* mean?

Definition

Yesterday our class visited the zoo; my favorite place was the **aviary**, or the large cage for birds.

- Find the definition of *aviary*.
- What does *aviary* mean?

Cause and Effect

Our town was so **engulfed** in snow, the superintendent announced that there would be no school.

- What makes this a cause-and-effect example?
- What does *engulfed* mean?

Strategies in Science and Social Studies That Link to Stronger Comprehension and Higher Reading Scores

It is hard to argue with the body of research that documents that explicitly teaching students comprehension strategies greatly improves their comprehension of nonfiction and fiction texts (Duke & Martin, 2008). Kathy Doyle, a fifth-grade teacher from Smith School in Tenafly, New Jersey, found that her students often needed to practice nonfiction strategies more than once and they needed to begin by using very easy text. Sometimes Kathy presents the class mini-lesson on the strategy, but she also works in small groups with students who need more support. It is helpful to give students a copy of the text, and also to display it with an overhead projector, document camera, or SMART Board. When students have a copy of the text, they can interact with it more easily and write directly on it. The hands-on experience helps their comprehension.

I created the following lessons to tie into some of the reading skills that students need to know for state tests. Once students have internalized the strategies, they will modify them, take short cuts, and use them much more quickly with the speed that timed tests demand. To demonstrate the strategies, I used two articles from *Scholastic News* that I downloaded from the Internet: "America the Beautiful" (Figure 4.2) and "Marine Invaders" (Figure 4.3).

• news map

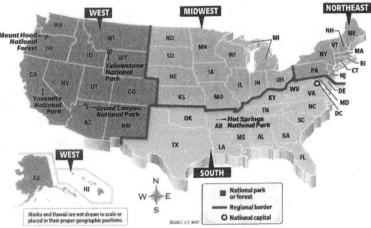

National Sites to Appear on New Quarters in 2010

Alaska and Hawaii are not drawn to scale or placed in their proper geographic positions.

SOURCE: U.S. MINT

- ■ National park or forest
- ▬ Regional border
- ✪ National capital

Yosemite Falls in California are the highest waterfalls in North America.

America the Beautiful

Scenic coins honor U.S. parks and other sites

Have you seen the wide red-rock valleys of the Grand Canyon? How about the tall snow-capped mountains of Yellowstone National Park? These are two of many national parks and sites that are part of the nation's landscape and history.

Now, 56 of those places are being honored in a special way. They are part of the America the Beautiful Quarters Program. The quarters will feature a national park or site from each state and U.S. territory. A portrait of George Washington will remain on the coin's other side.

The quarters "will help [renew] interest in our . . . national sites, as well as educate the public about their importance to us and our history," says Ed Moy of the U.S. Mint. That agency creates U.S. coins.

The first five quarters will be released this year. This year's coins honor Hot Springs National Park, Yellowstone, Yosemite National Park, the Grand Canyon, and Mt. Hood National Forest (*see map*).

Beginning in 1872, the U.S. has **reserved** beautiful parts of its landscape in the form of national parks. The U.S. was the first nation in the world to do that. Those parks, along with national forests and other sites, preserve what America values and respects.

—*Natalie Smith*

Word to Know

reserve (ri-**zurv**) *verb*. To save for a special purpose.

Figure 4.2

"America the Beautiful" article from *Scholastic News*

Marine Invaders

Lionfish are taking over the Florida Keys

There's another species invading Florida! The Sunshine State has already been dealing with invader snake species. Now, predatory lionfish have been found in greater numbers near the Florida Keys.

The colorful fish, with its striped headdress, is known for its beauty and is a popular pet among aquarium owners. But it poses a big danger in Florida waters. Lionfish are **voracious**. They eat up other fish, leaving few food sources for other species like grouper and snapper. Lionfish also eat species like the parrot fish, which does the important job of cleaning reefs. The result is stress to the fragile corals that live within the reefs.

"[Lionfish] eat until they are about to explode," Peter Kehoe, a fish salesman, told *The Miami Herald*.

Fighting Back

Officials are particularly concerned about the Florida Keys National Marine Sanctuary. The sanctuary holds the third-largest barrier reef in the world. Experts are removing lionfish from the sanctuary. The work is difficult because lionfish have no known marine predators in the Keys. Lionfish are native to the Pacific and Indian oceans, far from Florida's waters. In addition, the lionfish's fins are filled with venom, which can cause painful stings to humans and animals.

Scientists believe the lionfish got into the Florida Keys either after pet owners illegally discarded them or when the owners' homes were damaged during a hurricane.

—*Jennifer M. Walters*

> **Word to Know**
>
> **voracious** (vo-RAY-shuhs) *adjective*. Having a huge appetite.

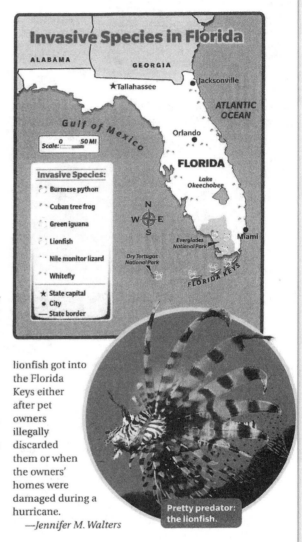

Invasive Species in Florida

ALABAMA · GEORGIA · ★Tallahassee · Jacksonville · ATLANTIC OCEAN · Gulf of Mexico · Orlando · FLORIDA · Lake Okeechobee · Everglades National Park · Dry Tortugas National Park · Miami · FLORIDA KEYS

Scale: 0 — 50 MI

N W E S

Invasive Species:
- Burmese python
- Cuban tree frog
- Green iguana
- Lionfish
- Nile monitor lizard
- Whitefly
- ★ State capital
- ● City
- — State border

Pretty predator: the lionfish.

Figure 4.3

"Marine Invaders" article from *Scholastic News*

Integrating Test Prep into Reading & Writing Workshops © 2011 by Nancy Jennison • Scholastic Teaching Resources

The chart below shows how I used each article to teach nonfiction comprehension strategies.

Nonfiction Reading Strategies	How the Strategy Helps Students	How to Model the Strategy Using "America the Beautiful"
■ Preview the text ■ Activate background knowledge ■ Make a prediction about what the article will be about	When readers preview the text, link it to what they already know, and make a prediction, they look more closely while reading to see if their prediction of the gist came true (Keene & Zimmerman, 2007).	Steps: ✓ Model how you preview and talk about the title and the subtitle. Link them to the article's other text features (photo, caption, map, and Word to Know), link them to what you already know, and write a prediction about the gist of the article (what the article is mostly about). ✓ Invite students to do the same orally with partners. Tell students, "Turn and talk with your partner about what the title, subtitle, and text features mean to you and link them to your prior knowledge." Confer with students while they work. ✓ Share a couple of the students' previews and point out what they learned. ✓ Ask students to talk to partners and write their predictions of the gist of the article on a sheet of paper. Continue to confer with students while they work. ✓ Tell students as they read the text to pause after each section, look back at their original prediction, and confirm it or revise it, based on what they read. ✓ Inquire about when students will preview a text, activate prior knowledge, and make a prediction when they are reading independently. Ask how this will help them grow as readers at school and at home.

Nonfiction Reading Strategies	How the Strategy Helps Students	How to Model the Strategy Using "America the Beautiful"
■ Paraphrase what the text is about as you . . . ■ Stop, think & say what it means ■ Continue to revise what the text is about	When readers stop and think about what they know, they can more easily monitor their understanding. As they paraphrase and say what the text means in their own words, they interact with the text and read more closely. They can then more easily link different parts of the text to one another as they revise and build meaning of the text (Harvey & Goudvis, 2005).	Steps: ✓ Read aloud the first paragraph of "America the Beautiful." Model for students how to read short paragraphs of easy nonfiction text, one paragraph at a time. "Now I will paraphrase what the text is about as I stop, think of what I know, and say what it means." ✓ Tell the gist of what the first paragraph is about and write it on a chart. ✓ Ask students to do the same with partners after reading the paragraph. Students continue to write the gist of each paragraph on sticky notes or notebook paper. They also discuss how the reading links and builds meaning with other parts of the text. Confer with students while they work. ✓ Discuss one or two of your students' paragraphs with the class. ✓ Release responsibility gradually to students. Once students understand what to do, they finish reading and discussing the article with partners while you continue to confer. ✓ Ask several students to share the gist of each paragraph and then write the gist of the entire article as a class. ✓ Inquire about what other texts students can use when they paraphrase, as they stop, think, and say what the text means. How do students think this helps them grow as readers in school and at home?

Integrating Test Prep into Reading & Writing Workshops © 2011 by Nancy Jennison • Scholastic Teaching Resources

Nonfiction Reading Strategies	How the Strategy Helps Students	How to Model the Strategy Using "America the Beautiful"
■ Determine what is important	When readers determine what is important, they use text features, topic sentences, key words, and concluding sentences to help them. As they reread one paragraph of the text at a time and underline or jot key words in the margin, it helps them interact with the text (Keene & Zimmerman, 2007). (Students who need more support can sketch a quick picture to signify what is important in the paragraph and label it with key words.)	Steps: ✓ Ask students to preview the text. ✓ Model how you tell something is important in a text. "I will read paragraph one slowly to make sure I understand it. I will underline just key words in the first two sentences and jot important ideas in the margin while I read." (I underlined *red-rock valleys*, *Grand Canyon*, *snow-capped mountains*, and *Yellowstone National Park*, and jotted famous parks in the margin.) ✓ Tell why those ideas you underlined and jotted are important to you. ✓ Invite students to determine what is important with a partner for the third sentence. Confer with students while they work on this. ✓ Students will tell why the ideas they underlined and jotted are important to them. ✓ Release responsibility gradually to the students as they continue to work with partners, read small chunks of the text, and determine what is important. ✓ Confer with students while they work, and then ask them to gather and share their work. ✓ Ask students how they can determine what is important with other texts on their own and how this will help them grow as readers in school and at home. (This lesson may be long, so you can break it down into several sections over several days.)

Nonfiction Reading Strategies	How the Strategy Helps Students	How to Model the Strategy Using "Marine Invaders"
■ Text structure: Cause and effect	When students look at the text structure, they can use it to better understand the text. If they know characteristics and signal words for the text structure, they comprehend the text more carefully (Harvey & Goudvis, 2000).	Steps: ✓ Preview the text with students and predict the text structure. ✓ Model how you notice the topic and ask yourself questions about why lionfish are invading the Florida Keys. Read the text with students to find the answers. ✓ Ask students to help look for signal words in the text that help organize information, such as: *because*, *as a result*, *since*, *therefore*, *caused*, *the result*, *the reason*, *the consequence*, *this is why*. ✓ Make a graphic organizer that helps students understand the article and matches the cause-and-effect text structure. (Example: Construct cause boxes, effect boxes, and an arrow in the middle connecting them.) ✓ Model how to ask questions and take notes inside of the cause-and-effect boxes. Here are questions to help you: *Effects answers*: What was the result? *Causes answers*: What came before or caused the result? ✓ Release responsibility gradually to students, and ask them to share ideas about causes and effects with their partners. Confer with students. ✓ Continue to meet with students as they complete the article and their own organizers independently. ✓ Share ideas as you and the students complete the organizer and talk about how cause-and-effect articles work. ✓ Ask students what they learned that will help them when they read on their own. Ask them how their understanding of cause-and-effect text structures helps them grow as readers in school and at home.

Nonfiction Reading Strategies	How the Strategy Helps Students	How to Model the Strategy Using "Marine Invaders"
■ How to read with inference: "This makes me think that . . ."	When students study important information from the article and link it to what they already know from their prior knowledge, it helps them make an inference. When students use the prompt "This makes me think that . . .", it helps them make a specific inference. It is key for students to make inferences that directly link to the text and strengthen their comprehension (Keene & Zimmerman, 2007).	Steps: ✓ Model how you preview the text and make an inference. Use the prompt "This makes me think that . . ." whenever you make an inference. Your inference should always strengthen your understanding of the text. For example: "I can see from the map that the lionfish are really concentrated around the Florida Keys. I know from prior knowledge to look closely at bold words in nonfiction texts, because the author thinks that they are important. My inference is that the Word to Know, *voracious*, describes lionfish. This makes me think that another reason that lionfish are such problems is because of their appetites. They keep eating huge amounts of fish that people in Florida could have used for their own food." ✓ Ask students to preview and make an inference with partners. Confer. ✓ Model how to look for key information in the first paragraph to use to make another inference. ✓ Ask yourself, "How does my inference help me to understand the text better?" ✓ Ask students to work as partners and read down to the end of the first section to make inferences. ✓ Confer with partners as they make their inferences and then share information. Their inferences need to help them better understand the text. ✓ Release responsibility gradually to students and ask them to complete the rest of the article with partners by making more inferences together. ✓ Ask students to share what they discovered. Ask them how they can use what they learned about making inferences with other texts and how this helps them grow as readers in school and at home.

Create Test-Prep Materials that Strengthen Students' Content Knowledge and Test-Taking Skills

The following section shows one of the ways that I created test-prep materials based on both our science and social studies curriculums. I did this for each grade level with which I worked. How did I locate materials to use? I asked teachers for relevant articles from their curriculum, and I used them to create questions similar to those used in released samples from New Jersey's state tests. The teachers loved receiving these.

- I created these packets after I studied the makeup of our state's reading test.

- Students' test-prep was more relevant to the curriculum, and students liked these materials more than commercial materials. Why? They liked to learn about the content that they already studied or would study in the future.

- It made test prep more authentic, more routine, and less frightening.

- Students recalled information from these articles that helped them in later content study.

- Students felt more confident about taking the state reading test since we coached them to improve, and they learned how to score well with these practice materials.

- We selected one of these packets to use as the preliminary demand tests to assess students' performances in each section. (I am borrowing the term "demand" from work done at the Teachers College Reading and Writing Project.)

- I provided examples of responses on several different levels with annotations, as well as the teachers' answer key for all materials.

Try It

Would your students enjoy reading content materials that are part of your curriculum for test prep? Consider how to create content test-prep materials for your students and link that work to your own professional development goals.

✓ Try working with another colleague to create test-prep materials that match your state test and your content areas.

✓ Select content passages that are approximately the same number of words as those that appear in your state reading test and use a similar format of questions.

✓ If you discuss this with your administrator, ask if you can receive some type of credit for doing this work, such as professional development hours.

✓ If you and colleagues each divide up this work, you can share materials and energize your test prep.

Integrating Test Prep into Reading & Writing Workshops © 2011 by Nancy Jennison • Scholastic Teaching Resources

Fueling the Future

by Paul Coco

People across the country are working to find newer and cleaner fuels and energy

WORKING WIND A wind farm in Southern California helps to create electricity.

Earth Day is April 22—a great time to think about how we can protect our planet in the future. Experts say finding new ways to bring fuel and power to people around the world is one of the most important steps toward preserving Earth's resources for years to come.

For example, can you imagine riding in a school bus that runs on fuel used for cooking? Or what about living in a home that is heated by turkey parts?

Finding new energy sources is more important than ever. According to a recent report, human activity is destroying about 60 percent of Earth's natural resources.

In an effort to protect those resources, some scientists are using sun and wind for energy. Others are using organic materials, such as corn and even animal parts to make cleaner fuels.

Fuel for Transportation

Fossil fuels—oil, natural gas, and coal—are used to create power for electricity or refined into gasoline to power cars, trucks, and buses. Fossil fuels can cause harmful pollution.

Recently, a group of college students from Vermont wanted to promote cleaner forms of fuel. They traveled across the U.S. in a bus fueled by biodiesel, a fuel made from vegetable oil. On the trip, the students filled the tank with cooking oil used at restaurants.

"Biodiesel greatly reduces carbon dioxide and carbon monoxide," says Stephen Swank, 22, one of the students.

Many people believe carbon dioxide and carbon monoxide cause global warming.

Another alternative fuel made from corn, called ethanol, is being used by people across the U.S. to fill up their cars. Ethanol is made by breaking down the sugar found in corn. Ethanol can be

word wise

- **organic:** (or-GAN-ik) adjective. To do with or coming from living things.

- **fossil fuel:** (FOSS-uhl FYOO-uhl) noun. Coal, oil, or natural gas, formed from the remains of prehistoric plants and animals.

Teaching Text Structures • 2007 by Dymock & Nicholson Scholastic 64

Figure 4.4

Grade 5 Demand Assessment Test Passage
("Fueling the Future" article from *Scholastic News*)

blended with gasoline to create a cleaner type of fuel. About 30 percent of all gas used in the U.S. last year was blended with ethanol.

The search for new kinds of fuel has led to even stranger ideas. One company is developing a process to make **organic** fuel from animal parts!

ORGANIC FUELS Corn can be turned into liquid fuel. Fuel can also be made from turkey parts.

Changing World Technologies (CWT) mixes turkey parts with grease and water. The mixture is heated to about 1,000 degrees and put under great pressure, which breaks down the turkey parts. CWT also uses tires and garbage to make cleaner fuel.

"If we take plastic, tires, and [turkey] bones and turn that into fuels, much less fossil fuel will need to be dug up out of the ground," says Brian Appel, who heads CWT.

Help From the Sun and the Wind

Some houses across the U.S. are powered by solar energy, or energy from the sun. Solar panels placed on the roofs of these homes collect sunlight and turn it into electricity, without waste or pollution. This electricity is used to heat and light homes, even when it is dark outside.

Some lawmakers in Los Angeles, California, want solar panels installed on about 30,000 rooftops by 2017. That much solar power would help reduce the amount of carbon dioxide in the air.

Like the sun, wind is another source of energy. Wind turbines, or windmills, are being used to turn wind power into electricity in more than 30 states. In states such as Minnesota, Iowa, California, and Texas, large numbers of windmills are built close together to form wind farms. As of this year, windmills created enough electricity to power about 1.6 million U.S. households.

"We need to think about using cleaner types of energy," Swank says. "Working on the problem now will reduce the harm people cause the earth."

Recycling Waste
Animal droppings are used to make paper

What do you get when you boil elephant poop, cut it, and press it flat? If you guessed sheets of paper, you are correct.

Companies in Asia, Africa, and Australia are recycling animal waste to make paper products. The Thai Elephant Conservation Center in Lampang, Thailand, is one place selling the poopy paper. The average elephant drops more than 100 pounds of poop each day, which can be made into about 115 sheets of paper.

To make the paper, workers wash and boil the poop for five hours. It is then dried, cut, and pressed into different types of paper. Best of all, no trees need to be cut down to make the paper.

Figure 4.4 (continued)

Grade 5 Demand Assessment Test Passage

DEMAND TEST

Grade 5 Nonfiction

"Fueling the Future"

Directions: Choose the multiple-choice response that is the BEST answer to each question.

1. Based on the article, what prediction would you make about the author's opinion on the importance of a wind farm in Southern California?

  Ⓐ The author would strongly agree that a wind farm helps to prevent pollution.

  Ⓑ The author would strongly agree that wind is an excellent fossil fuel.

  Ⓒ The author would not think that wind is an effective way to create electricity.

  Ⓓ The author would worry about how consistent the winds in Southern California are for producing electricity.

2. What do coal, oil, and natural gas all have in common?

  Ⓐ They have been created by scientists in laboratories in the United States.

  Ⓑ They are all alternative fuels.

  Ⓒ They have been formed from the remains of prehistoric plants and animals.

  Ⓓ They are fuels that will never be depleted by humans.

3. *According to the article*, why are scientists trying to use corn and animal parts to make cleaner fuels?

  Ⓐ The earth's climate is changing.

  Ⓑ The earth's deserts are running out of water.

  Ⓒ The earth's natural resource supply is great, and fossil fuels cause pollution.

  Ⓓ The earth's natural resources need to be protected, and fossil fuels cause pollution.

4. How is biodiesel different from fuels that most cars use today?

  Ⓐ Gasoline, which most cars use, is less toxic than biodiesel.

  Ⓑ Biodiesel is less harmful to the environment than gasoline.

  Ⓒ Biodiesel is more widely used than gasoline.

  Ⓓ Biodiesel is a fossil fuel.

5. If cars today used more biodiesel and less gasoline, what would be the result?

  Ⓐ Greatly reduced carbon dioxide and carbon monoxide resulting in less global warming

  Ⓑ Greatly increased carbon dioxide and carbon monoxide resulting in more global warming

  Ⓒ People would be frustrated with the biodiesel and would shop more often for gasoline.

  Ⓓ The pollution caused would be the same for biodiesel as for gasoline.

Figure 4.4 (continued)

Grade 5 Demand Assessment Test

6. How is it possible for corn to be turned into liquid fuel?

(A) Refined sugar is added to corn and then turned into gasoline.

(B) The sugar in the corn is directly made into gasoline.

(C) The corn is cooked to about 1,000 degrees and mixed with turkey parts to make gasoline.

(D) The sugar in corn is broken down into ethanol, which is blended with gasoline.

7. Why is CWT interested in plastic, tires, and turkey bones?

(A) CWT uses them in a process to make fossil fuels.

(B) CWT exports them to China for fuel economy.

(C) CWT turns them into organic fuels, resulting in less fossil fuels being needed.

(D) CWT experiments with them in solar energy sites.

8. Why is the use of recycling animal waste to make paper a good practice?

(A) This type of paper is far less expensive than regular paper.

(B) This type of paper is easier to produce than regular paper.

(C) This type of paper is used in industry.

(D) No trees need to be cut down to make this type of paper.

Teacher's Answer Key—Multiple Choice:

1. a, **2.** c, **3.** d, **4.** b, **5.** a, **6.** d, **7.** c, **8.** d

OPEN-ENDED QUESTION

9. The author discussed a number of ideas for fueling the future. Which ones might be helpful for the State of New Jersey to investigate? What do you think that the state could do to make a difference in helping New Jersey communities begin using newer and cleaner fuels and energy? Use information from the text to support your opinions.

Figure 4.4 (continued)
Grade 5 Demand Assessment Test

Integrating Test Prep into Reading & Writing Workshops © 2011 by Nancy Jennison • Scholastic Teaching Resources

SAMPLE 9A: EXAMPLE OF AN OPEN-ENDED RESPONSE THAT WOULD SCORE HIGH ON A STATE TEST

I think that the State of New Jersey should investigate using ethanol as an alternative fuel. The State could make a difference by building new State factories to manufacture ethanol. "Ethanol can be blended with gasoline to create a cleaner type of fuel." Gas stations could be forced to use gas made with ethanol. So, that means that there would be less pollution in our State . . . a big difference!

Secondly, the State could offer people who own homes money to build solar panels on their houses. Why? ". . . Solar power would help reduce the amount of carbon dioxide in the air." Carbon dioxide pollutes the air. Also, if people used solar power, their electricity bills would be less because sunlight would be turned into electricity. But also, the state would be making a difference in encouraging cleaner air.

Finally, the State could offer additional money to schools that would be willing to build solar panels or wind turbines. In other words, if our schools in Tenafly built wind turbines or added solar panels to the roofs of our buildings, we could get more State money for our schools! Money is a great reason to get people to do things. I think that the State can make a major difference in fueling the future by offering money to tax-payers and to schools for using solar panels and wind turbines. This would reduce New Jersey's use of fossil fuels. It is time for our state to become an environmental leader and a role model for other states.

Teacher Answer Key—Open-Ended Answer: 9A
Score = 4 out of a possible 4

Clear response: Each idea includes text evidence, as well as clear and complete explanations that strengthen the writer's opinions. Insightful thinking is present in the part about how cash incentives speak to taxpayers and schools, as well as how New Jersey could become an environmental leader.

SAMPLE 9B: EXAMPLE OF AN OPEN-ENDED RESPONSE THAT WOULD SCORE LOW ON A STATE TEST

I think that the State of New Jersey should investigate using ethanol as an alternative fuel. "Ethanol can be blended with gasoline to create a cleaner type of fuel." That would be a great idea.

Secondly, the State could offer people who own homes money to build solar panels on their houses. ". . . Solar power would help reduce the amount of carbon dioxide in the air." So, that would also help us.

Finally, the State could offer additional money to schools that would be willing to build solar panels or wind turbines. So, that would make a difference, too.

Teacher Answer Key—Open-Ended Answer: 9B
Score = 2 out of a possible 4

Although the ideas are correct and they include text evidence, the lack of clear and complete explanations, as well as a lack of insightful thinking, caused this answer to receive a 2. This sample is a watered-down version of sample 9A. Its purpose is to show students that they have to add explanations and insightful thinking. It also shows how poor their response sounds if they neglect to do this—they just have a shell of a response!

Food for Thought

▼

RESEARCH HAS SHOWN CLEARLY THAT WE CAN IMPROVE OUR STUDENTS' COMPREHENSION WHEN WE LINK READING TO WRITING FOR LARGER PURPOSES (DUKE & MARTIN, 2008). SO WHY NOT TRY TO PLAN UNITS OF STUDY THAT LINK READING TO WRITING, SO THAT THERE IS A LARGER PURPOSE TO YOUR WORK?

In this chapter you read about how we study fiction in reading workshop with our students so that they can write stronger fiction stories in writing workshop. Students' motivation to use the author's Golden Lines as a tool to read more carefully and their consequent growth in comprehension amazed fifth-grade teacher Jen Angerson. This chapter featured her comprehension work.

- Consider linking your reading to writing in the way that you teach fiction. Examine what third-grade teachers Melissa Erickson and Stephanie Tesorero did in Chapter 3 to increase their students' comprehension of characters (pages 46–60).

- Then link the teachers' work in Chapter 3 to Jen Angerson's description of Read How It Worked in this chapter (see pages 76–78). Melissa, Stephanie, and Jen worked to strengthen students' comprehension, and they offer great tips.

- Use the information on how to construct a fiction writing unit of study in Chapter 5 to help you link your reading workshop to your writing workshop. Jen Angerson's Read How It Worked (pages 108–113) is especially clear with regard to how she linked students' comprehension study of fiction to writing fiction. The student sample shows amazing growth.

CHAPTER
5

Mini-Lessons and Writing Units That Strengthen Students' Writing Skills for State Tests

Highlights

- Examine sample lessons for a persuasive writing unit of study and time-constraint suggestions.

- Consider lessons for a fiction unit of study and note how one teacher condensed the lessons for her class.

- Consider how revision can become a natural part of students' writing.

- Think about a middle school teacher's suggestions for improving word usage.

Do your students' opinions matter? When your students write persuasively, they empower themselves to feel the strength of their own words. They acquire a new zeal for writing when they realize their words can change others' opinions. I have found that teaching this unit is energizing, since students are so interested in expressing their views.

Teachers' Time Constraints

Are you under stressful time constraints, without much extra time to plan and complete this 14-day unit? Would you like to use a quicker plan?

✔ For a five-day persuasive writing plan: Consider these lessons: Days 2, 5, 6–7, and your choice of one other lesson.

✔ For an eight-day persuasive writing plan: Think about these lessons: Days 2–3, 5–8, and your choice of two additional lessons.

Lessons for a Persuasive Writing Unit of Study

This unit is one that can be taught during the school year, not only during test prep. It will help your students develop a firm foundation for essay writing that will benefit them on the state test. As you and your colleagues read through these lesson ideas, modify them to fit your students' needs and eliminate those that you do not need.

▶ Day 1 Focus: Writers learn characteristics of persuasive essays by studying the components of mentor essays.

Nancie Atwell, a noted writing teacher and author, always has her middle school students read well-written essays and list features that make the writing effective. She and her students create a list of "Characteristics of Well-Written Essays" to help her students understand how essays work (Atwell, 2002, pp.174–176). Christie Mortara and Arnold Almaguer, two creative special education and fifth-grade teachers from Mackay School, have followed Atwell's lead. They divided their class into cooperative groups and asked each group to study the same text by a mentor author, so they could brainstorm a larger number of effective strategies that the author used. The teachers used the persuasive essay "The Cruelest Show on Earth" by Paul Janeczko as a mentor text (2003) because it is well-organized, clear, and powerful (see Figure 5.1).

Integrating Test Prep into Reading & Writing Workshops © 2011 by Nancy Jennison • Scholastic Teaching Resources

Figure 5.1

THE CRUELEST SHOW ON EARTH?

By Paul Janeczko

When most of us hear the word *circus*, we think of clowns, high-wire acts, and wild animals. However, what many of us don't realize is that behind the excitement and glitter of the Greatest Show on Earth there is a dark side that the circus keeps secret. That is the world of abuse that circus animals must endure in the name of entertainment. It's time that we outlaw animals in the circus.

Travel can be a horrible experience for circus animals. Because the circus visits so many cities in all kinds of weather—some travel thousands of miles and are on the road for as long as forty-eight weeks per year. Circus animals are crowded into beast wagons that are often too small for them. Frequently, they travel through extreme weather. The animals are deprived of their social life that is so important in the wild. Elephants, for example, spend almost the entire day barely able to move.

Training is also a horror that these wild animals must endure. All training takes place behind closed doors. It can be brutal. Animals are often beaten and abused as part of their training. Standard practice is to beat, shock, and whip the animals to make them perform their ridiculous tricks. When the circus allows animal-rights organizations to observe training, they are really only allowed to see rehearsals, not the training process.

Circus people want us to believe that performing animals present an educational experience for customers, but this is not true. Animals are kept in an unnatural environment and made to perform unnatural tricks. Animals will run and jump in the wild if they want to, but elephants do not stand on their heads and horses do not walk on their hind legs in the wild. If we want to learn about animals, we are better off watching a wild-animal show that *was* filmed in the wild.

Many people believe that the circus performs a valuable conservation duty by breeding animals in captivity. A look at the facts shows otherwise. Many animals we see performing in the circus were taken from the wild. Elephant calves that wind up in the circus, for example, are often the survivors of culls, which are really the mass slaughter of adult elephants. And, not too long ago, some African traveling circuses were suspected of being "fronts for trafficking in endangered species" like parrots and chimpanzees.

The next time that the circus rolls into town, don't be blind to what is really going on under the big top. The circus is more than clowns and acrobats. It is a showcase for animals that are severely mistreated—animals that are denied the opportunity to live dignified lives, running free with their species. When the circus comes to town, just say, No!

However, you could also consider using a student sample. Although Paul Janeczko's essay is outstanding, sometimes students relate more to the work of one of their peers, since it may be more relevant and easier to understand (see Figure 5.2). Alice Rassam, a talented fifth-grade teacher from Smith School in Tenafly, New Jersey, taught a persuasive unit of study and shared Gal's essay below. How might you use this essay to demonstrate persuasive strategies to your students? Another option is to obtain released samples of persuasive essays from your state's education department Web site or gather samples from your students or your colleagues' students.

Lunch Outside of School
by Gal

Do you think TMS students should be allowed to walk to town for lunch? What if they had an accident? They could get hurt! Also, in town there are really long lines. Anyway, bringing lunch from home gives you more time, and is tastier. Perhaps you are one of those that believe that students should be allowed to eat lunch in town. I disagree!

A lot of accidents that happen in Tenafly occur in town. Students could get hit by a car when they aren't paying attention. This has happened many times before. Just 2 weeks ago, four seventh grade girls got run over by a car and were hurt very badly.

I think that in town the lines are way too long and take up most of your time. I know that when I go to town, the lines are extremely long, and I end up having very little time to eat. Students only get 22 minutes to eat. So they might not even get a chance to start eating.

Students might say, "Hey! There's good food in town, right?" Well, they might not like the food there. A good idea is to bring lunch from home. I know that a lot of people in my class—including myself—bring lunch from home and it tastes great. If they do this, they are saving time, money, and eating something that is healthier for them.

Up until a few weeks ago, I didn't think there was anything really wrong with going into town for lunch. Then I heard about what happened to those girls and started to change my thinking. Instead I want to enjoy my healthy lunches in the safety of the school cafeteria surrounded by my friends. It definitely allows for a more relaxed lunch.

Figure 5.2
Fifth-grader Gal wrote about eating lunch outside of school.

Integrating Test Prep into Reading & Writing Workshops © 2011 by Nancy Jennison • Scholastic Teaching Resources

Try It

What do you think about the issue of assigning your students a persuasive writing topic, versus allowing them to choose their own topic for writing? Fifth-grade teacher Kathy Doyle says, "When my students write persuasive essays about what they care about, they produce better writing."

✓ Brainstorm topics with your students on what they care about.

✓ Examine the suggestions for lessons in this chapter and select the ones that your students need.

✓ Consider how you'll use Paul Janeczko's piece (Figure 5.1), Gal's persuasive essay (Figure 5.2), your own student samples, or state-released samples as mentor texts.

▶ **Day 2 Focus:** Writers can generate ideas for persuasive essays by writing about things that interest them or issues that concern them that they want to change.

(*Suggestion*: If your students have not written essays in the past, you may want to have them write a simpler nonpersuasive essay about a topic of their choice before they write a persuasive essay.)

Model how to list several things that concern or interest you that you wanted to change when you were your students' age and show how you would free-write an entry about one of those things. Use the organizer and the frame on page 100. Teach students how to do the following:

■ Write a list of things that concern or interest them that they want to change (1) at home (home rules and chores, sibling rivalry, and so on), (2) at school (homework policies, length of school recess), or (3) social issues (ridicule about clothing or exclusion by peers).

■ Generate two entries about what concerns them that they want to change.

Teachers College staff developer Melanie Brown suggests that students use a graphic organizer to arrange their thoughts. Each organizer in the following lessons contains sample responses. After students write their ideas inside the organizers, they write an entry in their writer's notebook that relates to the organizer. (Students write one entry in school and another at home. See directions on the pages that follow.)

What Interests Me or Concerns Me That I Want to Change	Why I Want to Change It
It is wrong for people not to throw the football to players who are not good at football.	Everyone deserves a chance at catching the football. Just because someone didn't catch it in the past doesn't mean that he/she won't catch it on another occasion, and so on.

First, the student will use the above headings in the graphic organizer for jotting ideas. Next, they start each issue as a new entry on a new page in their writer's notebook and give each entry a heading like this:

Framework for My Notebook Entry:

An issue that interests and concerns me that I want to change is _____ because . . .

▶ **Day 3 Focus:** Writers of persuasive essays think about the possible audience and create arguments that are appropriate for that audience (Lane & Bernabei, 2001).

Model the following in a mini-lesson: "When I think of what I want to change that relates to school or home, first I need to identify my audience. Then it helps my ideas to be stronger if I think of the arguments that would be the most persuasive for convincing my audience about what I want. I can use this chart to help me organize my information in my entry to be the most powerful and convincing to my audience."

What Interests Me or Concerns Me That I Want to Change	My Audience	Three Reasons Why I Want to Change It
It is unfair that I have to go to bed at the same time as my younger sister.	My parents	I am two years older than my sister, and I should stay up later. I have no time to relax after I finish my homework. I have to hurry off to bed. I have no time to read at night, since I have so much homework and a strict bedtime.

- Demonstrate another example with reasons that do not fit with the audience.
- Ask students to help you fix your second example. Students will then write at least two entries at school or at home.

First, they will use the headings in the graphic organizer for jotting ideas. Next, students will start each issue as a new entry on a new page in their writers' notebooks and give each entry a heading like this: This is the topic that I'm concerned about and want to change.... These are the reasons why I want to change it. (Students will free-write several paragraphs about this topic and the reasons they want to change it.)

▶ **Day 4 Focus:** Writers of persuasive essays reread their entries about what interests and concerns them that they want to change. They select an issue to change that they will develop into a persuasive essay. They identify their audience and give reasons why the change is needed and important.

I refer to a chart that lists the steps and model the following:

Step 1: Reread your entries.

"So watch me as I reread my four different entries, so I can see which one I want to develop into a persuasive essay. My entries are: asking for more money for allowance, staying up later than my sister, stopping my brother from teasing me, and getting permission to eat lunch separately as fifth-graders."

Step 2: Think about your audience for each position and choose the position that is the most important to you.

"I'll think about my different audiences, and then I'll decide which position is the most important to me. That will be the entry that I will develop into a persuasive essay.

I've decided that my parents are my audience in the entries on staying up later, getting more allowance, and stopping my brother from teasing me, but my teacher and the principal are my audiences for fifth-graders eating separately in the cafeteria. The most important position for me is that fifth-graders should be able to eat lunch alone in the cafeteria, since they are the oldest students in the school. Every day this bothers me, and I want to change it. So that's my topic."

Step 3: Think of three new reasons to support your position and write them on your organizer.

"Watch how I can use a graphic organizer to help me rethink my ideas. When I begin writing now, I want to generate some different ideas. So watch me as I think aloud about what I already wrote and push myself to think of new, fresh ideas. Here is what I already wrote earlier in my chart in my notebook."

What Interests Me or Concerns Me That I Want to Change	My Audience	Three Reasons Why I Want to Change It
Fifth-graders should be able to eat lunch alone in the cafeteria, since they are the oldest students in the school.	My teacher and the principal	Fifth-graders should eat separately as a special honor. It is so noisy at lunch from the loud voices of younger students, many fifth-graders get stomachaches. Fifth-graders need a quiet lunch, so that they can talk about things going on at school.

"But here is how I can change it to think of more reasons that are even stronger! Watch how I can push myself to think harder and discover fresh new thinking to convince my audience. I will write it on this chart."

What Interests Me or Concerns Me That I Want to Change	My Audience	Three Reasons Why I Want to Change It
Fifth-graders should be able to eat lunch alone in the cafeteria, since they are the oldest students in the school.	My teacher and the principal	Fifth-graders are squished into two lunch tables because the younger students need so many tables. Fifth-graders hardly have room to eat. Many fifth-graders have lunch duties with other grade levels in the school, and they need to eat separately at lunch to save time. Allowing fifth-graders to eat separately would pay them back for all of the work that they do to help the teachers in the school.

Framework for Day 4's Notebook Entry:

My Sample Entry: *I could convince my principal and my teacher to agree with me about changing the fifth-graders' eating arrangements, so that fifth-graders can eat without other grade levels. My new reasons for wanting to change it are those that I listed on my chart.* (I mention them.) *My next step is to show you how I will free-write about my new reasons in my notebook, using this frame right now."* (I briefly demonstrate.) *I will confer with some of you today, as you start a new entry on a new page in your writer's notebook and give the entry a heading like this.* (I write the entry below on the board.)

Integrating Test Prep into Reading & Writing Workshops © 2011 by Nancy Jennison • Scholastic Teaching Resources

My Entry: My issue for my persuasive essay is _____. My audience is _____. These are the three new reasons why I want to change what concerns and interests me:

1. _____

2. _____

3. _____

▶ **Day 5 Focus:** Writers of persuasive essays select an issue for their essay. They outline their essay on a Persuasive Essay Organizer to make sure that the idea and supporting arguments are clear and logical. (See Figure 5.3 for a completed sample of the organizer.)

Figure 5.3

Sample of completed Persuasive Essay Organizer

Student's Name _____   Date _____

PERSUASIVE ESSAY ORGANIZER

What Interests Me or Concerns Me That I Want to Change: Fifth-graders should be able to eat lunch as a separate grade level, since they are the oldest students in the school.
Reason 1: Every school day, fifth-graders squish into two lunch tables and have no room.
Reason 2: Many fifth-graders have lunch duties and need to eat separately to save time.
Reason 3: Fifth-graders deserve to eat separately, since it pays them back for the work they do in the school.
Conclusion:

❑ I approve this.

❑ I disapprove.

Teacher's Signature_____

I model each of the following steps for students and write my essay position and reasons on the Persuasive Essay Organizer. Then I confer with students while they write their positions and reasons and meet with a small group if there is confusion.

Step 1: List your position about what interests you and concerns you that you want to change in the top box of the Persuasive Essay Organizer. Make sure that it makes sense and is clear to your audience.

- How can I make my position clearer?
- How can I make my position make more sense?

Step 2: Ask yourself the following question for each of the three reasons.

- Does my reason fit with and explain my position?

▶ **Day 6 Focus:** Writers of persuasive essays work with their writing partners to make sure that their reasons fit and explain their position. Then they revise their position and reasons in their Persuasive Essay Organizer.

Step 1: Make sure your reasons fit and explain your position.

Model how you ask yourself this question about each of your three reasons:

- Does my reason fit with and explain my position?

Step 2: Ask your class to be your writing partners, and demonstrate this lesson for students. Then have students do the same thing with their partners and apply what you taught.

Step 3: After students fill in their position and three reasons on the Persuasive Essay Organizer, but before they continue working, you need to approve their work to ensure that their positions and reasons make sense.

Students write only their positions and reasons now, and then in the Day 12 lesson they write the frame of their conclusion in the box on the organizer. Thanks to Medea McEvoy, former staff developer at Teachers College, for suggesting that students obtain teacher approval.

▶ **Day 7 Focus:** Writers of persuasive essays organize their reasons by using organizational tools to help them collect and store their ideas.

Model how to use the organizational tool using your position and show how you collected color-coded evidence and reasons that support your position. Demonstrate how you placed all evidence in color-coded manila envelopes:

"Watch how I use my Persuasive Essay Organizer to label all of my envelopes."

Integrating Test Prep into Reading & Writing Workshops © 2011 by Nancy Jennison • Scholastic Teaching Resources

"My issue is _____. I wrote it in red on my large manila envelope."

"See how I wrote my reason one in green on my smaller envelope?"

"See how I wrote my reason two in purple on my smaller envelope?"

"See how I wrote my reason three in orange on my smaller envelope?"

"I will label this fifth envelope in black as my conclusion envelope."

"Now I will take my evidence that I have gathered, reread it, and place it in the correct manila envelope. I made sure each piece of evidence on half-loose-leaf sheets or on index cards is color-coded with a dot at the top right corner to match the envelope."

Have students refer to their own Persuasive Essay Organizer and begin collecting lists of facts, quotes, anecdotes, firsthand observations, revealing details, statistics, and other evidence to support their reasons (Murray, 1998). Students collect supporting evidence in school and at home for each color-coded manila envelope.

▶ **Day 8 Focus:** **Writers of persuasive essays study a particular mentor text, such as "The Cruelest Show on Earth." They also can study a sample student essay.** (See Figure 5.1 for the essay and Figure 5.2 for the student sample.)

Students study the way that the author wrote the text and focus on one writing technique that the essayist used well.

▶ **Day 9 Focus:** **Writers of persuasive essays study the mentor essay's organization. Then they make sure that their reasons and elaboration fit their argument or thesis statement and decide on the order of the reasons. They write their drafts.**

For example, study how Paul Janeczko organized his essay, and then have students organize theirs.

Step 1: Study the organization of Paul Janeczko's essay with students.

Mr. Janeczko listed each reason in the first sentence of paragraphs two through five. All reasons clearly fit with his thesis.

Step 2: Reorganize your supports based on what you and the class learned from Paul Janeczko.

Say to students: "So, watch how I reorganize and prioritize the order of my supports to have the biggest effect on my audience like our mentor author showed us."

- "I want my first support to grab my reader's attention."

- "What support makes sense to add next? I could use Mr. Janeczko's strategy and find the support that fits best after the first support."

- "Next, Mr. Janeczko listed reasons that were important facts that people did not know about. So I will look for further supports that my readers might not know about."

- "Finally, which support should I place at the end that will resonate and stay with my audience to convince my readers that I am right? Mr. Janeczko grabbed our attention with his final reason by shocking us. I will look through my reasons and select the last reason that people will remember."

I continue to model how to do this and involve students in my decisions about how to order my reasons.

Step 3: Students work with partners and use the same strategies to reorganize their reasons.

▶ **Day 10 Focus:** Persuasive writers create leads that make a strong case for their issue and hook the reader. Then they use that lead to begin their draft.

Writing expert William Zinsser offered a great tip for students. He said a writer's most important sentence is the first one, and that each consecutive sentence in the lead must continue to hold the reader's interest (1998).

Step 1: Study the mentor author's lead.

Discuss how Paul Janeczko's lead paragraph captured your interest. Why did you want to continue reading? (Also ask students and list what they say.)

Step 2: Choose a type of lead that works for you.

I created the suggestions for leads that follow to fit with the circus piece. Select one or two to demonstrate for your students that you think fit their needs. Next, show how you would choose leads for your own essay, then circle the one that is better.

A Quote

A quote can be an excellent choice for a lead. Writing teacher Donald Murray says to "use a quotation to give authority to important points." (1985, p. 65)

"Circus life on the road is brutal for the animals," said the elephant trainer who wished to remain anonymous. "How'd you like to work all day and then be forced into a tiny pen until the next morning? The show must go on, but there's no glamour or comfort for circus animals," he added.

A Startling Fact

People who buy tickets to the circus think that what really matters is what happens under the big top. If they knew how circus animals were being mistreated behind closed doors, they might think twice about attending.

Integrating Test Prep into Reading & Writing Workshops © 2011 by Nancy Jennison • Scholastic Teaching Resources

An Anecdote

Every spring as a child, I turned page after page in the movie and theater sections of my local paper and scoured all of the ads. Finally, the day I had waited for arrived: the circus was coming to town. I had visions of dancing elephants, leaping tigers, and comical bears. But I might not have been so excited if I had known how the animals were being mistreated behind the scenes.

A Question

Is the way that trainers treat circus animals under the big top similar to how they treat the animals behind the scenes?

Step 3: Use your lead to begin your draft.

Model how you can begin your draft with your circled lead and how you write a paragraph of your draft. Use your persuasive organizer and details for the first reason as a guide.

Ask students to select two leads to try, circle the one that they like better, and then use it to begin their drafts while you confer with individuals and small groups.

▶ **Day 11 Focus: Model a lesson on how you continue to write your draft and match it with what your students need to remember, such as making sure that for each reason that matches the positions the draft includes clear details.**

▶ **Day 12 Focus: Writers study the mentor author's conclusion to learn about conclusion strategies. Then they write a conclusion in their Persuasive Essay Organizer that is clear, makes sense, and matches their position.**

Teaching: Study the mentor author's conclusion and rethink your conclusion. Say something like this:

■ "Writing expert William Zinsser states that the conclusion sums up the thoughts of the piece and concludes with a sentence that fits so well it amazes us" (1998).

■ "When we studied Mr. Janeczko's conclusion, we saw that he tried to persuade us by shocking us and adding an emotional plea that amazed us. I realize that my conclusion needs to be powerful. I will try to intrigue and persuade my readers with an emotional plea that amazes them."

■ "Watch how I read over my essay now and decide how to write my conclusion. I will tell you my idea for my conclusion, and then ask myself these questions: Is it clear and does it make sense with my position? Does it sum up the idea of the piece and intrigue or amaze my audience?"

Active Engagement: Say something like this: "Writers, now it is your turn to think about a strong conclusion. Turn and talk to your partner. Tell him or her one conclusion strategy that you learned from our mentor author. First, show your partner your position and reasons. Second, state your conclusion. Next, ask your partner, 'Is my conclusion clear and does it make sense with my position? Does it sum up the idea of the piece or amaze or intrigue my audience?' Then, write your conclusion at the bottom of your Persuasive Essay Organizer. Finally, tell your partner how you will elaborate your conclusion and write your conclusion on your draft."

▶ Day 13 Focus: Persuasive writers edit and publish their work.

As you assess your students' persuasive writing, model a mini-lesson on one editing strategy that their drafts indicate needs attention. After students edit their work, they practice presenting their essays out loud.

▶ Day 14 Focus: Persuasive writers have choices for how to celebrate their work.

Have students invite all of their audiences to come to the celebration or send the essay to a specific audience's address, if appropriate. You can also hold a celebration where persuasive writers share their essays in a whole group or small group. Those who listen to the essay will write a comment on how it convinced them to change their mind about the issue.

Help Your Students Write Amazing Fiction

Many state tests require students to write fiction. Teaching a fiction unit during the year will give your students the strong foundation that they need to do well on the state test.

 **Read How It Worked**

Studying Golden Lines in Stories Helped My Students Write Better Fiction

Jen Angerson, a fifth-grade teacher from Mackay School, set a goal to strengthen her students' fiction writing, but she had only a little bit of time to accomplish that feat. Since Jen had already conducted a fiction writing study earlier in the year, she decided in this fiction unit to focus on the lessons her students still needed for the upcoming

Integrating Test Prep into Reading & Writing Workshops © 2011 by Nancy Jennison • Scholastic Teaching Resources

state writing test, especially Golden Lines (Fletcher, 1999). (For more information on Golden Lines, see pages 76–78.) Jen describes below how we proceeded:

"Nancy and I condensed my fiction writing unit from the longer 13-lesson unit into only eight days of lessons. It saved me time and met my students' writing needs. I will list the focuses for each of my lessons. (See pages 114–121 for the discussion of the 13 lessons.) I believe that whenever I link my students' reading workshop to my writing workshop, their learning becomes more integrated and stronger."

- **Day 1:** Generate ideas to write a fiction story from events in your life.

- **Day 2:** Create your own character using an individual Character Organizer.

- **Day 3:** Writers use the Character Organizer to tell a story. Listeners ask the storyteller Inside and Outside Questions, and because of those questions, the storyteller discovers details to enrich the story.

- **Day 4:** Describe and stretch out the problem in the story and tell how the character deals with it.

- **Day 5:** Plan the fiction story.

- **Day 6:** Draft the story.

- **Day 7:** Demonstrate how to write Golden Lines and revise the story for Golden Lines that reveal the character.

- **Day 8:** Publish and celebrate.

Jen explained in the Read How It Worked in Chapter 4 how she used Golden Lines to strengthen her students' comprehension. Consequently, it made sense for her to use the descriptive writing that her students discovered in their mentor authors' books to study how those authors wrote so beautifully (Calkins, 1994; Calkins & Kesler, 2006).

Jen commented on her Gary Paulsen craft study: "Students explored Gary Paulsen's work like writers and looked for the writing craft techniques that he used. Most specifically, the students noticed how he repeats words, uses short sentences, and intensely describes feelings, scenes, and situations. So I created a graphic organizer where the students recorded moments when Gary Paulsen used the three specific strategies we were studying (see Figure 5.4). In the Wow! section, students noticed Gary Paulsen's Golden Lines and the amazing writing that appear in *Hatchet*. In the How? section, they analyzed Gary Paulsen's craft techniques. In the Why? section, they explained why he used that craft in his writing. Finally, in the Now . . . section, students applied Gary Paulsen's specific strategies to their own writing. Hence, this exercise helped them notice and study the author's use of Golden Lines and the power of Golden Lines.

"Having the students, as writers, identify our mentor author's Golden Lines helped make them realize the importance of character development. Students realized the great craft that is needed in their own writing in order for their readers to think and feel about their characters. Their readers should be able to *care* about their characters.

Gary Paulsen Craft Study

Wow!	How?	Why?	Now . . .
"GOING TO DIE, Brian thought. Going to die, gonna die—his brain screamed in the sudden silence. Gonna die." *Hatchet*—Chapter 3, p. 26	**Repetitive Words Strategy**—He repeats specific words or phrases poetically and in a rhythmic pattern.	For the reader to get inside the character's head, empathize with him or her, and experience the moment	Michael knew he had a test to study for, but he didn't study. He kept on making excuses, such as "I've got a baseball game," or "I'll study tomorrow." Now, Michael would pay the hefty price. He looked at the test and thought, "going to flunk. Going to flunk. Going to flunk." —Jonathon Amitai
"He was stopped. Inside he was stopped. He could not think past what he saw, what he felt. All was stopped. The very core of him, the very center of Brian Robeson was stopped and stricken with a white-flash of horror, a terror so intense that his breathing, his thinking, and nearly his heart had stopped. Stopped." *Hatchet*—pages 11–12	**Short Sentence Strategy**—He uses one, two, three, or four words in a sentence.	To make a point to the reader To point out the obvious answer after describing a moment To point out something important and meaningful	Mike sat there, in school, looking at the crowded sheet of paper. That paper was white and scary. All of the letters looked like little angry ants trying to bite Mike's skin. A test. —Itamar Schnitzer
"He was unbelievably, viciously thirsty. His mouth was dry and tasted foul and sticky. His lips were cracked and felt as if they were bleeding and if he did not drink some water soon he felt that he would wither up and die." *Hatchet*—page 43	**Intense Description Strategy**—He helps the reader to explore his or her senses and envision a particular scene or action by using detailed and intense description.	To give the reader a chance to experience two extreme sides of the same thing To help the reader envision (see the scene clearly in his or her mind) To make the reader feel as though he or she is experiencing the action	At that moment, POOF the power went out. Darkness. Pitch, black, darkness. Not the darkness like when you are sleeping, and not the darkness that your eyes adjust to. But darkness, so black you can't see a thing and you only hear the gurgling of rain rushing down the roof and the rumble of thunder shaking within the walls of the lonely house. That kind of darkness! —Jocelyn Dawson

Figure 5.4

Jen Angerson's fifth-grade students explored Gary Paulsen's writing craft and used his strategies in their own writing.

Integrating Test Prep into Reading & Writing Workshops © 2011 by Nancy Jennison • Scholastic Teaching Resources

As their teacher, I needed to help them make the leap from noticing Paulsen's craft moves to trying them in their own fiction writing. So here are the most important questions that I asked my student Aaron during conferring that helped them create Golden Lines in their fiction stories that revealed their characters:

- What is your character feeling right now?

- What is your character doing in this setting? (I wanted Aaron to think of action.) Describe the in-the-moment action that is taking place. (I wanted Aaron to describe it bit by bit.)

- What is your character thinking about?

- Is he/she distracted by other thoughts? What is really going on under the character's surface?

"After our conference, once Aaron was working independently, I told him to periodically stop and ask himself these same questions. I believe your students, as writers, should be able to answer all of these questions. Explain to them that the answers to these questions bring their characters to life in their writing. The answers help them develop the necessary Golden Lines needed for their readers to care about and empathize with their characters. I found that studying a mentor author's use of Golden Lines has truly heightened my students' awareness of character development while they read and write. They pay much more attention to the characters now. This work is meaningful, effective, and has tremendous depth.

"Please notice the differences in Aaron's fiction writing. Figure 5.5 shows the 'before' piece and Figure 5.6 shows the 'after' piece. I feel that my work with my students studying Golden Lines in Gary Paulsen's books has enriched their writing in ways that I have not seen before! Students put their own personal craft style into their pieces in powerful ways."

The Catch (draft)
by Aaron

It was the bottom of the sixth inning. Alan's team was hanging on by a thread. They were winning six to five against Montvale, the toughest team in the league. Alan threw the ball in left field warming up with his pulse racing. But he just focused on the ball twisting and turning out of his grasp. Finally the umpire called

"Balls in!"

Alan trembled as he saw the first batter step up to the plate, spit, and faced the pitcher with a dirty look. The pitcher fired the ball to home plate. It was like a ball of fire that was so fast, you couldn't see it!

"Striiiiiike one!" the umpire yelled.

One strike down, Alan thought to himself still shaking.

The pitcher hurled the ball back to the plate equally fast. Then Alan heard the ball go **SMACK!** And he saw it travel off the bat into center field.

The catcher yelled "no outs, one man on!"

The pitcher responded to the hit with three lightning fast strikes to the next batter. On the next batter the same.

Again the catcher yelled "two outs, man on first!"

But then Alan saw him. The batter stepping up was the most feared. He was a five foot tall monster with facial hair. He had already hit three homers in the game. The pitcher fired.

"Ball one!" the ump called.

"Settle down" Alan's coach yelled.

The pitcher set and through the fastest one yet.

CRACK! Alan saw the ball going. He raced back to the warning track. He focused on the ball and jumped. He felt the ball and squeezed with everything he had. After that he felt two things. Happiness and sadness. *Did I catch the ball*? Alan thought. He looked at his mitt. The ball was in it! He had won the game. Alan was jumped by his teammates and got piled on for making the game winning catch. He was the hero of the game.

Figure 5.5

Fifth grader Aaron tried to incorporate Gary Paulsen's craft strategies into his fiction draft after he studied the author's use of Golden Lines.

The Catch (final copy)
by Aaron

It was the bottom of the sixth inning. The hard New Jersey wind was hitting Alan's face. Alan's team was hanging on by a thread. The smallest thread. Ready to snap. They were winning six to five against Montvale, the toughest team in the league. The inning was about to start. Alan threw the ball from left field to his teammate in center field warming up with his pulse racing as fast as a horse at the Kentucky Derby. But he just focused on the ball twisting and turning out of his grasp. Finally the umpire called

"Balls in!"

Alan trembled as he saw the first batter step up to the plate, spit, and faced the pitcher with a dirty look. Not the kind of dirty look you give to someone who's annoying you, but a real dirty

Integrating Test Prep into Reading & Writing Workshops © 2011 by Nancy Jennison • Scholastic Teaching Resources

look. A look so dirty it was like he had daggers in his eyes. It was the kind of look a crazy, rabid animal might give. That kind of dirty look. The pitcher fired the ball to home plate. It was like a ball of fire that was so fast, you couldn't see it!

"Striiiiiike one!" the umpire yelled.

One strike down, Alan thought to himself still shaking.

The pitcher hurled the ball back to the plate equally fast. Then Alan heard the ball go **SMACK!** And he saw it travel off the bat into center field. The batter reached first base.

Single, Alan thought. *That's nothing. People hit hundreds of singles in our league.*

The catcher yelled "no outs, one man on!"

The pitcher responded to the hit with three lightning fast strikes to the next batter. Not one ball in between. On the next batter, the same.

Again the catcher yelled "TWO OUTS, MAN ON FIRST!"

That's when Alan saw him. The batter stepping up was the most feared. He was a five foot tall monster with facial hair, the best player in Little League. He had already hit three homers in the game. The pitcher fired.

"BALL ONE!" the ump called.

"Settle down!" Alan's coach yelled.

Don't hit it. Please don't hit it here. Anywhere but to me, Alan prayed as he stood in the outfield.

The pitcher got into position and threw the fastest one yet. No single pitch faster. As fast as a bullet. Fast enough to break the sound barrier. Alan heard a loud **CRACK!** He saw the ball going. He raced back to the warning track, almost slamming into the wall.

Just catch it! Please just let me catch it. Alan yelled in his mind.

He focused on the ball and jumped. He felt the ball and squeezed with everything he had as he hit the wall and fell to his back. After that he heard two things: moaning from one side of the field and cheering from the other.

Still on his back Alan thought, *Did I catch the ball? Did I win the game? Could I really have caught the game winner?*

Slowly, he turned, opened up his eyes that were tightly shut, and peered down at his mitt. The ball was in it! The ball was in his mitt! The ball. He had won the game! Alan ran to his teammates with an ear to ear grin. His teammates cheered and piled on top of him for making the game winning catch. Alan was the hero of the game. The hero.

Figure 5.6
After a conference with his teacher, Aaron revised his draft to include more of Gary Paulsen's craft strategies and added Golden Lines.

Lessons for a Fiction Unit of Study

▶ **Day 1 Focus: Generate ideas to write a fiction story from events in your life. Writers get ideas for their stories by thinking of events in their own lives and considering how they can change what happened to make the event into a fictional story.**

Barry Lane, a writing teacher and author, says that writers can create a character that solves a problem in a way that the writer may not (Lane, 2003). Special thanks to Teachers College Staff Developer Melanie Brown for format suggestions that I modified for the lessons on generating ideas.

Use true events from your own life that you can change. Lucy Calkins suggests that you write about events that occurred when you were the same age as your students (Calkins & Cruz, 2006). Here are examples I've used:

1. I abandoned my dog, Duchess, when I was eight years old.

2. I practiced a summer play that I wrote with friends when I was eight.

3. I stayed home from school to attend a clown party at my mom's preschool that was located inside of our house when I was eight years old.

Show students how you choose one of your three events and then jot down a description of how you can change the event on the Fictional Event Organizer (see Figure 5.7). Next, use the organizer to tell students how your story might go and begin writing an entry with the prompt, *I can write a story about . . .*

Then have students create their own list and circle one item on it. Next, they fill in their Fictional Event Organizers, and use the information from the organizer to tell partners how their stories would go, beginning with the prompt, *I can write a story about . . .* After each partner takes a turn telling his or her story, both write an entry in their writers' notebooks about how that story might go. For homework, they could select another true event and do the same thing.

As Figure 5.7 shows, I used the Fictional Event Organizer to model how I changed a true event from my life as a child to generate ideas for my fiction story. In the real classroom, I jot fewer notes than what appears in this table, because I explain as I write in front of the students.

Integrating Test Prep into Reading & Writing Workshops © 2011 by Nancy Jennison • Scholastic Teaching Resources

Figure 5.7

Fictional Event Organizer

A description of the true event in my life	What I wish happened	How I could make the result more positive	How I could make the event more exciting	How I could make the event take a different twist
My dog, Duchess, followed me on a bike ride. Two older boys blocked my street with sticks, forced me off my bike, and tried to hit my dog. Terrified, I rode my bike away. I did not realize that Duchess was not with me.	I wish that I drove my bike back and yelled at the boys. Then they stopped bothering Duchess and left me and my dog alone.	One of the boys' parents spotted her son bothering me, and she told both boys to come into her house.	A police car was cruising down Stratford Street. The boys stopped bothering Duchess, then ran and hid behind houses in the neighborhood.	One of the boys' older siblings walked by and ridiculed his younger brother for picking on a much smaller girl. The two bullies finally left.

▶ **Day 2 Focus: Generate ideas about how to write a fiction story from your story ideas. Writers can find story ideas by thinking about familiar aspects of their lives that they always wanted to write about.**

I model the process by making a list of the three ideas (from my childhood) that I wanted to write stories about:

1. Always needing attention: My friend Rita always wanted to be the best at everything and be the center of attention.

2. Feeling lonely: A boy in my class, Raymond, felt alone because the teacher continually embarrassed him and made an example of him.

3. Getting picked on by others: A boy in my class, Tyler, was bullied daily and didn't know how to stop it.

Then have students create their own list and circle one item on it. Ask them to begin writing their entry in their notebook with the prompt *I always wanted to write a story about . . .*

For homework, they could select another idea on their list and do the same thing.

Students fill in a Fictional Event Organizer on their own for the idea that they may want to develop into a story.

I use the Fictional Event Organizer shown above to model how I changed a true event from my childhood to generate ideas for my fiction story. In the real classroom, I jot fewer notes that what appears in this sample chart, because I explain as I write in front of students. I suggest that you do the same.

Figure 5.8

CHARACTER ORGANIZER

Directions: Answer the following questions about the character you are creating, keeping the following guidelines in mind:

1. Everything that you say must be believable.
2. The characters should be your age.
3. Write about a setting you know very well.
4. Keep the total number of characters in your story very small.
5. Select names for characters that are different from students at school.

Questions About My Character	Answers to My Character Questions
	Note to Teachers: Say most of your answers and shorten this list when you write.
Who is the main character? (name, age)	Jamie—8 years old
Who are just a few other characters? (name, age)	Tom and Larry—11 years old; Duchess—a small beagle
What is the setting? (name and describe the location)	Stratford Street, Boston, Massachusetts—a quiet street, shaded by many maple trees, a summer day
What details that are relevant to my story describe how the main character looks?	Jamie is 4 feet 8 inches tall and wears black glasses. She has long brown hair in a ponytail.
What does my main character like to do?	Jamie loves to ride her bike with her dog, Duchess.
What does my main character want to do most of all?	She tries to set the neighborhood record for how far she can coast down the hill on her street without touching the pedals of her bike.
Describe the supporting characters.	Tom and Larry are very tall boys who bother neighborhood children. They do hurtful things and usually get away with it.
What difficulties keep my main character from getting what he or she wants?	Tom and Larry dragged sticks across Stratford Street, so that Jamie and Duchess could not ride across it. Jamie stopped her bike in time, but Duchess kept on running, and the dog ran right into the boys. They hit Duchess with sticks. At first, Jamie didn't realize it until she turned around.
How does my main character solve the problem? Did the character change?	Jamie rode her bike back and started screaming at the boys to leave Duchess alone. A police car was cruising down Stratford Street, and the boys ran away from the scene. Jamie realized she needed to watch Duchess more closely.
What are my characters' traits and what proof can you give of these traits?	Jamie: adventurous—speeds on her bike down a steep hill; loyal: defended her dog Tom and Larry: mean—tried to hurt Jamie and hit Duchess Duchess: friendly—wagged her tail at Tom and Larry

Integrating Test Prep into Reading & Writing Workshops © 2011 by Nancy Jennison • Scholastic Teaching Resources

▶ **Day 3 Focus:** Writers use ideas generated from a Fictional Event Organizer and develop them using the Character Organizer. They use the Character Organizer to tell their stories to partners as a rehearsal for writing their drafts.

Step 1: I model how I read over the story plan of what I might write about (see the Fictional Event Organizer, Figure 5.7) and then show how I can fill in my Character Organizer (see Figure 5.8). I refer to the Character Organizer as I tell the students the story of my own character, who is the *same age* as my students. Students then evaluate my story for the five guidelines that appear at the top of the Character Organizer. I mention to students that Donald Graves said to avoid naming a character after a real student in school. He suggested pausing after each addition to your Character Organizer and asking students, "Does this make sense with what we already know about the character? Does the description ring true and sound like a real person?" (Graves, 2000)

Step 2: Students read over the ideas in their Fictional Event Organizer and fill in their Character Organizers, making sure they stick to the guidelines.

Step 3: Finally, students use their completed Character Organizers to plan their own stories. I then ask students to share their oral stories with partners. I let several students share with the class, and have the class evaluate them using the five guidelines on the Character Organizer.

(If this lesson seems too difficult for your students, you may want to insert a prior lesson where you complete a Character Organizer as a class to develop a class character.)

▶ **Day 4 Focus:** Writers plan the fiction stories by reading over their Character Organizers and writing scenes of their story inside planning boxes.

Planning boxes can be used for stories that contain a few scenes. Students name each scene at the top of a planning box. The first planning box is the beginning of the story, the second is the middle of the story, the third is the turning point of the story, and the fourth is the resolution or ending. Students write their scene ideas inside the boxes and use different sheets of paper for each scene.

Step 1: Reread your Character Organizer and show students how it helps you to fill in the planning boxes for the scenes of your story. After I reread my Character Organizer, I model how to label and write a scene for my story inside each planning box.

Step 2: Reread the scenes in your planning boxes and make sure that your story flows well. Ask students for comments.

Step 3: Students then do the same with their own stories and have their writing partners comment on the flow of the story.

▶ **Day 5 Focus:** **Draft a lead that matches a mentor author's lead. When writers study how different types of mentor leads create tension and engage the reader, it makes their drafts begin in intriguing ways (Lane, 2003).**

Step 1: Show students various mentor texts that you used as models for engaging the readers' interest in different types of leads for your story. (See Chapter 7, pages 157–161 for examples of different types of leads and lists of mentor texts that are useful for teaching how to write leads.)

Step 2: Model three different types of powerful leads to begin your story.

Step 3: Students each select several mentor texts and write three different types of leads to begin their drafts. Then they select the lead they think works best.

▶ **Day 6 Focus:** **Draft the story. Writers reread their planning boxes and their lead when they begin drafting their story.**

I model how mentor authors introduce the main character in a memorable way (Graves, 2000; see page 78, Chapter 4). I model using my story, making sure to introduce the setting and the problem early.

Step 1: I show how I reread the planning boxes before I begin to write the draft of my story and demonstrate how I use the lead I selected to begin my writing.

Step 2: I write a couple of paragraphs, showing how I introduced my character in a way readers will remember. (*Every Living Thing*, a collection of short stories by Cynthia Rylant, works well as a mentor text.)

Step 3: I point out how I introduce the main character, setting, and the problem early in the story. Afterward, students do the same.

▶ **Day 7 Focus:** **Writers read over their planning boxes and drafts and add tension in their stories by stretching out what the problem is and then describing how the main character solves it.**

Model each of the following in your mini-lesson:

■ Reread your own planning boxes about what your main character's problem is and how your character overcomes it. Read the section of your draft that deals with the problem and the solution.

Integrating Test Prep into Reading & Writing Workshops © 2011 by Nancy Jennison • Scholastic Teaching Resources

■ Model how to stretch out this section in your draft to add tension. Show students how you revise this to describe the tension in a bit-by-bit way. (See the Read How It Worked, pages 108–113 of this chapter.)

Students then repeat this process with their own drafts, stretching out the tension in the character's problem and solution and then reading that section of the story to a partner.

▶ **Day 8 Focus: Writers use questions from the audience to revise their stories. They strengthen character development and elaboration in their stories in an activity called Be the Character.**

When my students' stories need more details, I use this lesson to generate excitement in the middle of a fiction unit. Writing teacher Barry Lane suggests that the teacher model how to "Be the Character" and then have students ask what he calls "Inside and Outside Questions" to learn more details (2003).

Step 1: I read my story to my students and pretend that I am the main character. I talk and act and become the main character.

Step 2: While students listen to my story about my character, they jot down two types of questions about it:

   ✓ Inside Questions: questions about the character's thoughts or feelings—something that is not visible

   ✓ Outside Questions: questions about what they can see— how someone looked, and so on

Step 3: I jot down all of the students' Inside and Outside Questions. Then I model how to incorporate the answers to those questions into my second reading of the same story. The second version is much more complete because I demonstrate how I revise it to add details. I ask students to share with their partners what was different about the second version and how their Inside and Outside Questions helped with my elaboration and revision.

Step 4: Students do the first three steps using their own stories, switching turns with a writing partner.

▶ **Day 9 Focus: Writers revise the story by using what they learned from studying how mentor authors reveal characters to add character-appropriate language that moves the story along. They make sure that their drafts include a balance of dialogue, character's thoughts, and actions to reveal what the character is like.**

Step 1: I reread my draft to students and demonstrate how I added character-appropriate language to my story. I stress how dialogue that moves the plot along differs from speech that is not meaningful. Students then reread their drafts with an eye toward character-appropriate dialogue.

Step 2: I code and highlight my story to show that I used a balance of internal thinking, actions, and dialogue to reveal what my character is like. (See Chapter 7, pages 153–154 for more information on this process.)

Step 3: Students do the same.

▶ Day 10 Focus: Writers revise their stories for Golden Lines that reveal the character and study how mentor authors use Golden Lines and precise verbs to reveal their characters, then they revise their drafts by adding their own Golden Lines.

Show your students how your mentor author gave you ideas for writing Golden Lines to reveal your character. Then reread your draft for the students and add Golden Lines.

For example, in *The Tiger Rising*, Kate DiCamillo revealed what a bully named Norton was like in this Golden Line: "And then Norton came swaggering back and leaned over Billy and grabbed hold of Rob's hand, and with the other hand, ground his knuckles into Rob's scalp." Show students how you reread your verb choices and substituted more powerful verbs that revealed your character's actions. Students then study their mentor authors, reread their drafts, and revise them for Golden Lines. (See the Read How It Worked, pages 108–113 in this chapter for more strategies.)

▶ Day 11 Focus: Writers study the endings of mentor authors and revise their own endings to indicate changes in the character and to show if the problem was resolved.

Step 1: Model for students how you can reread your planning boxes to refresh your mind on how you planned to craft your ending.

Step 2: Then reread how your mentor authors ended their stories. Demonstrate those strategies for your ending and select one to revise the ending of your own story. (See pages 166–171 in Chapter 7 for different ways to write endings and for titles of books with notable endings.) Ask yourself, "Have I shown how my character changed at the end of my story? Is the resolution to my character's problem clear?"

Step 3: Students then do steps 1 and 2 with their own stories.

Integrating Test Prep into Reading & Writing Workshops © 2011 by Nancy Jennison • Scholastic Teaching Resources

▶ **Day 12 Focus:** Writers edit their stories for spelling errors and punctuation errors by finger pointing while reading aloud, with an eye toward the following common mistakes:

■ Omitted words, extra words, or incorrect suffixes

Show students how you edit your story by reading it *aloud* and pointing *under* each word as you read. This makes it easier to identify errors.

■ Difficulty punctuating sentences

Model reading your story aloud with exaggerated intonation and pausing often as a strategy for checking the punctuation. Students do the same thing on their own and then have their writing partners check their stories.

▶ **Day 13 Focus:** Writers publish their revised and edited copies and celebrate their accomplishments.

Plan a small celebration. You might divide students into groups of four and have them read their final stories to one another.

How Revision Becomes a Natural Part of Students' Writing

How can your students show their best writing when they are writing to a prompt in a timed writing test and may only have time to revise a couple of words? How do you encourage them to have a real interest in revision?

Janet Angelillo, an author and expert on revision, says that including revision strategies throughout the year in all writing units of study, and holding students accountable for using them, turns these strategies into a natural part of students' composition.

She believes that this will help students on the *state writing test* because they will need to make *fewer changes* to their responses. Why? Revision becomes "intuitive," and it is part of the students' good writing skills that they expand and strengthen in every writing unit all year long (2005b).

Another strategy that I have used to embed revision into writing units is to compose a cumulative list with the students of "What we know about revision" and add a new revision strategy to it after every revision mini-lesson. (In mini-lessons on editing, we constructed a chart titled "What we know about editing.") We held students accountable for these writing skills in all of their work, and we conferred daily to coach students.

Read How It Worked

A Middle School Writing Teacher Improves Students' Vocabulary and Word Usage

Amy Fabrikant-Eagan, a dynamic middle school creative writing teacher at Solomon Schechter Day School in New Milford, New Jersey, noticed that her students' writing lacked rich words. "Teaching vocabulary in writing workshop added a firm piece to the structure of writing workshop. However, in middle school, I was not able to give up the actual class time during writing workshop to teach it, since my writing classes were 45 minutes long. So that is why I asked my students to pull the unknown words that they wanted to define from their independent reading. They had the motivation. Because I expected them to use some of these words in their writing throughout the year, I saw a tangible change in their writing. They not only grew as independent readers, but they also grew as more vivid writers who used effective choices of words."

These are the steps that Amy took to launch her program:

1. She spent several weeks of vocabulary study with students by reading short texts. She and her students identified unfamiliar vocabulary words in the texts, words that vocabulary experts Isabel Beck, Margaret McKeown, and Linda Kucan define as Tier Two words. These are words that "mature language users" often encounter in their reading or in conversations, like *"coincidence"* or *"absurd"* (2002, page 8). When students located Tier Two words, it helped them with both their oral and written language, as well as with their reading comprehension.

2. Amy modeled how to create student-friendly definitions of unfamiliar words from short texts. (Student-friendly definitions use *someone, something, describes, if/you,* in a full sentence to clearly explain a word) (Beck, McKeown, & Kucan, 2002, 2008). For example, if you *examine* something, you look at it closely and carefully, or someone who is *clever* is good at figuring out things and solving problems.

3. She demonstrated how students could locate Tier Two words not only from school reading but also from their independent reading. Students chose unfamiliar words that they couldn't figure out from context clues. These words were important to understanding what they were reading.

4. Amy explained to students that they did not need to study Tier One words, since these are everyday, common words that they already knew (e.g., *door, desk*). Students also learned that Tier Three words are not often used except in specific content areas and were best learned in the context of content-area study (e.g., *photosynthesis, isotope*).

5. Students selected two Tier Two words from their independent reading books weekly and completed a Targeted Vocabulary Word Sheet independently. Students focused on learning the Tier Two words that impeded their understanding of the passage. Amy said, "I assessed the sheets weekly with a check plus for two words done well, <u>or</u> a check for one word done correctly or two words not done exactly the way we specified. Many students did extra vocabulary work to bring up their grades. It was easy for me, and it took five minutes per class to assess. I never gave my students a vocabulary test. Instead, I asked students to use their words in writing assignments. They weren't stressed about learning their new words, and we all really enjoyed the activity."

Rachel

Targeted Vocabulary Word abhor   Total of times word is heard/ used for week:
Student friendly definition: If you hate something you abhor it.

Used in **school** discussions. (Write the sentence.)	The teacher abhors when a student hands in homework late.	The students' abhor when they get a lot of home work.
Used in **home** discussions. (Write the sentence.)	You don't abhor your brother and never will.	I abhor that store because the music's so loud I can't hear anythi
Used in **notebook** entries. (write the sentence)	I abhor my life.	You don't abhor your life, but abhor the situation.
Heard the **word** used. (Write the sentence.)	My mom abhors waiting at the doctors office for more than an hour.	My parents abhor paying taxes.

Targeted Vocabulary Word abrogate   Total of times word is heard/ used for week:
Student friendly definition: If something is cancelled it's abrogated.

Used in **school** discussions. (Write the sentence.)	The whole class was extatic when the test was abrogated.	The teacher abrogated the midterm.
Used in **home** discussions. (Write the sentence.)	My parents had to abrogate our vacation because my brother was sick.	We had to abrogate our ski trip because my grandpa got sick.
Used in **notebook** entries. (Check and tally.)	I'm sorry your vacation was abrogated.	You don't have to abrogate your plans because of your mom.
Heard the **word** used. (Write the sentence.)	My favorite TV show was abrogated.	Do to the weather my brother's hockey game was abrogated.

Figure 5.9

Targeted Vocabulary Word Sheet

Rachel, an eighth-grade student, used innovative strategies on her own for learning new words that she selected from her independent reading. She recorded them once a week on this sheet.

What Amy expected students to do:

■ Students recorded hearing their targeted words used in school discussions, home discussions, or in other conversations, and they tried to use the words in their writers' notebook entries.

- Students kept their Targeted Vocabulary Word Sheets for reference and maintained a running list of the words they were learning. (See Figure 5.10.)

- Students used some of the new vocabulary words in their writing. (See Figure 5.11, where Kayla uses *irreducible* in her poem titled "A Halo Above Us.")

Kayla
Grade 7
Ms. Eagan – Creative Writing

My Vocabulary Words from My Reading

condone
sullen
catalyst
idle
clot
irreducible
ricochet
curvaceous
molehill
prodigious
reminisce
ambiance
lithe
influx
incumbent
frigid
encompassed
invigorated
illuminate
untrammeled
illustrious
dread

Figure 5.10

Targeted Vocabulary Word Sheet

Kayla, a seventh-grade student, kept a running list of new words from her independent reading that she studied on her own.

A Halo Above Us
Kayla

Tall, lean, strand of grass
Sprouting from the clot of dirt underneath it
Rising Towards the heavens
Reaching for the stars
Wanting to float on the gray clouds

Stretching, trying to go as far as it can go
Past the horizon
Where the sun rises and sets each day
Feeling so confident and irreducible
Nothing can stop it from going up

Wanting to lash every piece of grass around it
Having them fly across the field
The angel above it whispering "grow, grow"
God's haloed helper glowing in the darkness
Keep on going up, up

Figure 5.11

Teacher Amy Fabrikant-Eagan asked middle school students to use their new vocabulary words in their writing. Note how Kayla used the new vocabulary word, *irreducible*, in her poem.

Food for Thought

WHEN I MET WITH MY COLLEAGUES AND STUDIED THE RELEASED STUDENT SAMPLES THAT OUR STATE SENT TO US, WE ALL GAINED A STRONGER UNDERSTANDING OF WHAT STUDENTS NEEDED TO KNOW IN ORDER TO SCORE WELL ON THE STATE WRITING TEST. WHY NOT THINK ABOUT MEETING WITH YOUR COLLEAGUES TO ANALYZE YOUR STATE WRITING SAMPLES AND BRAINSTORM HOW YOU CAN IMPROVE THE FICTION AND PERSUASIVE WRITING UNITS THAT YOU TEACH DURING THE SCHOOL YEAR?

- Study your state's released writing samples and discuss what skills your students need to score well on the persuasive and fiction writing segments of the test.

- Circle the lessons in each unit of this chapter that match what you and your colleagues think your students require.

- Modify the lessons that you select to match your students' needs and develop additional lessons based on your assessments.

CHAPTER 6

Plan for Differentiation: Improve Scores on the Reading Test

Highlights

- See why independent reading is an important key to developing stronger readers.

- Try simple suggestions for how to differentiate reading instruction.

- Examine solutions for common reading problems that interfere with students' success on the state test.

- Consider reading strategies to help solve three important issues: lack of reading stamina, loss of focus and meaning while reading, and lack of motivation to read.

- Read about three proven lessons to teach students main ideas.

How do we help our students develop strategies that result in the most effective preparation for state reading tests? When we help our students develop strategies to become stronger readers, we give them the most effective preparation for state tests. Researchers at Teachers College found that students who read at high reading levels with strong fluency and stamina perform much better on state tests.

Independent Reading—An Important Key to Developing Stronger Readers

A key to developing strong readers is to make independent reading an untouchable block of time in our classes, a time when students read appropriate self-selected texts so they can develop fluency and strengthen their skills (Gambrell, 2009).

The research of Lucy Calkins and her colleagues showed that students need to independently read texts that match their reading levels daily for one half hour in order to maintain their rate and level of reading. If students are reading below grade level, they need more than 30 minutes a day and may need help in structuring how to achieve this, whether at home or in other reading support activities at school (Teachers College Reading and Writing Project Reading Curricular Calendar, Grades 3–5, 2009–2010).

During this block of independent reading time, when students are reading, we can coach small groups and confer with individual students or partnerships. Conferring tips appear on pages 129–130. Small-group coaching strategies appear on pages 57–60. This chapter focuses on strategies you can use to help your students overcome common reading problems that impede their performance on state tests. After you read this chapter, list the names of students who need help in reading issues addressed in the chapter and plan your follow-up instruction.

Planning How to Differentiate Your Reading Instruction for State Tests

Here are some proven suggestions for how to differentiate reading instruction:

- **Determine your students' reading levels.** Assess your students and match them to the right texts. If you have no assessment materials, visit the Web site, www.fountasandpinnellleveledbooks.com, created by reading experts Irene Fountas and Gay Su Pinnell and select several texts that match levels you think your students can read. The site describes the equivalent grade level for Fountas and Pinnell's A-to-Z reading levels, and numerous books are listed on each level. (My school district subscribed to this Web site, but individuals can also subscribe for a small fee.) Another choice is to examine the reading assessments available at the Web site of the Teachers College Reading and Writing Project: http://rwproject.tc.columbia.edu.

- For a quicker assessment while your class reads independently, ask each student to read aloud 100 words to you and count their errors. Check comprehension and ask the student to retell what he or she read. Ask a few inferential and explicit questions. For a text to be a just-right match, students need good comprehension, fluency, and accuracy.

- Experts have different ideas on what constitutes just-right text. In the past, many teachers followed the leadership of New Zealand reading expert Marie Clay, who explained that a just-right text is one that students can read at 90–94% accuracy—meaning no more than six to ten errors for every 100 words read aloud (Clay, 1979).

- However, in recent years, Richard Allington and other reading experts have recommended instruction with easier texts (2002). They advocate the idea that students should read texts with nearly 99% accuracy, which means one error in 100 words (2006).

■ **Plan large-group, small-group, or individual teacher-directed strategy lessons and mini-lessons based on your assessments.** Use the lesson ideas in this chapter to help you. For example, if you have a couple of students who do not read fluently, then follow the fluency suggestions in this chapter on pages 130–135 for how to work with them for a couple of minutes per day.

■ **Consider whether you should present a large- or small-group lesson to the students who need your help.**

✓ If approximately one-half of your class is having trouble with a particular reading strategy, present one or more whole-class lessons. I did this with a fourth-grade class where more than half the class had trouble with reading and following directions.

✓ In contrast, in a fifth-grade class, only six students had difficulty with determining the main idea, so I coached these students in a small group.

✓ Lastly, in a third-grade class, only one student had fluency issues, so I worked with him one-on-one.

■ **Select the right texts for your coaching and strategy lessons.** We want students to be able to focus on the skill that we are teaching, not wrestling with trying to decode difficult words in the text. Reading expert Richard Allington states that one of the reasons why some students never become fluent is that they regularly read texts with less than 95%

to 98% accuracy, which means that students make more than three to five errors in 100 words (2009). He echoed the need for "high-success reading," which means that when we coach readers, they need to read text at a minimum of 99% accuracy.

- **Meet with small groups to save time if your assessment reveals groups of students with similar reading issues.** For example, if you have students who do not detect changes in the character in your read-aloud, then meet with that group and talk about how authors reveal characters, as well as which signal words denote important changes in the read-aloud text.

- **Confer with individuals and reading partners daily.** Teachers College reading expert Kathleen Tolan says to make your reading conferring and small-group work as concrete as possible (2004). Here are some of her tips that I use when I confer with students:

  ✓ **Ask students to show you proof from the text** to support their thinking about a book they have read. For example, they could show the page in the text that caused them to think a certain way.

  ✓ **Ask students to write the relevant page numbers** on sticky notes to substantiate their thinking. Students then point to evidence in the text.

  ✓ **Keep on hand a "tool kit" of one or two familiar read-alouds** that you know inside and out and have already read to the class, so you can easily make a teaching point on a text that you know. Why? Some teachers have trouble making a teaching point with an unfamiliar text.

  ✓ **Confer with partners and small groups to save time** if your students are on the same reading level and reading the same book in partnerships or small groups. For example, if two of my students are reading and discussing *Hatchet* together, I confer with both partners together.

  ✓ **Do a mini-lesson showing students how you expect them to be ready for a conference with you.** This simple lesson can save you many minutes of wasted time by eliminating conferences that last too long! My students love it when I model for them what not to do, as well as what to do to get ready for a conference. Always let students know that you expect them to state their opinions concretely by providing plenty of proof to back up their ideas. For example, if the topic is a character from their independent reading book, say, "What do you know about _____? How do you know that? Show me your proof."

  ✓ **Keep records on your students' reading progress.** A quick way to keep conferring records is to have a whole-class chart listing each student's name in a box. This way, you can easily see which students you haven't met with yet, because their boxes on the sheet are empty. When conferring with individuals or groups, start by modeling a teaching point based on your observations of what the students need, then have them try what you just taught. Record your teaching point and how the students responded. Students are always accountable for the strategy or skill that you taught. When you record what you taught in the small group or conference, you can refer to your notes before your next meeting with the student to save time.

Examine Solutions for Common Problems That Interfere With Students' Performance on the State Reading Test

Teachers and I brainstormed what was getting in the way of our students' success on state reading tests. We implemented the following solutions in our classes for those problems.

PROBLEM Overcoming a major reading-test roadblock: slow reading caused by too-difficult text. Students cannot read fluently enough to be successful on the reading test.

POSSIBLE SOLUTION Improve fluency by conducting a one-minute reading-aloud session each day with readers who need help.

Teachers often tell me with forlorn looks on their faces that one of their main concerns is that some of their students, especially English language learners (ELLs), will struggle to finish reading the timed selection of the state test in time to answer the questions on the passage, and their scores will suffer. There is a solution to this problem: fluency training.

If you start daily fluency training early in the year with your below grade level students or slower readers, you can help them dramatically improve their reading before the day of the state test.

Strengthen Your Students' Reading and Comprehension Through Fluency Work

Repeated readings, for just one minute a day, have been proven to raise students' fluency, not only with texts that they have practiced reading but also with unfamiliar texts. The National Reading Panel validated repeated readings as a strategy for improving both fluency and general reading development (Allington, 2009). In addition, repeated readings also improve overall reading achievement (Young & Rasinski, 2009).

Kylene Beers, a well-respected reading researcher and teacher, suggests that students read a passage that is one level below their independent level in their daily one-minute practice sessions as a way to improve fluency (Beers, 2007).

Preparing for Fluency Training: Assemble the Fluency Packets

My fluency reading packets use the A–Z national reading levels created by Irene Fountas and Gay Su Pinnell, which are accessible on their leveled book Web site for trade books, www.fountasandpinnellleveledbooks.com. I only needed to assemble a few pages of each text, since students only read orally for one minute. I also needed to determine the instructional level of each individual reader according to the Fountas and Pinnell reading levels. If, for example, a student was reading at the end of grade 3 or the beginning of grade 4 it signifies level P for "instruction," which means that the "easy" reading level is O (approaching the end of grade 3). A student's easy level is below the instructional level. Using the suggestion of Kylene Beers, who recommends conducting fluency practice on the level below the easy level, I begin fluency training on level N with this student, which means using much easier grade 3 books. To locate level N texts that I can obtain in my school library, I simply scroll down the list of N texts on the Fountas and Pinnell Web site.

After I assembled the fluency packets, the student read the passage aloud for one minute as I took quick notes on the student's errors, fluency rate, and final word count. I counted any deviation from the text as an error.

- Omissions (a skipped word = a deviation from the text)

- Insertions (an added word = a deviation from the text)

- Substitutions (a different word than the text word = a deviation from the text)

- If the student just repeated the text word, I noted it, but did not count it as an error. Why not? It did not deviate from the text.

After one minute of oral reading, I told the student to stop and asked for a retelling of the text. (I had already taught students how to retell a text before I started this fluency work.) For five days, I met with the student, and we followed the same procedure with the same text. The next week, we did the same thing using a different text packet.

What are the criteria for fluent readers?

Richard Allington, an expert on fluency, cited the following criteria for fluent readers (words per minute): grade 3—100 words; grade 4—110 words; grade 5—120 words; grade 6 and up—140 words. Once the student can read at the targeted rate of fluency, make the passage harder (Rasinski, 2003). But before you make the passage more difficult, check the student's comprehension.

Directions for Fluency Work: One Minute of Oral Reading per Day

Before beginning the work each day, briefly demonstrate for your student what good reading sounds like (Moskal & Blachowicz, 2006).

1. **Create one leveled fluency text packet for the student** using text that is one level below the easy level text. When I made my packets, I marked the 100th word before I copied each packet to speed the process.

Your student marks the date on his or her own packet and notes how far he or she reads orally in one minute. (Each packet lasts for one week.)

2. **Make a copy of the student's text for yourself.** On it, note the date and use a slash to mark where in the text the student finished reading in each of the five sessions.

3. **Jot notes as you listen to the student read the same packet to you for one minute for a week.** The student tries to increase the number of words accurately read daily, while also improving reading fluently and with meaning. Be sure to jot errors and keep a tally of errors. Assess and record the students' fluency and retelling. Please see the accompanying rubrics and the recording sheet for each in Figure 6.1, Figure 6.2, and Figure 6.3.

Fluency Rubric Rating Scale

✓– = Poor Fluency	**Showed a number of the following:** The reader made many errors while reading and struggled to decode certain words, read with a slow or choppy speed, did not read in phrases, had poor expression and failed to stress certain words that were meaningful, and ignored the punctuation in the passage repeatedly.
✓ = Just OK Fluency	**Showed some of the following:** The reader made some errors while reading and struggled with a word or two, read with a moderate speed, read in phrases for some of the time, had fair expression, stressed only a couple of words that were meaningful, and ignored some of the punctuation in the passage.
✓+ = Very Good Fluency	**Showed the following:** The reader made very few errors while reading and read effortlessly without any struggle recognizing or decoding words, read with an appropriate speed most of the time, read in phrases most of the time, had excellent expression most of the time, stressed certain words that were meaningful, and noticed the punctuation and paused to reflect on the meaning of the punctuation and the passage most of the time. (Beers, 2003; Griffith & Rasinski, 2004)

Figure 6.1

Use the Fluency Rubric Rating Scale to score your student's fluency after he or she reads for one minute aloud daily.

Integrating Test Prep into Reading & Writing Workshops © 2011 by Nancy Jennison • Scholastic Teaching Resources

Narrative Retelling Rating Scale

✓ − = Poor Retelling	Includes only a few details about events in the story that may be out of order, mentions only a few characters just briefly, and doesn't grasp what the passage was about.
✓ = Just an OK Retelling	Includes more details about events in the story in the correct order, tells more information about the characters and what they are like, may include information about the setting, and has a satisfactory grasp of what the passage was about.
✓ + = Very Good Retelling	Includes many details about events in the story in the correct order, tells comprehensive information about the characters, includes information about the setting, has a strong grasp of what the passage was about, and may exhibit thinking at a higher level and make an inference. There is a degree of certainty and confidence that is apparent in this retelling.

Figure 6.2

Use this Narrative Retelling Rating Scale to score your students' oral retelling after he or she reads for one minute aloud during fluency training. Modify it for nonfiction.

 Read How It Worked

Fluency Training Made a Major Difference for a Fifth-Grader Reading at the Beginning of Grade 2 Level

Arnold Almaguer and Christie Mortara are two fifth-grade regular and special education teachers at Mackay School in Tenafly, New Jersey. They offer a remarkable account of how fluency training helped one of their fifth-grade special education students.

"How would one of our special education students, let's call her Noreen, possibly do well on the fifth-grade New Jersey state reading test, when she was reading at the beginning of Grade 2 level? Our fluency work made a major difference! We began in late October. Figure 6.3 shows a sample of our fluency work with Noreen during a three-month period. Although we only met an average of two to three times per week and were not able to meet often in December, we are still amazed at how the fluency training helped Noreen.

"For example, at the beginning of the year, Noreen had difficulty with reading punctuation that affected her comprehension. She read right through the periods and linked sentences together. When she made errors, they resembled the first letter

Assessing a Student's Fluency and Comprehension

Date	Title of Text	Text Level	#Errors in #words read in one minute	Fluency Score Rate: ✓+, ✓, or ✓-.	Retelling Score Rate: ✓+, ✓, or ✓-.
10/26	*Little Bear's Visit*	J	1 error in 86 words	✓	✓
10/27	*Little Bear's Visit*	J	0 errors in 100 words	✓+	✓
10/28	*Little Bear's Visit*	J	1 error in 126 words	✓	✓
11/2	*Little Bear's Visit*	J	1 error in 136 words	✓	✓
11/4	*Little Bear's Visit*	J	3 errors in 136 words	✓	✓+
11/16	*Henry and Mudge and the Sneaky Crackers*	J	3 errors in 77 words	✓	✓
11/18	*Henry and Mudge and the Sneaky Crackers*	J	1 error in 89 words	✓	✓+
11/19	*Henry and Mudge and the Sneaky Crackers*	J	1 error in 100 words	✓	✓+
11/23	*Henry and Mudge Get the Cold Shivers*	J	1 error in 58 words	✓	✓
11/24	*Henry and Mudge Get the Cold Shivers*	J	0 errors in 67 words	✓-	✓
11/30	*Henry and Mudge Get the Cold Shivers*	J	0 errors in 78 words	✓	✓
12/1	*Henry and Mudge Get the Cold Shivers*	J	1 error in 105 words	✓+	✓+
12/2	*Henry and Mudge Get the Cold Shivers*	J	0 errors in 105 words	✓+	✓+
1/20	*Frog and Toad All Year Down the Hill*	K	0 errors in 104 words	✓	✓
1/21	*Frog and Toad All Year Down the Hill*	K	1 error in 134 words	✓	✓-
1/22	*Frog and Toad All Year Down the Hill*	K	0 errors in 138 words	✓+	✓
1/25	*Pinky and Rex Get Dressed*	L	3 errors in 110 words	✓	✓-
1/27	*Pinky and Rex Get Dressed*	L	2 errors in 110 words	✓	✓
1/28	*Pinky and Rex Get Dressed*	L	2 errors in 122 words	✓	✓

Figure 6.3

Note the progress that Special Education teacher Christie Mortara's fifth-grade student made after three months of fluency work. By the end of the school year the student improved by two grade levels. The text levels that you see on the chart refer to the national A–Z text levels developed by Irene Fountas and Gay Su Pinnell.

of the text word and made no sense. She read at a very slow pace and with no expression. Her comprehension was only literal with sparse details; she had difficulty with all types of inference. She always selected books that were much too hard for her and did not participate in classroom book discussions.

"Now, she is a very different reader! She chooses books that she can read with confidence and is more interested in reading. Now, at the end of the school year, Noreen is reading on fourth-grade level. She talks confidently with her read-aloud partner about our current read-aloud. Noreen realizes when she does not comprehend and has strategies in place to get her comprehension back. Now, she reads with expression, easily reads punctuation correctly, and reads at a good reading rate. Also, she is able to add inferences on her own in her retellings. She is excited about reading and gladly reads aloud for 40 minutes at home every day.

"We found it helped our students if we had a weekly focus for our fluency work. So, weekly, we made one of the issues that Noreen struggled with a focus for that week. For example, now our focus is on inferential thinking, since Noreen already improved in everything else related to fluency. That means that before Noreen reads aloud the fluency passage to us, we remind her to think about why the character is acting a certain way. It is a quick reminder before she begins her fluency work.

"It takes us only five to ten minutes per session with Noreen, and that includes our focused reminder, her reading aloud for one minute, and her retelling what she read. The rubrics helped us a lot, so the scoring went much faster. As Noreen reread her new text three times per week, at the end of each week we expected to record fewer errors, stronger fluency rates, and stronger retellings. From week to week, we expected to see greater overall fluency.

"A question that we ask ourselves as fifth-grade regular class and special education teachers is, 'if we don't help our students with fluency and comprehension, who will?' We found that a tiny investment of our time has reaped amazing rewards for a below grade level reader."

Three Important Problems That Interfere with Students' Reading Improvement and Performance on State Tests

As I met with teachers in my school district, we targeted students' lack of reading stamina, loss of focus and meaning while reading, and lack of motivation to read as major reading issues that impeded their reading growth and success on the state test. I developed suggestions for how to improve each in the following examples.

LACK OF READING STAMINA

PROBLEM Students tire in the reading test.

POSSIBLE SOLUTION Implement concrete, routine procedures and mini-lessons. Confer with students to raise their stamina.

Use the chart in Figure 6.4 as a tool to help you think about your students' reading stamina.

Figure 6.4

Improve Your Students' Reading Stamina

Reading Problem	If you see this . . .	It could be . . .	What you can do to help
Lack of reading stamina	Student's inability to concentrate during independent reading time	The book is too hard.	Determine your students' reading levels and confer to check on book choices. See suggestions on pages 127–130.
	Students who make no progress with stamina in reading	Student has not set stamina reading goals.	Implement book logs and confer about stamina. See section below.
	Student's reading log shows no progress in numbers of pages read or time spent reading.	Student is distracted in reading location.	Do a mini-lesson on being distracted and confer with student on reading location. See section below.

SUGGESTIONS FOR HOW TO IMPROVE STUDENTS' READING STAMINA AT SCHOOL AND AT HOME

State testers expect all students to have enough reading stamina to stay focused and read all parts of the test. Here are six practical tips based on Lucy Calkins' work:

1. **Locate appropriate leveled texts that match your students' reading levels and interests.** At the beginning of the year, when you are trying to raise stamina, encourage students to read easier texts so they will want to continue to read.

2. **Time how long your students read independently in school.** Chart and celebrate accomplishments in increasing that length. For example, you might create the following chart:

   Title: Watch our Stamina Grow!

   Entries: September 14th—read 15 minutes, September 15th—read 17 minutes, and so on

3. **Ask students to set stamina goals.** Your students will steadily increase their reading stamina if you encourage them to set goals. While other students read independently,

Integrating Test Prep into Reading & Writing Workshops © 2011 by Nancy Jennison • Scholastic Teaching Resources

meet with each reader to help him or her set a clear, specific, and realistic goal. For instance, Joanna's first stamina goal stated, "I will read my independent reading book for 20 minutes at home six days a week and record how many pages I read."

4. **Use concrete materials to help students with stamina.** For example, Lucy Calkins suggests (2001) a number of goal-setting strategies to help increase students' stamina. If students set a page goal, ask them to put a sticky note on the page they want to reach each day at school before they start to read. If students set a time goal for number of minutes read, ask them to write yesterday's time and date on a sticky note and then set a new goal for today before they start to read.

Example: "You can push yourself to read longer at home and at school. Place your sticky note on the deadline page that you want to reach after you write School or Home on the sticky note and the date." Time students' independent reading in school to help them feel more confident and excited about improving their stamina.

5. **Ask students to record independent reading information in book logs,** so that you can see how much reading they are doing at school and at home. Lucy Calkins suggests conferring with students during independent reading to check on their book logs, book choices, and comprehension.

Possible categories include the following: **date, title, author, genre, time spent reading, page started, and page ended**; **S** or **H**—for reading at school or at home.

6. **Do a mini-lesson showing what you do when you get distracted or lose interest while reading.** Make a chart with students listing things you do and they do to foster reading stamina. Ask students to brainstorm other ideas to add to the chart. Here's an example from a chart that fourth-grade students and I constructed during a stamina lesson:

How to Keep My Stamina Strong When I Read

- Sit in a reading position that helps me to be attentive. (Students found it very funny when I modeled how I fall asleep reading in a too-comfortable lying-down position.)
- Read at the same time of day when I have lots of energy (not when I am exhausted and ready for bed).
- Choose a quiet home location where I will read (away from the TV and phone).
- Select a quiet location in school where I will read (an area of the classroom away from my close friend).
- Use a sticky note and place it at the end of the page number or chapter as a stamina goal for my reading.
- Get a glass of water if I need a quick stretch break.
- Place a fiction or nonfiction book on deck (next book to read) in my desk.

[Lucy Calkins (2001) created the concept of a book on deck.]

Loss of Focus and Meaning

PROBLEM Students lose focus and meaning while reading and have difficulty with comprehension.

POSSIBLE SOLUTION Teach students strategies for regaining comprehension.

Use the chart in Figure 6.5 as tool to help you analyze whether or not your students lose focus and meaning while reading.

Figure 6.5

Analyze Whether or Not Your Students Lose Focus and Meaning While Reading

Reading Problem	If you see this . . .	It could be . . .	What you can do to help
Student loses focus and meaning.	Student does not notice important changes in the story.	Student does not notice key signal words that denote change.	Teach the role of signal words and ask the student to reread the text and point to the change (see page 163). Then teach the student to stop and periodically retell.
	The student is confused about the characters.	The student reads part of the story quickly and does not pay close attention to the characters.	Teach the student how to jot notes about characters' names and relationships.
	The student misses an important revelation about the character communicated through dialogue.	The student does not recognize that dialogue often reveals character motivation.	Teach the student how to change the pace and read dialogue more slowly. Then ask the student to para-phrase what it revealed about the character.

SUGGESTIONS FOR HOW TO HELP STUDENTS IMPROVE READING FOCUS AND BETTER UNDERSTAND THE MEANING OF WHAT THEY READ

State testers expect students to stay focused and comprehend the meaning of what they are reading during a test. Here are some practical tips for how to improve your students' focus and ability to make meaning of what they read:

- Develop a chart for your class with the title of **When I Am Confused, I Can . . .**
- Present a series of mini-lessons in which you demonstrate and think aloud what you do when you become confused in your reading. Possible examples include the following (Tovani, 2000):

    ✓ Stop and think about my confusion.

✓ Look back and locate the part in the text where I lost focus, or where I didn't understand what was happening.

✓ Reread and retell what that section is about before I go on.

✓ Continue rereading if I still don't understand how that section fits with what I have read so far.

✓ Jot notes in the margin about the gist of what I read.

✓ Continue reading and stop periodically to retell what I read.

✓ Visualize what I am reading and also visualize changes in the text as they occur.

✓ Ask questions about the text and look for answers while I read.

✓ Change my reading speed to fit the text. Slow down at tricky parts.

✓ Think about what I already know about how fiction and nonfiction texts work. (Also see Chapter 3, page 48.)

LACK OF MOTIVATION TO READ

PROBLEM Students are not excited about reading and may have negative attitudes about it.

POSSIBLE SOLUTION Determine the root of the student's lack of interest in reading.

Use the chart in Figure 6.6 as a tool to help you interest your students in reading.

Figure 6.6

Analyze Your Students' Motivation to Read

Reading Problem	If you see this . . .	It could be . . .	What you can do to help
Student is not motivated to read.	Student groans when you say it is time for independent reading.	The student was assigned an independent book.	Give the student choice in selecting an independent reading book.
	Student says that he or she hates to read.	No books relate to the student's interests.	Ask your students to complete an interest inventory, and borrow books of interest for the student (see page 140).
	Student becomes angry and frustrated while reading.	The book is too hard for the student.	Determine the student's reading level and make sure the student reads books on that level (see pages 127–128).

SUGGESTIONS FOR HOW TO HELP STUDENTS IMPROVE IN MOTIVATION TO READ

1. **Administer an interest inventory and obtain books or magazines from the library that interest your student.** Here are some sample questions:

   What are your hobbies or what do you like to do in your free time?

   What sports do you enjoy?

   What do you want to learn more about?

   What are your favorite topics to study or read about?

   Do you have a favorite author?

   Why do you like that author?

   Do you have a favorite genre that you like to read? (fiction, biography, and so on)

   What magazines do you like to read?

   Do you have a favorite place to go or a favorite vacation location?

2. **Obtain an assortment of books on the level that your student can read.**

   Guide your student to make careful book choices from an assorted group that you know he or she can easily read.

3. **If the student reads below grade level, consider obtaining high-interest low-vocabulary books on your student's reading level.**

   Sixth-grade students with whom I worked in Fairfax County, Virginia, loved reading sports stories. Their favorite was *The Jesse Owens Story*, a high-interest, low-vocabulary book that did not look easy but worked well for below-grade-level readers.

Try It

Have your students taken an interest survey yet this year? Take a few minutes to administer the survey that I showed above and obtain more books and magazines that relate to your students' interests to increase their motivation to read.

✓ What does the interest survey reveal about your students' interests?

✓ Can you make categories of their interests, favorite genres, and favorite authors?

✓ How can you supplement classroom texts with texts from the library?

✓ Once you collect the new texts for your classroom library, how can you share these with students to generate excitement?

Integrating Test Prep into Reading & Writing Workshops © 2011 by Nancy Jennison • Scholastic Teaching Resources

PROBLEM Students are not accumulating information from one chapter to another and they forget what they read.

POSSIBLE SOLUTION Model strategies for retaining information.

New Jersey fifth-grade teacher Kathy Doyle modeled the following strategies to help her students accumulate and recall information. She had noticed from her conferring work, that her students were not linking current parts of their book to earlier parts. Some students were treating each chapter as a separate entity, because they did not know how to link information from one chapter to information in another.

Kathy solved her problem by using teacher modeling prior to the read-aloud. At the beginning of every day's read-aloud, Kathy modeled what she, as a proficient reader, does to recall what she read the day before. The list below begins with Kathy demonstrating the most teacher support and ends with the least teacher support and more student interaction. She did the following:

- Thought aloud and retold the previous chapter for students as she paged through it.

- Encapsulated the main parts of the previous chapter for students.

- Summarized the main parts of the previous chapter but invited students to fill in the gaps.

- Looked back at the last few pages from the read-aloud and thought aloud about what happened on those pages.

- Looked back at the last few pages and invited students to help her tell what happened on those pages.

- Asked student to retell the previous day's chapter before beginning the new chapter.

PROBLEM Students have difficulty reading and following directions in the state test. They often lose points for misinterpreting the directions.

POSSIBLE SOLUTION Develop reading strategies with students on following directions.

Use the following strategies consistently across all subject areas throughout the year. When my third-grade students had difficulty with following directions, over a period of time I read different types of directions to them (in different content areas first, and later using test-like directions). To model how to read directions, I thought aloud while reading and demonstrated what I did to carefully follow the directions. I used *motions* to help third-grade students recall the steps.

For example, I used this set of directions as a demonstration for students: *Write the title and author of your independent reading book on the top line of the next blank page of your notebook. Then, skip a line and write its genre.*

Here are the four strategies that I showed the students. They participated by acting out each phase with me, and then they worked independently applying the strategies on their own in partnerships with different sets of directions. They also noticed if they used any other strategies they discovered on their own to read directions. We added students' ideas to my ideas on the chart below.

Strategies for Reading Directions

- First, reread the directions and underline key words—especially action words and words that tell what is important that I must do. (Students joined by motioning what to underline.)

- Second, box little power-packed words, such as <u>and</u>, <u>or</u>, <u>at least</u>, <u>more than</u>, <u>most</u>, and anything to do with amounts and location. (Students joined by motioning as I boxed words.)

- Third, visualize, sketch, or use hand motions to help understand the directions. (Students joined me with their hands in the air, motioning the steps of what the directions meant.)

- Fourth, say, "That means that I am supposed to," after each step of the directions, and restate the directions in your own words. (Students watched me say the directions in my own words after each step, and then they practiced the same thing in partnerships.)

TEACH STUDENTS HOW TO READ BETWEEN THE LINES IN READING TEST QUESTIONS

Later, when I teach students about reading-test strategies, we use a strategy called Read Between the Lines. This teaches students reading strategies that help them carefully think about what the test questions are asking them to do. Here is an example of a simple open-ended question: *Describe how Atalanta is similar to and different from typical princesses.*

Step 1: Count the number of parts in the directions.

I teach my students to read between the lines and figure out how many parts there are in the directions; in this case there are two. The word "and" means there must be two parts in the answer: how Atalanta is similar to but also how she is different from, the typical princess. I tell students to write and circle the number two beside the directions as a reminder that they need two parts in their answer.

Step 2: Decide if you need to use the dot strategy.

I have had success with having students make a light dot on their answer sheet (in this case halfway down the sheet in the left margin) since there are two parts to this response.

Integrating Test Prep into Reading & Writing Workshops © 2011 by Nancy Jennison • Scholastic Teaching Resources

Students erase the dot when they complete their answer. (If there were three parts to the answer, then they would use two dots, so it divides the paper into three parts.) Why is this strategy helpful? Before I taught the dot strategy, students struggled with organizing their space for their responses on state answer sheets. This became a major problem for wordy writers, since often they would write so much in the first part of a two-part answer that they ran out of room for the second part of the answer.

PROBLEM Students need additional practice in learning to follow directions well.

POSSIBLE SOLUTION Play a game: the *Read Between the Lines* activity.

For many of my students who had difficulty with interpreting state open-ended reading test directions, this game made a major difference! Classes loved to play it.

Materials:

- Several sample open-ended test-like questions written on a piece of paper and placed in a jar or paper bag

- 5 slips of paper labeled Person 1, Person 2, Person 3, Person 4, Person 5 with each person's job described on the back of the sheet. (See below for a description of each job.)

Procedures:

Step 1: Write the questions on slips of paper and place them in a paper bag or jar.
Sample question: *Use two words to describe how the main character changed from the beginning to the end of the story. Use information from the text to support your ideas.*

Step 2: Assign jobs to groups of five students. Give each group of students a different open-ended question. Each person has a job, plans together with group members, and then performs, explaining what the open-ended question asks them to do.

- **Person 1:** Quickly box and underline key words in the question. Say what the question means.

- **Person 2:** Read between the lines and figure out how many parts there are to the directions and figure out whether you should use the dot strategy on your answer sheet. If you use the dot strategy (above), tell how to do it.

- **Person 3:** Read between the lines and figure out what you should think about while reading. (For example, with the above question the student thinks about how the main character *changes* and thinks of two words to show it.)

- **Person 4:** Read between the lines. Figure out if you need to code while you read. If so, how will you do it so you can do it really quickly? (In other words, for this example, think of a code for the two words to save time—perhaps, *angry* and *happy*—and then write **A** for angry in the sections of the text that show that the character is angry, and write **H** for the parts of the text that show that the character is happy.)

- **Person 5:** Think of how you would begin the first line of your answer as if you have read the story or article. (Often students have trouble getting started with their answers on the real reading test. This activity offers them easy strategies for how to use words from the question stem in their answer.)

PROBLEM Students cannot determine the main idea.

POSSIBLE SOLUTION Use a series of differentiated lessons on main ideas. Select the lessons to match your students' needs.

If your students have serious issues identifying the main idea, do all three lessons that appear below. These lessons progress from the easiest to the most difficult. You can implement them with the whole class or in small groups.

Lesson 1: Main idea collage (suggested by Kathleen Tolan, Teachers College Reading and Writing Project, Columbia University)

To prepare for your lesson: cut pictures out of magazines that have a similar theme and create a collage on 8½-by-11-inch paper. When I did this for my students who needed more support with figuring out the main idea, I told them to study the pictures and asked, "When you look at all of the pictures, what are they mostly about?"

I found pictures of people doing all sorts of exercising and made a set to show the benefits of exercise. In another set, I showed healthy foods versus unhealthy foods. The students loved guessing different main ideas, and they enjoyed backing up their opinions by pointing to all of the pictures that validated them. As long as they could offer logical evidence for their guesses, I accepted their ideas.

Lesson 2: Types of headings

I adapted this idea from suggestions from Kathleen Tolan. Take a very simple magazine article from a publication like *Scholastic News*. Teach your students about the three different types of headings:

Giveaway Heading: clearly matches what the text is mostly about (main idea) and gives it away

Question Heading: asks a question and usually answers it in the text that follows

Snazzy Heading: a "cool" heading that grabs your interest but doesn't match what the text is mostly about

Integrating Test Prep into Reading & Writing Workshops © 2011 by Nancy Jennison • Scholastic Teaching Resources

Demonstrate the three different types of headings for students from past issues of *Scholastic News*. Take additional articles, show the headings, and ask students to identify and write the type of heading on a sticky note: draw a hand on the sticky note for a giveaway heading (because it hands you the meaning of the heading); draw a series of question marks on the sticky note for the question heading; and draw a series of *zzzzzz's* on it for the snazzy heading. Ask students to work with a partner and use sticky notes to label the different types of headings in the magazines or easy content materials that you distribute.

Focus on the giveaway headings, since they reflect the gist of the article. Ask students in partners to find examples from the text to justify each time they labeled a heading as a giveaway.

Lesson 3: Using main ideas as a tool to better understand content texts.

Begin with easy content text and progress as you teach the same lesson with gradually more difficult texts.

Display a very simple science or social studies text so that the title shows but keep the words of the first heading covered. This text should contain giveaway headings, those that reflect the main idea of the text.

Demonstrate for students how you can use the following strategies to determine the main idea of a paragraph in order to write a heading:

✓ Study and talk about the title of the chapter or text. Tell what the words mean.

✓ Read the text in chunks or small sections.

✓ Read the first chunk aloud. It is missing a heading, since you covered it.

✓ Reread the first chunk, and ask yourself:
  What is the first chunk mostly about?
  Are there any words that JUMP out that are really important? (For example, words in bold, or key words that are repeated throughout the chunk)

✓ Underline important words and facts.

✓ Bracket the chunk. Name what it is mostly about by using a few key words.

✓ Say what the chunk is mostly about in your own words.

✓ Write a heading using only a few words. (Do not write a sentence for the heading.)

✓ Check to see if you are right: Ask yourself: Does my heading match what the section is MOSTLY about? Here are the steps to answering that question: Reread each sentence in the paragraph. Put a check beside the sentences that match your heading. If you check most of your sentences, your heading works.

✓ Unveil the original heading and see how your heading is the same as or different from the original.

Reina Pattner is a talented fifth-grade teacher at Maugham School in Tenafly, New Jersey. A few of her students had difficulty with how to determine the main idea, so I modeled lesson 3 with her class, and we created main idea strategies. Once the students used these with partners, they learned how to figure out main ideas. I used three different types of texts over a period of days with this group of students, starting with very easy text. All texts had headings covered. For several students who had the most difficulty, small-group coaching was most helpful. Students discovered that if they followed the steps in order, especially using the checking step, they could be most successful in determining the main idea and writing a good, appropriate heading!

Fifth-grade students watched me model how to write main idea headings, created the list of steps with me, as shown in Figure 6.7, and used the steps on their own to determine main idea headings. Two students discovered that step eight was most important!

Figure 6.7

Strategies for Writing Main Idea Headings

1. Read the paragraph at least twice.

2. On the second reading, stop and talk about the text. Say what it means.

3. Notice if there is a key word that jumps out.

4. Underline important words and facts.

5. Bracket the paragraph. Name what it's about by using key words.

6. Explain what the paragraph is mostly about.

7. Write a heading with a couple of words.

8. Check if the heading matches what the paragraph is mostly about by rereading your paragraph and placing checks where the ideas match the heading.

Integrating Test Prep into Reading & Writing Workshops © 2011 by Nancy Jennison • Scholastic Teaching Resources

Food for Thought

▼

USE THIS CHAPTER AS A TOOL TO HELP YOU ORGANIZE AND PLAN FOR DIFFEREN-
TIATION TO STRENGTHEN READERS' SKILLS FOR THE STATE TEST. AS YOU SURVEY
THE PROBLEMS AND POSSIBLE SOLUTIONS THAT I DETAILED IN THIS CHAPTER,
WHICH ISSUES MATCH THOSE WITH WHICH YOUR STUDENTS STRUGGLE?

In Chapter 3, I showed how I conducted a small-group coaching session with
four students who were struggling with comprehension activities connected
to character relationships. I constructed the chart that appears on page 51
to keep track and differentiate comprehension follow-up activities with third-
grade students in Stephanie Tesorero's class. This type of chart may work
well for you.

- How can this chart help you in planning for follow-up differentiated
  instruction? What follow-up charts work well for you?

- How can you adapt my suggestions in this chapter to match your
  students' needs?

- As you look at your follow-up assessment chart, how will you organize
  your follow-up lessons, small-group conferring and coaching, and
  individual or partner conferring?

CHAPTER 7

Plan for Differentiation: Improve Scores on the Writing Test

Highlights

- Plan how to differentiate writing lessons needed to produce higher state test scores.

- Learn from writers' problems on actual state tests and examine possible solutions that include lessons, activities, and games.

- Explore different types of leads and endings and mentor text suggestions.

- Examine and adapt the all-purpose writing lesson.

- Improve your students' revision with a game they will love.

Integrating Test Prep into Reading & Writing Workshops © 2011 by Nancy Jennison • Scholastic Teaching Resources

No matter what state writing test students take, effective writing is effective writing. A comparison of various states' writing rubrics shows that major similarities exist. For example, writing skills that students need to be able to use include the following:

- write a powerful lead

- present a clear, focused main idea

- write a coherent piece that flows well with effective transitions

- write a unified piece with ideas that support the focus

- develop a logical progression of ideas with interesting elaboration

- choose effective words—especially strong verbs and nouns

- use words and images to show what you mean (show, not tell)

- write with a distinct style and voice

- demonstrate clarity of thought

- incorporate sentences of varying lengths

- use conventions of mechanics, capitalization, usage, and proper spelling

- include a memorable ending

Your more capable writers can try their hand at more sophisticated techniques such as the use of humor, literary devices, and realistic dialogue that moves the piece along.

This chapter gives you tips on how to differentiate writing instruction to help students score higher on the writing test.

Plan How to Differentiate the Writing Instruction Needed for State Tests

Here are some suggestions for how to use the lesson ideas in this chapter to differentiate writing instruction:

- **Incorporate some of the writing skills listed above into your writing units during the year.**

  For example, incorporate writing leads into a beginning-of-the-year unit on personal narrative writing. (A lesson on writing leads appears in this chapter on pages 157–161.)

  Differentiate as you customize your instruction when you confer and meet in small groups with writers. For tips on how to conduct small-group sessions, see Chapter 3, pages 57–60. For tips on conferring, see Chapter 5, pages 108–113.

- **Plan specific lessons to use with certain groups of students either during an earlier writing unit or during test prep.**

  For example, a humor lesson may be a perfect match for a small group of your best writers, since humor is a challenging compositional risk. When unskilled writers try to be funny, their manner may make scorers think the writing is abrupt or doesn't make sense.

- **Teach a lesson to your whole group of students, but have different expectations for different writers.**

  For example, evaluate the endings lesson on pages 166–171 and choose several different ways of writing endings that you feel matches what most of your students need.

  - Conduct this lesson after you note the types of endings students have already written in drafts and think about what the class needs to see you model.

  - Refine your choices as you narrow your focus to just one or two types of endings for your students who need more support. For example, some writers find it easier to write gliding and action endings, since they are so straightforward. After students try writing the endings that you modeled, have them select the ending that fits and sounds better, and insert it into their piece of writing.

- **Display writing lessons at centers during test prep to review what you have taught earlier in your writing units of study.**

  For example, construct a Literary Device Center with different types of literary devices that you taught earlier in the year. (See the lesson on literary devices in this chapter, pages 154–156.) During this review class, students can go from one center to another and review key writing skills you have taught them (Heard, 2002). This can be a fresh and unique way to start your writing test prep. To differentiate instruction, you can ask certain students to be sure to visit certain centers.

- **Use games to teach writing skills and differentiate your instruction within the game.** A number of games appear in this chapter (see pages 173–175).

- **Teach writing lessons during test prep** in whole-class mini-lessons based on your analysis of students' practice tests, aka demand tests. (I am borrowing the term "demand" from work done at the Teachers College Reading and Writing Project.)

  - What skill do most of your students still need to practice?

  - Plan small-group follow-up for students who need support. For example, if you have a group of five students whose papers do not flow well, a transition-word lesson for that group may be just what they need (see pages 161–163).

Examine Possible Solutions for Common Problems That Interfere With Students' Performance on the State Writing Test

PROBLEM Students are not including a problem in their stories.

POSSIBLE SOLUTION Review what a problem is and improve students' story planning.

Read a narrative picture book with your students and make sure that they can identify the problem and solution; for example, read and discuss the problem and solution in *What You Know First* by Patricia MacLachlan. Then give your class a story prompt and have students work in partnerships to *plan* a story together on a pre-writing planning sheet. Emphasize the word *problem* in the planning: c = character, s = setting, w = wants, p = problem, sol = solution. Students then tell the story together, based on the plan they created, as the class evaluates if they included a problem and solution.

PROBLEM Students are not getting to the problem soon enough in their stories.

POSSIBLE SOLUTION Customize your writing sheets to include the problem early.

Arnold Almaguer, Kathy Doyle, and Christie Mortara designed sheets of lined paper for some of their students that clearly reminded them where the problem must be added. If your students can use three lined-pages during the state writing test, design your practice pages like this:

- *The lead and introducing the characters and problem*: These take place on up to three-quarters of the first lined page. The teachers helped students remember by photo-copying paper that showed a line drawn three-quarters of the way down the page, labeled "Problem."

- The character changes in the longest scene that starts to get to the solution—from the three-quarters point of page 1 to the end of page 2. This section is called "Getting to the Solution."

- And the place when the student solves the problem and then writes a powerful ending—called "Solution and Interesting Ending"—goes from the end of the second page on to page 3.

- In Figure 7.1, Ean, a fifth-grader, responds to a practice test prompt created by Tenafly Language Arts Staff Developer Meredith Alvaro: *Imagine that it is almost the end of the year and your classmates want to throw a class party. Write a story about this experience.*

Figure 7.1

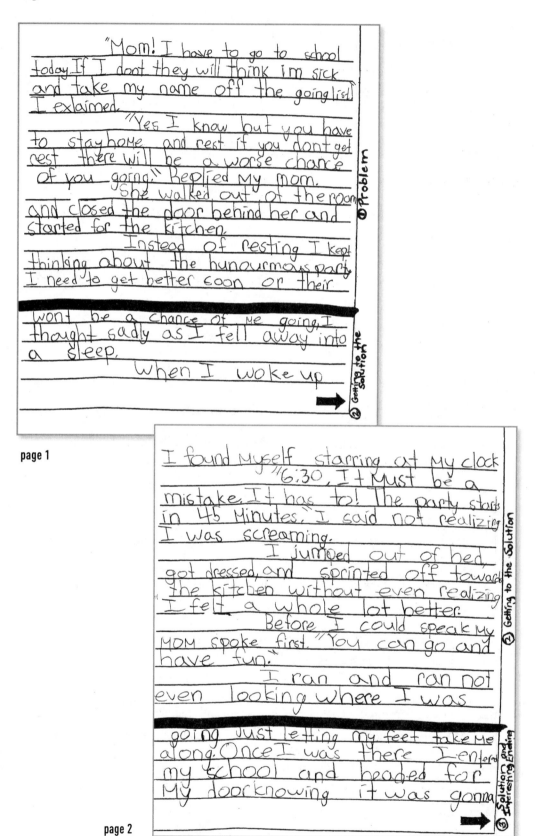

page 1

"Mom! I have to go to school today. If I dont they will think im sick and take my name off the going list" I exlaimed.

"Yes I know but you have to stay home and rest if you dont get rest there will be a worse chance of you going." Replied my mom.

She walked out of the room and closed the door behind her and started for the kitchen.

Instead of resting I kept thinking about the hunourmous party. I need to get better soon or their

— ① Problem

wont be a chance of me going, I thought sadly as I fell away into a sleep.

When I woke up

— ② Getting to the Solution

page 2

I found myself starring at my clock "6:30, It must be a mistake. It has to! The party starts in 45 minutes." I said not realizing I was screaming.

I jumped out of bed, got dressed, and sprinted off toward the kitchen without even realizing "I felt a whole lot better.

Before I could speak my mom spoke first. "You can go and have fun."

I ran and ran not even looking where I was

— ② Getting to the Solution

going just letting my feet take me along. Once I was there I entered my school and headed for my door knowing it was gonna

— ③ Solution and Inferential Ending

Integrating Test Prep into Reading & Writing Workshops © 2011 by Nancy Jennison • Scholastic Teaching Resources

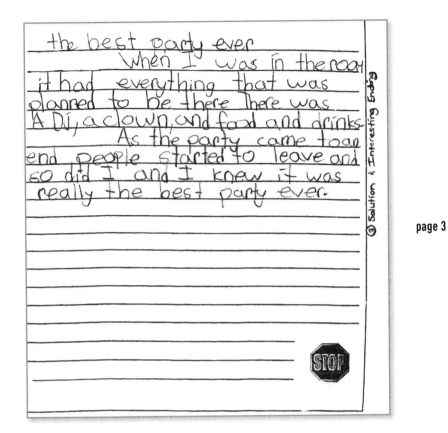

the best party ever
 When I was in the room
it had everything that was
planned to be there. There was
A DJ, a clown, and food and drinks.
 As the party came to an
end people started to leave and
so did I and I knew it was
really the best party ever.

③ Solution & Interesting Ending

page 3

STOP

Figure 7.1

Ean used a specially designed writing sheet that helped him organize his thinking
and prompted him to include a problem, solution, and an interesting ending.

PROBLEM Students are not using effective elaboration in their stories—they need to achieve a better balance of dialogue, internal thinking, action, and setting.

POSSIBLE SOLUTION Use a mentor text as a model and have students highlight dialogue, internal thinking, action, and setting using different colored markers, first with the mentor text and later with their own writing.

Arnold Almaguer, Kathy Doyle, and Christie Mortara helped their regular education and special education students by selecting excellent texts that showed this balance to students—*Journey* by Patricia MacLachlan and the short story "The Bike" by Gary Soto (but a text that you select would also work well). They had students use highlighter pens to color-code parts of *Journey* and "The Bike" to show how each author used dialogue, internal thinking, action, or setting to elaborate, and then students did the same with their own writing as a revision technique. Students had a simple way to see exactly how to improve elaboration when they used the following colors to highlight their writing:

- Yellow: use of elaboration with dialogue

- Red: use of elaboration with internal thinking

- Pink: use of elaboration with action

- Green: use of elaboration with setting

PROBLEM Students are not noticing editing errors.

POSSIBLE SOLUTION Do a mini-lesson on how to edit using the finger-pointing/pencil-pointing strategy.

Ramon, a sixth-grade student at Rolling Valley School in Springfield, Virginia, was a superb content writer, but as I looked at his composition I noticed he had 13 editing errors in spelling, word omissions, and use of improper tenses. After I showed Ramon how to reread his writing aloud while he finger-pointed or pencil-pointed under each word, he located and fixed all 13 errors on his own. He remembered this technique later, when he took the state test. He reread his composition during the test to himself, rather than aloud.

This is what Ramon did when he edited his writing *before* the test:

- He pointed under each word, moving his finger or a pencil directly under each word as he read his composition aloud.

- As Ramon pointed to words, he questioned the tenses, asking himself, "Does that sound right?"

- He looked closely at his words, thinking about whether they looked strange because he had made misspellings or left one out, and asked himself, "Does that look right?"

Ramon felt that taking the time to edit was worth his effort.

PROBLEM Students are not using literary devices in their writing.

POSSIBLE SOLUTION Use activities and a game to help students understand how to use literary devices effectively.

Suggestions for literary device activities for students include the following:

- Create literary devices to come up with a positive description of classmates and the teacher, for example, "My teacher is so smart, she is a walking computer!"

- Use literary devices to describe the main character in your read-aloud. Demonstrate how mentor authors use literary devices to make writing more descriptive. Ask students to describe the main character using literary devices.

Integrating Test Prep into Reading & Writing Workshops © 2011 by Nancy Jennison • Scholastic Teaching Resources

- Co-write with the class ordinary versus poetic descriptions of objects (Heard, 1999). Have students co-write a description of an object using poetic language containing literary devices and then write a contrasting version using everyday language.

- Ask students to reread their drafts to see where a literary device fits. Coach students on how to use the devices to enhance their writing pieces: make sure the stories make sense and that your students select images effectively, tastefully inserting only one or two devices into their writing.

A GAME TO TEACH LITERARY DEVICES

Special education teacher Joan Shayne and third-grade classroom teacher Judi Feinberg of Smith School in Tenafly, New Jersey, taught literary devices in an exciting way that both special and regular education third-grade students simply loved. Joan and Judi made one sign for a sentence and another sign for the literary device. The students matched the sentence to the correct literary device during Morning Meeting. Another idea is to ask students to do the same activity independently at their seats and time them. They never tire of trying to beat their own time.

- The gang of girls giggled and gabbed. (alliteration)

- Six seals swam in the sea. (alliteration)

- The waves crashed and splashed against the rocks. (onomatopoeia)

- Swish, swish, swish went the leaves. (onomatopoeia)

- The breeze laughed and called to me. (personification)

- My rocking chair looked happy to see me. (personification)

- The boy was as silly as a clown. (simile)

- She was as loud as a thunderstorm. (simile)

- The angry boys were a swarm of noisy bees. (metaphor)

- The dog was a hungry bear. (metaphor)

Once your students all understand how to use simile, onomatopoeia, personification, metaphor, and alliteration, you can teach more sophisticated literary devices, such as hyperbole, to your top students.

When I work with writers who need more support, I want them to know how to recognize all literary devices, but I have found that for some of my students, teaching them how to write all five devices was difficult. So I focus on helping them become very proficient at using several of them, for example, how to write an effective simile.

PROBLEM Students do not understand how to write a clear paragraph with effective details.

POSSIBLE SOLUTION Play a game called "Talk About a Classmate!" and follow up with whole-class paragraph writing. Once students understand the basics, provide coaching to match more sophisticated writers' needs in small groups.

A GAME TO TEACH PARAGRAPHS: TALK ABOUT A CLASSMATE!

This game helps students with learning the structure of a paragraph, as well as how to create topic sentences, supporting detail sentences, and closing sentences. Use more sophisticated variations, such as including dialogue as a detail, for differentiating instruction.

Materials:

- A container for each cooperative group of 5 students
- 5 red slips of paper, 5 green slips of paper inside each container

Procedure:

- Inside a jar (or other type of container) place five red slips of paper labeled: topic sentence person, first detail sentence person, second detail sentence person, third detail sentence person, and concluding sentence person. Write the names of five different students on each of five green slips and place them inside the jar.

- Divide students into teams. Five students make up a team. Each team works together to create an oral paragraph. Each student selects a red slip of paper. Then each team chooses a green slip of paper with a classmate's name on it. The team's job is to create a paragraph about the student whose name is on the green paper by saying something that is kind and true about the classmate. Here is an example:

Topic sentence person: "Joanna is very athletic."

First detail person: "She runs very fast in PE."

Second detail person: "Every day Joanna jogs for a mile."

Third detail person: "She entered the Run for Life race with her mother and finished the race."

Concluding sentence person: "So, Joanna continues to impress all of us with her sports talents."

At the end, say together: "Let's hear it for Joanna!" Everyone applauds!

Integrating Test Prep into Reading & Writing Workshops © 2011 by Nancy Jennison • Scholastic Teaching Resources

- Expect students' sentence structure as well as their details to become stronger and more descriptive the more you play the game. Modify the game to reflect your mini-lessons. For example, after you have taught literary devices, add a condition that one detail sentence has to include a literary device that fits well and enhances the paragraph. Or, after you have taught types of leads, ask students to begin the paragraph with a dramatic lead.

PROBLEM Students are not using effective leads that hook the reader.

POSSIBLE SOLUTION Teach students strategies for writing different types of leads in earlier writing units before the test-prep unit. Have them identify the types of leads that mentor writers use and then practice writing various types of leads of their own.

How to Differentiate Teaching Effective Leads

This lesson helps everyone in the class with strategies for writing leads, since I adapt the type of leads I teach to match my students' needs. For example, if I find that my students' leads do not grab the readers' attention, I teach them dramatic leads. The strategies that I demonstrate simply give students more ideas to keep at their fingertips. First, I use labels for a variety of different leads suggested by writing experts, then I prepare my own written examples of each type to share with the students.

As you read through this list of possible ways for your students to write leads on their drafts, think about the mentor texts that you have and the kinds of writers you have, so you can effectively match your mentor texts with your writers' needs. Lucy Calkins suggests choosing only a few to model (Calkins & Martinelli, 2006).

Differentiate your instruction by matching choices of leads to groups of writers in your class. Begin by teaching just a couple of leads, then ask students to practice them and insert them into their drafts, where appropriate. As you confer, you will get ideas for how to group writers. For example, for students who easily wrote the type that you demonstrated, select another type to show them that might fit better. On the other hand, for students who need more support, work with them in a small group and use brainstorming and drama to add easier leads, such as using sound effects or a question.

I wrote the leads that follow as examples. The story centers on a boy named Chris, who is in competition with his twin brother, Max, a basketball star.

Types of Leads

A DIALOGUE LEAD

Writers captivate readers' interest as they begin their writing with a line or two of dialogue that is important to the piece (Lane, 1999).

"You're acting like a loser!" Max said to his twin brother, Chris. Max grabbed the basketball and tossed it easily through the hoop. "That's how to do it, so practice more and stop feeling so sorry for yourself." Max flipped the ball back to Chris and whistled while he walked away.

A QUESTION LEAD

Writers grab the audience's attention as they ask a question that they hope readers will read on to answer (Fletcher, 1993).

What is this? I practice twice as much as Max does, and I just get worse. What am I doing wrong?

A DRAMATIC LEAD

A dramatic lead grasps the audience's attention and often includes tension (Fletcher, 1993 & 1999).

The ball missed the basket for the eighth time in a row, and Chris slammed it against the garage door. His stomach was in knots as he visualized another game, another benching, and another humiliation.

AN ACTION LEAD

Writers use an action lead to show (not tell) the main character or another character doing something that is very specific that catches the reader's attention (Calkins & Martinelli, 2006).

Max dribbled the ball down the court, stopped near the foul line, jumped and shot the ball cleanly through the basket. Chris, Max's twin brother, watched from the bench and thought to himself, *There he goes again. Mr. Perfection.*

Discuss with students why adding the sentence *I'll never be as good as he is* at the end of the action lead gives away too much, too early in the story.

A SETTING LEAD

Writers begin with the setting to set the story up for their readers, and create a mood so that the audience can picture where it is taking place (Calkins & Martinelli, 2006).

Integrating Test Prep into Reading & Writing Workshops © 2011 by Nancy Jennison • Scholastic Teaching Resources

In *A Critical Handbook of Children's Literature* (1999), Rebecca Lukens, speaks of integral settings that are crucial to the story, and she contrasts them to backdrop settings, which are of less importance to the story.

Buzzing mosquitoes bounced against the window screen. As darkness overtook the evening sky, Chris flicked his finger at the screen, causing the mosquitoes to scatter. The light over his garage shone on the driveway and made the dreaded basketball hoop clearly visible.

A SOUND EFFECTS LEAD

A sound effects lead catches the audience's interest by causing readers to wonder about the source of the sounds and what is happening. It is key that the sounds matter to the story in some way. Ralph Fletcher speaks about the power of using sound effects as a lead in his children's book *Live Writing: Breathing Life Into Your Words* (1999).

SSSSSSsssssssssSSSSSsssssssssSSSSSSssssss. The basketball hissed, while the air streamed out of it, changing its shape from round to oval. That sound gave Chris a sharp pain in the pit of his stomach. *It's all over for me now,* **he thought to himself.** *I never should have smashed my basketball on the jagged rocks. Now, I can't even practice.*

ADDITIONAL ACTIVITIES THAT HELP TEACH STUDENTS ABOUT USING DIFFERENT TYPES OF LEADS

Insert leads into a class scenario. The students and I think of a scenario that will enable us to compose examples of each different type of lead. For example, one class and I wrote a variety of leads about what went wrong on an imaginary class trip.

Use drama to open students' minds and renew their interest. To differentiate teaching leads for students who need more support, I have found that drama opens students' minds and renews interest and excitement about the task at hand. Model a specific type of lead and dramatize how the lead looks. Invite students to dramatize other sample leads. Once you complete the drama, co-write with students other examples of leads that you dramatized. This is a bridge that gets students ready to work independently.

Identify leads in mentor texts and read-alouds. Take copies of your favorite read-alouds and identify their leads. See which types match your categories, as well as those that belong in other categories. There is a list of additional resources in Figure 7.2.

Recommended Fiction and Nonfiction Mentor Texts for Teaching Leads

Dialogue Lead

On My Honor by Marion Dane Bauer

Charlotte's Web by E. B. White

Ida B by Katherine Hannigan

Esperanza Rising by Pam Muñoz Ryan

The Gold-Threaded Dress by Carolyn Marsden

Question Lead

Sarah, Plain and Tall by Patricia MacLachlan

Animals Nobody Loves by Seymour Simon

Hottest Coldest Highest Deepest by Steve Jenkins

Dramatic Lead

Three Cups of Tea: One Man's Journey to Change the World . . . One Child at a Time by Greg Mortenson & David Oliver Relin

Wringer by Jerry Spinneli

Wilma Unlimited by Kathleen Krull

Clementine by Sara Pennypacker

The Underneath by Kathi Appelt

Spider Boy by Ralph Fletcher

The Hundred Dresses by Eleanor Estes

Action Lead

Journey of the Sparrows by Fran Leeper Buss

Sisters & Brothers: Sibling Relationships in the Animal World by Steve Jenkins & Robin Page

Setting Lead

Pale Male: Citizen Hawk of New York City by Janet Schulman

When the Wolves Returned: Restoring Nature's Balance in Yellowstone by Dorothy Hinshaw Patent

Holes by Louis Sachar

Night in the Country by Cynthia Rylant

The Emperor's Egg by Martin Jenkins

The Watsons Go to Birmingham—1963 by Christopher Paul Curtis

Twilight Comes Twice by Ralph Fletcher

Down, Down, Down in the Ocean by Sandra Markle

Fireflies! by Julie Brinckloe

Hatchet by Gary Paulsen

Sound Effects Lead

Bridge to Terabithia by Katherine Paterson

Into the Sea by Brenda Z. Guiberson

Figure 7.2

The chart lists texts that contain examples of the types of leads I introduced in this section.

Integrating Test Prep into Reading & Writing Workshops © 2011 by Nancy Jennison • Scholastic Teaching Resources

Link the leads to students' authentic writing. I always link my lesson on leads to authentic writing. I ask students to use the leads of their choice to write their drafts in several different ways. Author and writing expert Donald Murray advises letting your students write different types of leads and then asking them to tell each writer which lead interested them the most. Murray feels that leads are vital because writers only have three to five seconds to capture the reader's interest (1985). Students and I recall and list the types of leads that we have studied in mentor texts and notice additional techniques other authors use. We keep those in mind as we revise future drafts of fiction and nonfiction.

PROBLEM Students are not using effective transition words, so their writing does not flow well and lacks coherence.

POSSIBLE SOLUTION Teach the different types of transition words, observe and highlight how professional writers use them, and ask students to highlight appropriate places in their own writing to insert them.

I found that my students were not using transition words effectively to make their writing more coherent, so I developed this lesson to remediate the problem. You may already have lists of transition words like the list in Figure 7.3, which consists of common transition words that I compiled and used with students. Feel free to modify this list.

HOW TO TEACH A TRANSITION WORD LESSON

I modeled how I could use a transition word example in a sentence (see the chart in Figure 7.3) and asked students to generate other examples in partnerships. They listened to one another's oral examples and raised their hands when they heard the transition word mentioned in each sentence. As a group, we evaluated the transition word sentences and made sure that they sounded smooth and not stilted.

- Next, I showed students an example of text from their current read-aloud that had transition words embedded effectively. I asked students to raise their hands for the transition words in the read-aloud, then I had partners locate and circle more transition words on a copy of the text.

- Finally, I asked students to reread their own writing and to highlight places where they could make their writing more coherent by adding more effective transitions. Students added transitions to those areas.

DIFFERENTIATE FOR STUDENTS WHO NEED MORE SUPPORT WITH TRANSITIONS

If your students still need more help with understanding how to use transition words, consider doing what a creative teacher did. Fourth-grade teacher Stacey Bailey, from Stillman School in Tenafly, New Jersey, asked her students to cut out newspaper articles and bring them to school after they highlighted transition words. Stacey also asked students to notice transition words everywhere in their environment. The students loved to share and talk about what they found. Using transition words was easy for Stacey's students because it became part of their thinking early in the school year. Consequently, they wrote coherent writing pieces that were full of appropriate transitions.

PROBLEM Students' sentence structures are lackluster and have no voice.

POSSIBLE SOLUTION Use sentences from mentor texts to show your students how varying sentence length is a tool to show voice.

I have conducted this lesson with students as early as grade 3. It energizes them to think like authors, to notice what authors have done in writing sentences with voice, and then to try to write similar sentences themselves. I found that when I re-examined familiar classroom books with a critical eye toward sentence structure and considered reasons why the authors had written sentences in a certain way, I discovered that many of these old favorites took on a newfound sense of voice in their sentences. I invite you to make a similar reappraisal of the books on your classroom shelves.

For example, in a picture book *Come On, Rain!* by Karen Hesse, a third-grade class and I saw the excitement and tension building with the author's use of short sentences as the characters in the story wait for the rain to begin. We noticed how Ms. Hesse's use of repetition in the following example creates tension.

> *"Is there thunder?" Mamma asks.*
>
> *"No thunder," I say.*
>
> *"Is there lightning?" Mamma asks.*
>
> *"No lightning," Jackie-Joyce says.*
>
> *"You stay where I can find you," Mamma says.*
>
> *"We will," I say.*

In another scene, when the children are holding their mammas' hands and dancing in the rain, the author uses longer sentences. The students and I felt that these long sentences seemed to stretch out the enjoyment, so that it felt like it was going on and on.

> *"We twirl and sway them,*
>
> *tromping through puddles,*
>
> *romping and reeling in the moisty green air."*

Figure 7.3

Six Common Types of Transition Words and Phrases

1. Time Transition Words

Time transition words help let the reader know how time is passing.

"*As soon as* I get to school, I get ready for my wonderful students."

Examples of Time Transition Words: about, after, afterward, as soon as, as, before, eventually, finally, first, immediately, later, meanwhile, next, next week, *number words*—first (and so on), often, once, previously, rarely, second, soon, then, third, till, today, tomorrow, until, usually, when, while, yesterday

2. Compare and Contrast Words

These transitions show what is the same or different.

"*Although* I enjoy eating apples, pears are my favorite fruit."

Examples of Compare and Contrast Transition Words: as, also, although, and, another, at the same time, but, conversely, even though, however, in the same way, like, likewise, nevertheless, on the other hand, otherwise, rather, similarly, still, too, yet

3. Summarizing or Drawing Conclusion Words

Use these words to sum up what you are saying.

"*All in all*, I believe the third- and fourth-grade classes can use transition words very well."

Examples of Summarizing or Drawing Conclusion Transition Words: accordingly, all in all, as a result, because, consequently, finally, for, in conclusion, in other words, in short, in summary, lastly, since, so, so that, that is, therefore, to sum up

4. Place or Location Words

These transition words show where something is located or placed.

"Your pencil is *beside* the globe *on top of* the counter."

Examples of Place or Location Transition Words: at the bottom, at the left, at the right, above, across, adjacent, against, behind, beside, beyond, by, close, down, farther on, here, in, in back of, in front of, inside, into, near, nearby, next to, off, onto, on top of, opposite, outside, over, surrounding, there, throughout, to the left, to the right, under

5. Words That Make a Point Clear

Use these transition words when you want to make your point clear to the listener or reader.

"*Truly*, you are the best class I have ever had!"

Examples of Transition Words That Make a Point Clear: above all, again, also, besides, certainly, for example, for instance, for this reason, furthermore, indeed, in fact, in other words, in truth, really, specifically, surely, that is, to emphasize, to illustrate, to repeat, truly

6. Words that Add Information

Use these transition words when you want to add something to what you said or wrote.

"*Another* benefit of teaching these students is that they learn so quickly."

Examples of Transition Words that Add Information: Again, additionally, along with, also, and, another, as well as, besides, equally important, finally, for example, for instance, in addition to, in fact, likewise, moreover, next, not only-but also, therefore, too

HOW TO TEACH A VOICE LESSON USING SENTENCE STRUCTURE

To prepare for a lesson on sentence structure, simply reread books that are familiar to students that you think are written well, and notice the types of sentences that the author uses. Ask yourself, "Why did the author use this length of sentence here? Did it set a mood or develop a feeling in the reader?" Select the texts you will use as mentor texts.

■ Use a document camera or make a transparency (or a copy) of the short sentences from the mentor book and contrast them with longer sentences that the author has used. Next, begin by modeling for students why you think the author chose to write like that. Be explicit and clear on your thinking.

■ Invite students to think of other reasons why the author made the choices he or she did.

■ Display other examples in the text of both short and long sentences. Ask students to think of why the author wrote them. (They are insightful in what they discover!)

■ Show students a section of your own writing where you've deliberately used short sentences. Once students are familiar with your piece, ask them to tell you why they think you used the short sentences. Listen to their amazing ideas!

■ Implement the suggestions of Janet Angelillo, who recommends an activity that is especially helpful for students who need more support. She suggests asking your students to think of and substitute other words that you could have used in the short sentence section of your piece. This activity is a scaffold that enables students to see that writing short sentences is something they can do successfully, so it gives them confidence (Angelillo, 2005a).

■ Invite students to reread their drafts and see how they can build tension by using shorter sentences or stretch out moments with longer sentences. (*Come On, Rain!* by Karen Hesse is fabulous mentor text for showing this.)

Once students understand why authors use a variety of sentence types to show voice, they can write powerful sections of their own texts by controlling the sentence length. Other books that I have used for this lesson are the classic *Owl Moon* by Jane Yolen and *Fireflies!* by Julie Brinckloe.

PROBLEM Students' word choices are either too simple, inappropriate, or they do not fit the intended message or enhance the piece.

POSSIBLE SOLUTION Create and display Vocabulary Ladders to raise students' consciousness about word meanings.

A vocabulary ladder (Greenwood, 2004) is a strategy that I have used in training teachers about vocabulary enrichment and in working with students. When I created ladder-type charts with students' help, the goal was to demonstrate a continuum of meanings for common words, but it also functioned as a concrete tool that helped students to choose exact words (Angelillo, 2005b). By posting this chart and making it into a ladder that shows a range of word meanings from mild to extreme (see Figure 7.4), students learned subtle differences that helped them to be more precise both in writing and in speaking. They referred to these ladders throughout the year and used them as a reference in their writing. To make vocabulary ladders part of daily activities, you can model how you refer to the chart in selecting the most appropriate word to use in conversations with students.

HOW TO USE A VOCABULARY LADDER

This strategy has been successful in classes when teachers have used it as follows:

- Once you have constructed a continuum of shades of meaning with students for one word, make a list of other words that you could develop in a similar manner. This is your chance to move students beyond overusing those same tired-out words that drive you crazy!

- Divide students into partnership groups and ask them to create their own vocabulary ladder at home on one of the words.

- On the next day, ask students to each share the vocabulary ladder of the same word with their partners and prepare to share their final list with the whole class. Partnerships share their continuums on ladder-like charts large enough so that they can be displayed in the classroom.

- Make copies of each partnership's different vocabulary ladder and ask students to paste them inside their writers' notebooks to increase word consciousness.

- Continue to demonstrate all year long how you use a vocabulary ladder for writing precise words in your writing and show students how to do the same.

- Ask students to verbalize how they will use this knowledge when writing and how they will refer to the ladder continuum sheets in their writers' notebooks.

- As an assessment check, ask students to highlight words from the continuums in their own writing to demonstrate that they are using them. Also, ask them to place a check beside each word that they use that is on a continuum and periodically ask to see this list when you are conferring.

- Differentiate as you modify the vocabulary ladder depending on your students. You may want to make the continuum briefer if students need more support. In writing your definitions for the continuum, try to include the words *something*, *someone*, or *describes* in your explanations to make the definition more student-friendly and clear. Explain the meaning in everyday language, so students can understand the meaning of the word with ease. Write the definition of how the word is typically used, and students will more easily understand its meaning (Beck et al., 2002, 2008). A sample vocabulary ladder for the word *angry* is shown below.

Figure 7.4

Example of a Vocabulary Ladder Using Student-Friendly Definitions

ANGRY	
annoyed	Someone who is annoyed is bothered by something that has happened or that someone has said, and this may have occurred more than once.
heated	Someone who is feeling heated is starting to get mad and beginning to show her anger.
exasperated	Someone who is exasperated is very angry because something unpleasant keeps happening.
furious	If someone is furious, you can tell by his expression that he is extremely mad about something.
fuming	Someone who is fuming is feeling very mad about something that happened but may not have said anything about it yet.
infuriated	If you infuriated someone, you did something to make that person very angry at you, and she looks it!
irate	Someone who is irate cannot keep her anger to herself. She is so angry that she may lose control of herself.
outraged	You are outraged if someone has done something that is so cruel or offensive that it made you extremely upset.

PROBLEM Students' endings are lackluster and make no impression on the audience.

POSSIBLE SOLUTION Study endings used by mentor writers, and teach students a few techniques for writing different types of endings and for using appropriate ones in their writing.

SUGGESTIONS FOR TECHNIQUES FOR TEACHING ENDINGS

Endings are what readers carry with them and recall about a piece of writing (Murray, 1985, Calkins & Martinelli, 2006). If your students do not know what important points they want readers to carry away with them, try what Lucy Calkins and Marjorie Martinelli suggest. Have your students reread their drafts and then have them ask themselves, "What is the important message I've conveyed?" Then ask students to highlight places in the text which seem very important. As they reread those highlighted places, students make their endings relate to those places (2006, p. 97).

HOW TO DIFFERENTIATE WHEN YOU TEACH ABOUT ENDINGS

- As you read through this list of possible ways for your students to end their stories, think about the mentor texts that you have and the kinds of writers in your class, and select the endings that best exemplify your mentor texts and match your writers' needs. Locate endings in texts that conclude by implication, so that the reader comes to the conclusion that the writer wants (Murray, 1985).

- If you do not have mentor texts, consider writing your own examples of each ending, or use the samples on pages 168–170. Choose only a few types to model and differentiate by matching the endings that you select to groups of writers in your class.

- Another way to differentiate is to select a small number of types of endings for students who need more support from you to try. Also, select the endings that you feel would be easier for these students and coach them in small groups.

GLIDING ENDING VS. CRASH ENDING FOR YOUNGER INTERMEDIATE WRITERS

When I work with younger intermediate-grade writers, I select a gliding ending to model for students who needed more support, since their pieces often end abruptly. I instruct these students very explicitly and directly (De La Paz, 2007) by showing a poster with a movable paper airplane that glides down on the runway. I compare that image to a crash ending, which sounds as brief as "the end." To help younger intermediate-grade writers visualize the differences between a gliding and crash ending, I ask them to pretend that their hand is an airplane, and we glide down together and come in for a landing. Students easily understand that image. When I work with students who need more support, I modify the example so it is easier to grasp. Here is the revised easier ending that matches the gliding sample on page 168: *As Chris lay in his bed wide-eyed, too excited to sleep, he still could not believe that his basket actually scored the winning point at the Greenfield Middle School championship game. A smile crept over his face as he heard the crowd cheering his name, again and again and again. This was a day made in heaven.*

SOME TECHNIQUES FOR WRITING ENDINGS

There are many different techniques for crafting endings; here are a few that my students have used that work well in state tests. I incorporated teaching endings earlier in the year so that students were less stressed by having to craft powerful endings during the test-prep unit right before the test. They already had a choice of strategies for writing endings, and they knew what worked well for them. When they tried to write different types of endings, it was always for an authentic purpose. That is, they selected the ending that worked the best in their piece of writing.

You may already know of other strategies for writing endings that work well for your students. As you read over the examples below, feel free to modify them for a closer fit to your students' needs.

Types of Endings

A GLIDING ENDING

A gliding ending slowly glides to a close and sometimes refers back to the topic. It prepares the audience by making the story sound like it is coming to a close, but it doesn't rush through the ending.

Many texts have this type of ending. Here is an example of an alternative ending for the Chris and Max scenarios that I featured in the section on leads earlier in this chapter on pages 158–159:

As Chris lay in his bed wide-eyed, too excited to sleep, he still could not comprehend that his basket actually scored the winning point at the Greenfield Middle School championship game. A smile crept over his face as he heard the crowd cheering his name, again and again and again. *They said my name; they actually said my name. I don't know how I did it; they thought I was a hero. Maybe I was just lucky, but I'll take it. Being a star feels fine!*

AN EMOTIONAL ENDING

An emotional ending leaves a sharp emotional feeling that stays with the reader when the paper is finished. It might be happy, sad, or funny, and so on. Or it may just make the audience think really deeply and feel things from the writing. It is one type of ending that readers remember (Fletcher & Portalupi, 1998).

Here is another example from the Chris and Max scenario:

As Chris lay in his bed wide-eyed, too excited to sleep, he still could not believe that his basket actually scored the winning point at the championship game. His grin said it all. *The crowd roared my name, not Max's.* **But an instant later his smile suddenly vanished, and his eyes swelled with tears as he wondered . . .** *but, how can I keep the cheers going?*

Integrating Test Prep into Reading & Writing Workshops © 2011 by Nancy Jennison • Scholastic Teaching Resources

Teaching Suggestion: Kathy Doyle recommends *Journey* and *Fireflies!* as excellent texts for showing your students how settings help to create emotion. She also suggests having them revise the Chris and Max example above with an eye toward using setting to make it emotional.

AN IMPORTANT MESSAGE ENDING

An ending with an important message occurs when you write an ending so skillfully that your audience realizes something new and meaningful from the text.

Kathy Doyle believes students need to be careful with this type of an ending in order to avoid sounding too preachy. To demonstrate the differences for students, rewrite this ending below so that it does sound too preachy, then ask students to compare the two versions and revise the moralistic one. Here is another example from the Chris and Max scenario:

As Chris lay in his bed wide-eyed, too excited to sleep, he pictured his ball scoring the winning point in the championship game. He heard his father cheer, "Chris! You did it, Chris!" A smirk crossed his lips, as he replayed the crowd's earlier boos for his brother, when Max fouled out. *Now I know what it's like to be Max. But is being like Max so great? One minute the crowd applauds you and the next minute they boo. Is this what I want?*

AN ACTION ENDING

An action ending uses an important movement that reminds readers of the entire story they've just read (Calkins & Martinelli, 2006).

Lucy Calkins and Marjorie Martinelli suggest that students reread their drafts and think of the "important messages" that are in them, and then read again as they highlight "important actions" that can be incorporated into their endings (2006). Here is another example from the Chris and Max scenario:

Coach Myers hurriedly motioned to Chris and said, "Get in the game." Chris bounded out on the court. A Deerfield High guard swung both arms in front of his face, so Chris couldn't get the ball. Quickly, Chris spun and ran into the corner, eluding his guard, and received a sideline pass. Now he got a chance to shoot. He steadied himself and then launched a one-handed jump shot. The crowd's cries and cheers said it all. Chris had shot a perfect basket. The buzzer sounded and the scoreboard showed that his team had won. Chris felt slaps on his back. Proudly, he smiled as teammates carried him around the court on two players' shoulders. He wondered if it was all just a dream.

A DIALOGUE ENDING

Use a dialogue ending when the dialogue relates to what the piece was really about and is a whole-story reminder (Calkins & Martinelli, 2006).

Kathy Doyle adds that "in between the dialogue, I always tell my students to put a bit of action or something to show setting. It sounds better and keeps the balance of action, setting, and dialogue more even." Here is an example from the Chris and Max scenario:

As Chris walked on air toward his brother, Max stopped him. "Hey, Chris, you really showed them tonight, didn't you?"

Chris responded, "So, Max, ah, you didn't mind that I scored the final points?"

Max slapped Chris on the back and answered, "We kept it in the family. Maybe we need to work together like that more often . . . you and me, I mean. What do you think?"

Chris glanced again at the final score on the scoreboard and said, "Max, do you really think I can pull my weight? I mean you are the one that the fans always want."

Max smiled and said, "So, why can't they want both of us? After breakfast tomorrow, how about a game of hoops?"

Try It

Why not consider adding the use of mentor texts to your lessons on leads and endings? Read over the lists of assorted mentor texts for teaching leads and endings that appear in this chapter.

✓ Decide on the types of leads and endings that you will teach to your students.

✓ Obtain samples of the suggested mentor texts from your school or local public library.

✓ Use the mentor texts to show students examples of leads and endings. Study the different techniques that the mentor authors used with students.

✓ Demonstrate how you use those techniques in your writing.

✓ Guide students to incorporate similar techniques in their own drafts.

Recommended Fiction and Nonfiction Mentor Texts for Teaching Endings

A Gliding Ending

When the Wolves Returned—Restoring Nature's Balance in Yellowstone by Dorothy Hinshaw Patent

Spider Boy by Ralph Fletcher

The Tiger Rising by Kate DiCamillo

Wolfsnail: A Backyard Predator by Sarah C. Campbell

Because of Winn Dixie by Kate DiCamillo

The Buffalo Storm by Katherine Applegate

An Emotional Ending

Charlotte's Web by E. B. White

A Taste of Blackberries by Doris Buchanan Smith

The Escape of Oney Judge: Martha Washington's Slave Finds Freedom by Emily Arnold McCully

The Miraculous Journey of Edward Tulane by Kate DiCamillo

An Important Message Ending

Three Cups of Tea: One Man's Journey to Change the World One Child at a Time by Greg Mortenson and David Oliver Relin

The Hundred Dresses by Eleanor Estes

Holes by Louis Sachar

Barack Obama: Son of Promise, Child of Hope by Nikki Grimes

Mission Save the Planet: Things You Can Do to Help Fight Global Warming by Sally Ride and Tam O'Shaughnessy

Freedom Summer by Deborah Wiles

Coretta Scott by Ntozake Shange

An Action Ending

Fig Pudding by Ralph Fletcher

Because of Winn-Dixie by Kate DiCamillo

Dream Weaver by Jonathan London

Sisters & Brothers: Sibling Relationships in the Animal World by Steve Jenkins & Robin Page

A Dialogue Ending

Yolanda's Genius by Carol Fenner

Clementine by Sara Pennypacker

Esperanza Rising by Pam Muñoz Ryan

Ida B . . . and Her Plans to Maximize Fun, Avoid Disaster, and (Possibly) Save the World by Katherine Hannigan

Hatchet by Gary Paulsen

The Gold-Threaded Dress by Carolyn Marsden

Lavender by Karen Hesse

Figure 7.5

The All-Purpose Lesson! Use Contrasting Examples

Use two contrasting examples of the same piece of writing that match your teaching point, one well-written piece and one that needs work. When I share these samples with small groups of students, I can customize my lesson to address exactly where students need help, and my teaching point is more easily seen.

A SAMPLE LESSON FOR STUDENTS WHO NEED HELP USING VIVID WORDS

If my students are not including vivid words in their writing, I do the following:

- Ask students to bring their pieces of writing, highlighters, extra sheets of paper for revising, and a pencil, and come meet with me in a small group.

- Show two different versions of a short writing sample to the group. Often, I write student-like samples myself, making the weaker sample reflect precisely what the group needs to revise in its writing.

  For example, I write a very short piece for sample one. Its length is a paragraph or two, and it contains vivid words that enhance the piece and fit well. Sample two is the same piece of writing as sample one, but I modify it to fit my teaching point. In this instance, I watered down the vibrant words.

- Ask the students to read over both pieces with me, and I tell them that I want them to notice how one piece is different from the other.

STUDENTS TURN AND TALK TO THEIR PARTNERS

- I ask students to turn to their partners and tell what they notice. Their comments must be very specific, and students need to refer to the pieces to prove what they say, for example, "In sample one, the author used the word *hurled*, which is much clearer than the word *threw* used in sample two. *Hurled* helped me to see that the boy in the story was angry."

STUDENTS SHARE WHAT THEY NOTICED

- The students and I brainstorm other reasons why the first sample is much better than the second.

- We discuss what students have learned that they can apply immediately to revising their own writing.

STUDENTS APPLY THE STRATEGIES TO REVISE THEIR OWN WRITING

- Students reread their writing, highlight words to revise, and replace them with more vivid ones.

Integrating Test Prep into Reading & Writing Workshops © 2011 by Nancy Jennison • Scholastic Teaching Resources

- I begin to confer with each student in the group, and together we look at one or two places where he or she has added more vivid words, and I offer support.

- Students return to their seats and complete their revisions. I read over their writing that evening and jot my comments for them on sticky notes.

 ## Read How It Worked

Improve your students' revision strategies when they play the Make it to Hollywood game.

This stimulating activity was developed by two fifth-grade teachers at Mackay Elementary School in Tenafly, New Jersey. In this collaborative classroom, Donna Klein is the special education teacher, and Jennifer Angerson is the regular fifth-grade teacher.

"Our game is modeled after the TV show *American Idol*. You could use it with any genre of writing. We used this in conjunction with our test-prep writing unit, but next year we will also use it earlier with writing other genres. When our students wrote their fiction stories, they used a checklist for speculative writing that Nancy Jennison created for us, and it reflected what our state expects our students to do. This checklist made the New Jersey State Writing Rubric much easier for students to understand. Since the New Jersey State Writing Rubric was on a five-point scale, we decided to create a game that was on a five-point scale and that would excite students about writing well." Students' reactions to the activity included, 'It was fun,' 'Cool!' and 'You got other people's opinions to help you.'"

Materials:
- Speculative Writing Checklist (Figure 7.6)
- A student who volunteers to read his/her writing aloud
- Three judges
- A set of 5 number signs for each of the judges: 5, 4, 3, 2, 1
- 3 whiteboards for the judges
- Sticky notes for the rest of the class

Procedure:
Three judges sit at a special area. To judge the piece of writing, they use a speculative writing checklist that is familiar to them and to all students. The student reads the story aloud and displays it on a screen. The three judges jot comments on individual whiteboards. Each judge then votes by holding up the appropriate number sign, along with his or her specific comments on the whiteboard.

Example: "4—Great lead that grabbed me, but lengthen the ending!" Students at their seats write their own evaluations on sticky notes. Both the judge and the students must be able to justify their scores by writing specific reasons for the score and by writing suggestions for what the writer needs to do to improve.

The writer hears the three judges' comments and then also collects the comments of the students in their seats. A writer needs a score of "5" to "Make It to Hollywood."

Speculative Writing Checklist

	Yes	No	Suggestions for making it better
❐ I used a clear, inviting lead that pulled the reader in.			
❐ My topic was focused, clear and well-developed, and it related to the speculative prompt.			
❐ I included specific details and developed them through show not tell, as well as through the use of literacy devices.			
❐ I used a logical organization that moved my reader through my story.			
❐ I made sure that I included a problem and resolved it at the end.			
❐ Transitional words helped my reader connect paragraphs and ideas.			
❐ I used clear and varied sentence lengths for different purposes.			
❐ I used vivid words that fit well.			
❐ I capitalized, spelled, and punctuated correctly.			
❐ I wrote a powerful ending that will linger in the reader's mind.			

Figure 7.6

I created the Speculative Writing Checklist for fifth-grade students to show them ideas of what the state expects in their state writing test.

Take Two

This is the revision and editing part of the game. After the writer gets the scores from the judges . . . perhaps he or she wants to still go to Hollywood but hasn't received the highest scores of 5 from all three judges. Then that night, the student can "Take Two." That means that he or she takes two chances to Make It to Hollywood. The student simply takes the piece home, revises and edits it with the suggestions in mind, and faces three different judges the next day!

Food for Thought

▼

PLANNING YOUR WRITING UNITS OF STUDY WITH COLLEAGUES CAN SAVE YOU TIME AND MINIMIZE YOUR STRESS IN CURRICULUM PLANNING. WHY NOT THINK ABOUT ADMINISTERING A DEMAND NARRATIVE TEST AT THE BEGINNING OF THE SCHOOL YEAR, AND THEN USING THE STATE RUBRIC TO SCORE STUDENTS' WRITING, SO THAT YOU CAN GLEAN SOME VITAL INFORMATION?

- Look at the assortment of lessons listed in this chapter and make a data retrieval chart. List the topic of each type of lesson across the top of your chart.

- List the names of your students at the left side of your chart. Evaluate your students' writing and place checks beside the names of students who need one or more of the lessons that appear in this chapter.

- Think about what writing units you will teach this year, and brainstorm with your colleagues when you will insert the lessons from this chapter, as well as others that students need.

  For example, after you assess your students' demand tests, you discover that a majority of your students are weak in writing leads. You can insert the lead lesson from this chapter into your first writing unit and revisit leads later in the year.

- By doing this and planning your lessons strategically, you can ensure that your students will be more prepared and less overwhelmed when you begin your test-prep unit.

CHAPTER 8

Create a Test-Prep Unit in Reading Workshop That Matches Your State Test

Highlights

- Use state resources and a demand reading test to assess your students and to plan test-prep instruction.

- Raise students' confidence by using study packets for state tests.

- Teach students test-prep strategies that help raise reading test scores.

- Teach students strategies for success with multiple-choice and open-ended questions.

- Teach students time-management tips for the reading tests.

- Examine one teacher's daily schedule for one week of reading test prep.

Pressure is building, since the date for the state test is right around the corner. Your administrator has just returned from meeting with the superintendent and told your staff that he expects your school to raise its scores this year. You want your reading test-prep unit to build on and reflect the work you have done all year during reading workshop, but you are not sure of where to begin. This chapter will give you the tools to make your test-prep work power-packed and on target.

Assess Students and Plan Test-Prep Instruction

Begin with a study of your state test to help plan your test-prep unit.

■ List the various parts of your state's reading tests.

■ Visit your state's Web site and locate released samples of reading tests. Think about which reading test component is the easiest for your students and start there.

■ Think of the last reading unit you completed in your reading workshop. Which part of the test is most like that reading unit? Start your test-prep studies with a topic that is familiar to your students.

■ Decide which part of the test you will practice first and select a released sample that you can use and administer for the demand test. Again, a demand test is the test students take before any test-prep instruction. (I am borrowing the term "demand" from work done at the Teachers College Reading and Writing Project.) If your state has time limits for students, then administer a timed demand test with the same time limits as the state test.

OBTAIN A DEMAND TEST FROM INTERNET RESOURCES

Reading test experts agree that the more you know about how your state's reading test works, the more strategic your test-prep instruction will be, and the more your students will benefit. In addition, when you and your students analyze and plan strategies for test items, they feel more ready to perform well on the state test (Fuhrken, 2009). If your state has not released any test samples of past state reading tests, there are several options:

One option is to go to other states' Web sites and select samples of released tests that are most like yours. New York, Texas, and Massachusetts, as well as other states, have all have released samples on their respective Web sites (see a list of links in Chapter 1, page 24).

CREATE A DEMAND TEST THAT MATCHES YOUR CURRICULUM

Another choice is to create your own test with colleagues using your district's content materials. I have created demand tests and test-prep materials for my school district that all tie to grade-specific content curriculum.

For example, since students in grade 4 study batteries in science and immigration in social studies, I created test-prep materials for fourth-grade teachers using text excerpts from trade books on these subjects. I wrote test questions similar to those that the state uses: multiple-choice and open-ended. From that group of materials and also from narrative test-prep materials that I created, I decided which tests were the demand tests. A sample test that I created for fifth-grade teachers that matches their science curriculum appears on pages 89–94.

ADMINISTER AND SCORE THE DEMAND TEST

The demand test is a baseline which can be used to assess your students' strengths and areas where they need support. Based on that initial assessment, you can begin to plan your test-prep mini-lessons and small-group work. If you have students who read below your grade level, you may want to administer an easier demand test for those students. For example, some of my special education colleagues used an easier demand test that their students read more easily, so students felt more confident.

Note the types of questions where students are having difficulties: multiple-choice, open-ended, or both. In some states, open-ended questions are called open-response or constructed-response questions.

■ Notice what reading skills were tested in the problematic questions: recognition of central idea, identifying supporting details, forming opinions, and so on. (See pages 11–21 and 23, for more information.)

■ Make lists of students who had difficulties and group them according to the types of lessons that they need.

■ Plan follow-up instruction on those reading skills, test formats, and time-management tips.

Get Ready for Your Test-Prep Unit: Create a Student Study Packet

I created study packets for each grade level, so that students would have a summary of state test components, formats, strategies for doing well, and time frames. I used them during test prep to introduce each section of the state test, and I also used them to help students review information. It helped them feel prepared, confident, and ready to take the test. Their parents appreciated the helpful tips on the study packets, too.

Creating simple study sheets for your student study packet helps students organize the information in their heads and feel more in control. The study packet informs students about the formats of each test. Once students learn about the sections and components of the test, many of their concerns disappear and their confidence improves (Calkins et al., 1998). When asked to name what was most helpful in preparing for the reading test, Tia, a fifth-grader from Tenafly, New Jersey, responded, "The Student Study Packets helped us remember tips to get a good score. These helped because when the actual test came around, I was relaxed and knew what to do. In my mind, I had a little angel reminding me what to do."

CREATE STUDENTS' STUDY SHEET FOR TEST PREP

As you look at Figures 8.1 and 8.2, notice how I designed the grade 5 study sheets to describe the New Jersey tests' components and students' strategies to do well. You can see that both tests are reading tests on informational and narrative reading passages and that they also contain multiple-choice and open-ended questions. Modify these study sheets to fit your state tests. In order to do so, this is what you need to know:

- The name for the specific section of the test
- The timing of the test
- The reading genre
- The types of questions
- Students' time-management strategies
- Students' strategies to get the highest score

Test-Prep Strategies for Students That Save Time and Raise Scores

These are the four proven strategies that I teach in my classes during our test-prep unit to help students raise their test scores. If your state test has time limits, these ideas may be just what you need to help your students save precious minutes.

1. Encourage students to read the reading test questions first.

Reading experts say it is crucial for students to read the test questions first and think about them while they read the test passage (Calkins et al., 1998). This way they have a genuine purpose for reading.

Figure 8.1

GRADE 5 NJ ASK | Nonfiction Informational Reading
STUDY SHEET

Test time: 30 minutes
Multiple-Choice Questions and an Open-Ended Question

Strategies for Managing Your Time

First: Read each <u>question</u> and underline or box KEY WORDS. Say, *"That means that I am supposed to think about _____ while I am reading."* (Do not read the answers yet.)

Second: Next, read the passage, while keeping in mind the questions that you just read. Underline answers to the questions in pencil while you are reading.

Third: Answer the multiple-choice questions. Check each answer before you mark it by *quickly* going back to what you underlined to make sure that it is the BEST answer.

Now go to the Open-Ended Question. Remember, this question is worth up to 4 points! Be sure that you do a GREAT job on this question!

Strategies: ROPE Your Answer

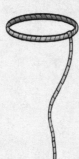

R = *Read* the question carefully, box or underline key words, and use some of the words from the question to begin your answer.

O = Give your ***opinions***.

P = *Prove* your opinion with a quote or reference to the text.

E = *Explain* your answer fully. Explain your own thinking and use insight.

To Get the Highest Score

- Use **specific information from the text** to support your explanations or opinions.

- **Add your own thinking** to tell more about each piece of proof, so you can show that you *really thought* about your answer.

- **Link your thinking back to the text** to explain how your **insight fits**.

- **Answer all parts** of the question.

Figure 8.2

Test time: 30 minutes
Multiple-Choice Questions and an Open-Ended Question

Strategies for Managing Your Time

First: Read each <u>question</u> and underline or box KEY WORDS. Say, *"That means that I am supposed to think about _____ while I am reading."* (Do not read the answers yet.)

Second: Next, read the story, while keeping in mind the questions that you just read. Underline answers to the questions in pencil while you are reading.

Third: Answer the multiple-choice questions. Check each answer before you mark it by *quickly* going back to what you underlined to make sure that it is the BEST answer.

Now go to the Open-Ended Question. Remember, this question is worth up to 4 points! Be sure that you do a GREAT job on this question!

Strategies: ROPE Your Answer

R = *Read* the question carefully, box or underline key words, and use some of the words from the question to begin your answer.

O = Give your *opinions*.

P = *Prove* your opinion with a quote or reference to the text.

E = *Explain* your answer fully. Explain your own thinking by adding insights.

To Get the Highest Score

■ **Use specific information from the text** to support your explanations or opinions.

■ **Add your own thinking** to tell more about each piece of proof, so you can show that you *really thought* about your answer.

■ **Link your thinking back to the text** to explain how your **insight fits**.

■ **Answer all parts** of the question.

After learning this strategy, a Tenafly fifth-grader named Michael said, "I had completely forgotten about reading the questions first. It helped me to know what to expect on the questions. It really gave me an advantage in answering the questions."

2. Coach students to underline or box key words in the question.

When Lucy Calkins and her colleagues examined how students with reading troubles performed on state reading tests, they discovered something surprising. When researchers compared text excerpts in the state test to other passages that were not well written, students had the most trouble reading and understanding the tasks embedded in the test questions (Calkins et al., 1998).

In other words, teaching students how to read test questions is crucial. I coach them and model how to underline or box key words. I also discuss which words are important and why, including question words, number words, *s* on words (since *s* denotes more than one and may signify more than one task for the student), "and/or," specific directions such as "at least, the same as, in contrast to," and so on. Then I encourage students to say to themselves, "That means that I am supposed to think about _____ while I am reading." Students who perform well on state tests have a clear understanding of the tasks and translate them into "kid talk" (Greene & Melton, 2007, p. 9). Paul, a fifth-grade student in Tenafly agreed: "Boxing and underlining the questions helped, because I understand the questions more." Here is an example of one student's boxing and underlining on a practice reading test:

10. What would the author's opinion be about what Jessica learned by the end of the story?

(A) Jessica learned she made life better for a disabled person, just by taking the time to think about how to solve a problem that another person faces.

(B) Jessica learned that if she smiles at her sister, Kerry, that they can get along much better.

(C) Jessica learned that sometimes disabled brothers or sisters are favored most of the time by their parents.

(D) Jessica learned that it is important for her mother to pay attention to her, even though she is busy caring for Kerry.

3. Review how to determine what is important in the text.

After students have a clear understanding of strategies for answering questions, I review how to underline key words that are important in the text. I had already taught students how to do this earlier in the year, based on the ideas of reading experts Ellin Keene and Susan Zimmerman. (1997, 2007) (See the lesson on how to determine what is important on page 85.)

Integrating Test Prep into Reading & Writing Workshops © 2011 by Nancy Jennison • Scholastic Teaching Resources

4. Jot quick notes in the margin.

Once students know how to determine what is important, they can underline or jot key words in the margin during test prep. These jottings are clues to where the answers to the questions appear. Once you start your test-prep timing practice, coach students about how much time they have for each section of the test. Underlining saves time when students need to refer to the text to verify an answer choice. Students can visualize where they underlined or jotted and then quickly turn back to a particular section. Josh, a fifth-grader, from Tenafly, found this strategy very helpful. "A reading lesson that helped me was underlining places in the text that relate to the multiple-choice questions. It helped because in my mind I could remember the answer easier."

At the beginning of your reading test prep, if your students have difficulty with recalling which question goes with the underlined sections, show students a simple scaffold. Write the number of the reading test question in the margin directly next to the sentences that the students underlined. During the actual test, do not ask students to write the test item numbers in the text margins unless they take the test untimed and still need this support. Otherwise, it may slow them down, and every minute counts.

Strategies for Success With Answering Multiple-Choice Questions

I include a lesson on strategies for answering multiple-choice questions during test prep. After students complete the demand test, I share the study sheet with them for the specific reading test that we are studying, and we begin our study of strategies for answering multiple-choice questions (see Figure 8.1, Figure 8.2, and Figure 8.3).

MULTIPLE-CHOICE QUESTIONS: PLANNING A LESSON WITH STUDENTS

- Discuss the section titled "Strategies for Managing Your Time" in Figure 8.1 or 8.2.

- Help students understand the strategies for answering multiple-choice questions (see Figure 8.3).

- Distribute students' scored demand tests and examine the multiple-choice questions and answers.

- Reread a couple of multiple-choice test questions in the demand test that students have taken and demonstrate how to box or underline important words in the question. Discuss which words are important and why (question words, number words, *s* on words since *s* denotes more than one, "and/or," specific directions such as "at least, the same as, in contrast to," and so on).

Figure 8.3

Strategies for Answering Multiple-Choice Questions

✔ Read the test questions first before you read the reading passage.

✔ Underline or box key words in each question.

✔ Say in your own words what the question means: "That means that I am supposed to think about _____ while I am reading." That sets a purpose for your reading.

✔ Underline each part of the text that answers the questions as you read the text.

✔ Reread each multiple-choice question, predict your answer, and then read all answer choices.

✔ Use the process of elimination. That means to eliminate the answers in the multiple-choice questions that could not be correct or do not make sense, and check which one of the remaining answers makes the most sense with the text evidence in the passage (Fuhrken, 2009). (Help students think through why certain answers could not be correct and why only one makes the most sense.)

✔ Check your answers when you are done. If time is running short, check the *hardest* questions first. Jot down the numbers of the hard questions as you answer them so that you can quickly check those first (Calkins et al., 1998).

■ Ask students to practice boxing or underlining important words in the other multiple-choice questions with a partner.

■ Set a purpose for reading. Paraphrase what a test question means. Model how to look at what you boxed and underlined in the multiple-choice test question and state what the question means in your own words: "That means that I am supposed to think about _____ while I am reading." Ask several students to verbalize to you how they paraphrase what questions ask them to do. Write down what they say and ask the class to see if it makes sense. This is very important, since students who incorrectly interpret a question often get answers wrong.

Integrating Test Prep into Reading & Writing Workshops © 2011 by Nancy Jennison • Scholastic Teaching Resources

Use Small-Group Strategies With Multiple-Choice Questions to Differentiate

Help your students who need support become successful in answering multiple-choice questions by doing the following in a small group:

■ Examine students' demand tests to see where they had difficulties. Look at what students boxed, highlighted or underlined in test questions, what they underlined in the text, and where they made their errors. Design the lesson to match where they struggled.

■ Distribute a short piece of easier text to students that contains one or two multiple-choice questions similar to those that students found difficult.

■ Watch each student box and underline key words in the questions.

■ Listen to students paraphrase the new question/s in their own words. Ask them to use this sentence when they explain what the question means: "That means that I am supposed to think about _____ while I am reading."

■ Begin reading the short text and ask students to raise their hand when you read a section that answers one of the questions and to underline that part in the text. Discuss why each section answers or provides clues to the answer.

■ Ask students to write the number of the question that the text answers in the margin. (On the day of the test, if the test is timed, students do not write the number of the question in the margin of the text.)

■ Have students continue reading and working independently while you coach. Move from student to student in the group and offer support.

■ Encourage students to share their thinking about their answers and determine why each answer is correct or incorrect and continually use text evidence. Point out that for some answers, students make inferences by linking their own thinking to the text evidence to select the best answer.

- Ask students to examine several other multiple-choice questions and answers with you. Have students discuss, write down, and share with their partners what the test writers expect them to think about for each question. Make sure that they correctly interpret the questions.

- Read aloud the demand test passage and ask students to raise their hands when something that you read answers a multiple-choice question. Demonstrate how to underline the words in the reading passage that relate to or answer the multiple-choice questions. (Students usually need coaching on not underlining too many words.)

ALERT STUDENTS ABOUT WRITERS' TRICKS IN MULTIPLE-CHOICE TEST QUESTIONS

- Always read all answer choices. For example, one student who answered the first multiple-choice question quickly selected option A and then moved onto the next question. Had she taken a few more seconds to read all the answer choices, she would have seen that option D made much more sense.

- Consider what the question is asking, and don't be tricked if facts in the text passage appear in answer choices. In other words, just because part of the text is quoted in an answer choice, it doesn't mean that answer is correct (Calkins et al., 1998).

- Read back copies of your state's released tests to see if they contain tricky language. Tricky language means questions with *not, most likely, least likely*, and so on in them. For example, "Which of the following is NOT an example of a simile?" Make a list of the words that might be confusing for your students and routinely use them in classroom conversations and in questions about classroom texts.

- Teach students that they must be able to defend their answers. It is vital that students refer to the text to support their ideas. A prominent reading test writer stresses that no argument can make an incorrect answer choice correct (Fuhrken, 2009). Help students to think this through.

Strategies for Success With Answering Open-Response Questions

When students score well in answering open-response questions, it can greatly improve their overall reading scores on state tests. For some readers this is the hardest part of the reading test. I think if you closely examine the proven strategies and tips that I have provided in this section on open-response questions and modify them to fit your students' needs, you will be amazed with your students' results.

Teach Students to Code the Text in Answering Open-Ended Questions

Another strategy that has worked well for improving students' scores in answering open-response questions is coding the text. I suggest that you teach coding the text, explained below, *early* in the year and use it all year with your students. Here is how it sounds during test prep. Suppose a science question from a content passage sounds like this: *Contrast the differences among igneous, sedimentary and metamorphic rocks and use evidence from the text to support your opinions.*

A Sample Lesson for Teaching Students How to Code the Text

(I credit the names of the sections of this lesson to Lucy Calkins.)

▶ Connection:
Connect the lesson to past work, name your teaching point, and tell how it will help students.

"The state test is just around the corner, and today we are reviewing a strategy that we used this year called coding. You have already seen how coding helps us remember important information. We just used this strategy when we read about the human body. It helped us easily locate facts about what the organs do. It is pretty awesome that you will also be able to use coding during the state reading test, because you can write directly on the test. So, when you want to locate key facts and save time, you can just carefully examine how you coded the text in the margin.

"Yesterday, when we underlined and boxed the reading test question in this sample state test, we saw that it asked us to tell the differences among igneous, sedimentary, and metamorphic rocks. Coding helps me remember the details that I can use in my answer. Today we will see how we can use coding to help us remember key information when we take the state test."

▶ Teaching:
Demonstrate for students.

"When I code, I think of a quick abbreviation for each word. One way to code is to think of the first letter or two of each word. So, in this case, I thought of I for Igneous, S for Sedimentary, and M for Metamorphic. Then, while I am reading the test passage, I underline the very important parts in the text that relate to each kind of rock, but I code the text by writing the initial letter for each rock in the margin, right beside the part of the text that refers to that type of rock.

"Why do I bother to do this? I do this to save time during the test. When I begin to write my test answer, I quickly return to each section to look for my coding and my underlining and get ideas to use in my answer about the differences among the rocks. Coding helps me write specific information in my answer to raise my score. Watch me as I code the text. But keep in mind that we are coding to answer this question:

Contrast the differences among igneous, sedimentary and metamorphic rocks and use evidence from the text to support your opinions."

(Next, I read the text aloud and underline important parts about the rocks and think aloud about what code to use. I demonstrate how much underlining is too much underlining versus an amount that is just right. Also, I show students how I look for key words and facts to underline. I gradually release responsibility to students. They help me determine what to underline and what to code.)

▶ Active Engagement:

Tell students to turn and talk in partners and practice what you modeled.

"Now it is your turn. Let's see how coding the text helps you notice and quickly locate important information. Read the next paragraph of the text to yourself. Think about what you should underline about igneous, sedimentary, or metamorphic rocks that is important, and discuss it with your partner. Next, underline what's important. Then discuss what to code and write your code in the margin next to the important section." (While students are working, I confer with partnerships and coach them about coding.)

I share an additional teaching point that I think is relevant to everyone: "Coding helps you quickly locate information, but we need to be careful not to underline too much information. Look how Cindy and Mack first thought that all of the words in this paragraph were important. See what they first underlined: lots of words and sentences. But notice how smart they were to realize that underlining everything wouldn't help them to know what was important. They asked themselves, 'What facts are important that will help me with my answer?' That helped them to erase extra sentences that they did not need. Let's give a round of applause to thank Cindy and Mack for sharing."

▶ Link:

Link the lesson to the students' work of the day.

"So, students, you have seen me show you how to code. When you code, you can use any abbreviation that you want. The abbreviation that works for me is just thinking of the first letter or two of the word that I am coding. You saw how I underlined important facts and details about igneous, sedimentary, and metamorphic rocks that will help me to write my

Integrating Test Prep into Reading & Writing Workshops © 2011 by Nancy Jennison • Scholastic Teaching Resources

answer. You also saw what Cindy and Mack taught us: underline only key words, and do not underline everything. Your job now is to finish reading the article about rocks on your own, underline important facts, and code in the margin. Remember, you are coding so that you can answer this question: *Contrast the differences among igneous, sedimentary and metamorphic rocks and use evidence from the text to support your opinions.*

"When you are finished doing this, I want you to talk to your partner and jot down ideas from your coding to use in our answer." (I confer with students and coach them while they work independently and I record their progress on a conferring note sheet.)

Try It

Are your students underlining important text and correctly coding it as a time-saving strategy for answering their open-response questions? If your answer is no, you may want to incorporate some of these ideas into your plans.

✓ Examine your students' demand tests and note if they underlined and coded correctly.

✓ Assess their answers to open-ended questions and list the students who had difficulty. Contrast the quality of their responses to how well they underlined and coded.

✓ Select text that is suitable for students to use their coding strategies on more easily and meet with them in a small group to reteach the strategies.

✓ Help them see how underlining important words and coding can improve their answers. Practice answering an open-response question linked to the easier text with students.

✓ Ask students to re-answer the same open-response question in the demand test independently and show you how their underlining and coding will improve their answer.

STATES EXPECT DEEPER THINKING IN STUDENTS' OPEN-ENDED RESPONSES

The type of critical thinking that states expect from students in writing constructed or open-ended responses is consistent. It is deeper thinking. Often, students offer opinions, draw conclusions, synthesize the passage, and make insights that give more meaning to the text. These questions receive many more points than multiple-choice questions. Sample open-response questions appear in Chapter 1, page 23. Here is an example of an easier narrative question:

What three traits would you use to best describe Nora? Use the words in the semantic map or use your own words. Support your ideas with information from the text.

curious	impolite	knowledgeable
patient	ignorant	caring
determined	creative	thoughtful

Students need a different strategy for answering open-ended questions than what they use for multiple-choice questions. The ROPE strategy is effective for answering such questions.

ROPE: A Strategy for Answering Open-Ended, Constructed Reading Responses

ROPE is an acronym that helps students craft the best possible open-ended responses. (See page 54.) Please see the section about ROPE on the Nonfiction Reading or Narrative Reading Study Sheet (see Figure 8.1 or Figure 8.2). Examine the second half of the form that addresses open-ended questions. Notice what the steps are for ROPE. Read the additional tips listed under "To Get the Highest Score." Encourage your students to express their ideas or opinions in their answer and always back them up with specific information from the text that supports their thinking. Focus on adding insightful thinking, because when students include insight as part of their responses, it shows test scorers that they thought deeply about their answer and linked that thinking to the text. Chapter 3 contains a thorough explanation of how to use ROPE in a mini-lesson (pages 52–56), small-group coaching (pages 57–60), and conferring (pages 62–66).

Small- or Large-Group Reading Lessons for Answering Open-Ended Questions Effectively: Problems and Possible Solutions

Below, I list the five problems that I repeatedly encounter with students' answers to open-response questions, and I share the solutions that have made major differences for my students. I conduct these lessons for the whole class, if most of the students have difficulties, or I teach them in small groups if a few students need further support.

PROBLEM Students cannot get going, are disorganized, or their answers are off track.

POSSIBLE SOLUTION Co-write an answer with your class and use the I ROPE Hamburger.

Teaching Point: Say: "Students who take tests want to make each part of their open-ended response flow well and make sense. Notice how the I ROPE Hamburger shows us different words to use to give an opinion, offer proof, explain, and add insight. Test takers use these words as a resource when they write their response so they will know what to say and can provide a response that's complete."

Students' Follow-Up Work: (Students had already co-written a class open-ended response using the I ROPE Hamburger as a resource after they wrote their own response earlier.) Say: "Now, reread your own open-ended response to see if it is complete and clear, by checking it against what the open-ended question asked you to do. Compare the words that you wrote to the words in the I ROPE Hamburger and use the words in it to make your response flow better and make more sense."

PROBLEM Students' open-ended responses remain lackluster and their revision did not help much.

POSSIBLE SOLUTION Teach writing partners how to coach each other while you confer with students who need the most support.

Teaching Point: Say: "Students who take tests work with writing partners who use resources as tools to coach each other to revise open-ended responses. Notice how the Student-Friendly Open-Ended Response Scoring Rubric shows what a perfect score includes (see Figure 8.4). I created this rubric to match the scoring system of the state rubric. Notice how the I ROPE Hamburger shows us different words to use to give an opinion, offer proof, explain, and add insight. Your job as a student editor is to use these resources as tools to offer suggestions to make your writing partner's response stronger."

Students' Follow-Up Work: Say: "Read aloud and show your open-ended response to your writing partner. Ask your partner to score your response using the Student-Friendly Scoring Rubric and to make suggestions on how to make it better. Ask your partner to use the I ROPE Hamburger to make your response flow better and be more complete. Jot down all your partner's suggestions and think about them. Switch turns and then both of you revise your answers."

Figure 8.4

Student-Friendly Open-Ended Response Scoring Rubric

USE THIS TO SCORE ANSWERS TO OPEN-ENDED QUESTIONS

4 = Perfect Score
Includes all of the following:

❏ Evidence of ROPE (Opinion, Proof = reference/quote, Explain with insight)

❏ The student answered the question COMPLETELY.

❏ The answer was very clear.

❏ The student included an insight that linked to the text and was powerful!

3 = Very Good
But something is missing.

❏ All parts of the question were answered.

❏ The thinking is clear.

❏ This answer did not go far enough to make it complete. It may need either more explanation, proof, or insight.

2 = Pretty Good
But it has several problems.

❏ Some questions were not answered.

❏ The thinking doesn't make sense.

❏ The answer has only a few details and explanations.

❏ There is not a clear link to the text.

1 = Needs Work
Just one or two things were correct.

❏ Only one or two things are included, and the answer still needs work.

0 = Oh, No!
Nothing is correct!

PROBLEM Students' responses show very little deep thinking.

POSSIBLE SOLUTION Revise a student's response that lacks insight with the class to make it insightful. (Get permission from your student and ask him or her to help you.)

Teaching Point: Say: "Students who take tests push themselves to use Minds on Fire thinking strategies to think more deeply when they write or revise their answers. Use Minds on Fire Thinking strategies with your classmate's answer to make it more insightful." (See Chapter 3, page 70.)

Students' Follow-Up Work: (Each partnership has a copy of one classmate's response that the teacher and class started to revise.) Say: "Continue to revise the same response with your partner after you discuss how to use Minds on Fire Thinking strategies to make it reflect deeper thinking. Then take your own response and revise it by using the same strategies to add insight. Finish by sharing your response with your partner, and then get your partner's reaction."

PROBLEM A number of students still do not show deeper thinking in their open-ended responses.

POSSIBLE SOLUTION Play Go for the Gold and then play the Minds on Fire games (pages 71—73).

As you think about your students' progress in improving their open-response answers, it is far better to ask students to revise and improve their work than to have them do more and more practice tests. When students revise their open-ended answers, they develop an innate understanding of how to achieve the highest open-ended scores. See Chapter 3 for suggestions about how to confer with students on open-ended responses. (I borrowed the term "Minds on Fire" from work done at the Teachers College Reading and Writing Project.)

Teach Students Time-Management Tips for the Reading Test

If your students have a limited amount of time to take a reading test, their understanding of how to manage their time is a vital key to their success. This knowledge empowers them to feel more confident, because they know what part of the test they should be completing when the teacher announces the time segments. It gives students more assurance that they will finish the test on time and do well.

To begin teaching time management, administer another sample reading test, time your students, and discuss time-management tips for the actual reading test, using the tips listed in Figure 8.5. Modify these time-management tips to fit your state's time restrictions. When we practiced using these tips during test prep, my students understood how to manage their time much better. I told students that these were *approximate* times.

Figure 8.5

> ## Time-Management Tips for 30-Minute Narrative and Informational Reading Tests
>
> ### Amount of Time Remaining in the Test . . .
>
> **30 minutes:** Read the multiple-choice and open-ended questions and think about what they are asking you to look for while you read, but *do not read* the answer choices.
>
> **25 minutes:** Read the text and underline and/or code possible parts that will answer the questions.
>
> **20 minutes:** Finish reading the text, underlining, and/or coding possible parts that will answer the questions. Then begin answering the multiple-choice questions and refer back to what you have underlined to help you.
>
> **15 minutes:** Answer the open-ended question remembering to use ROPE strategies and adding insightful thinking.
>
> **10 minutes:** Continue answering the last part of the open-ended question. Check to make sure it is complete.
>
> **5 minutes:** Revise and edit your open-ended response, and then quickly check your multiple-choice responses. Make sure that you answer all multiple-choice questions.

 ## Read How It Worked

Examine a Daily Schedule for One Week of Narrative or Informational Reading Test Prep

Kathy Doyle conducts a reading workshop that is recognized and featured in talks and videos by Lucy Calkins and other leaders at the Teachers College Reading and Writing Project. However, she has many of the same fears that millions of other teachers do, as all of us prepare our students for state tests. As the New Jersey state test loomed on the horizon, Kathy began to worry about how she could design

Integrating Test Prep into Reading & Writing Workshops © 2011 by Nancy Jennison • Scholastic Teaching Resources

a test-prep schedule for reading that would meet her students' needs and, build on the work she had done all year in reading, but not take over her curriculum. Kathy and I designed this schedule.

Sample Week's Test-Prep Schedule to Prepare for a State Reading Test

Monday

Kathy gave the reading demand test to students and timed them in a manner similar to her state test's time restrictions. (To view a sample of a demand test, see pages 89–94.) After students completed the test, Kathy used the test results to begin her test-prep instruction in reading. She used the Narrative Reading Study Sheet (Figure 8.2) as a reference for herself and for the students while she modeled the following test-taking strategies for her class:

- Read the test questions first (not the answers) before you read the test passage.

- Box or underline key words in the test questions. Say to yourself what the question means. Kathy modeled these, and her students all practiced with partners.

- Underline key sections of the text that answer the questions as you read, and code certain parts if needed. Picture in your mind what you underlined so that you can quickly turn back to that text section when you answer questions.

- Use multiple-choice strategies when answering multiple-choice questions. Make sure that you always consult the parts in your text that you underlined or coded when you answer these questions. Kathy discussed each multiple-choice question and answer on the demand test. (Later that day, Kathy scored the open-ended responses so she could use them for revision work the next day. She also wrote each student's feedback on a sticky note describing ways to improve the response.)

Tuesday

Kathy evaluated her students' open-ended responses from the demand test, noticed that they needed quite a lot of revision, and decided to model how to write an open-ended response with the class. Later, she asked students to work with partners on how to revise their responses to the demand test's open-ended questions.

- Review the second half of the Narrative Reading Study Sheet (Figure 8.2) and teach and share the ROPE Your Answer study sheet (page 54) with students.

- Write a class response to the demand test's open-ended question. Use the I ROPE Hamburger (Figure 3.6) to help students learn how to write a complete response. Show students different ways to add insightful thinking to the class response.

- Teach students how to use the Student-Friendly Rubric (Figure 8.4). Divide the students into five cooperative groups:

   O = Opinion

   P = Proof (a referral group—students cite text evidence in their own words)

   P = Proof (a quote group—students cite text evidence as quotes)

   E = Explain

   I = Insight (an insight is part of, or added onto, the explanation)

- Read aloud one sentence of the class response at a time, and have students in one of the five groups that the sentence represents raise their hands. Each time they raise their hands, their topic receives a point. (Example: "I think Aunt Alix and Codie have a very close relationship." Members of the opinion group raise their hands, since this sentence is an opinion. They receive one point.)

- Tally the response's points. (Example: "This response has three opinions, two referrals, one quote, three explanations, and two pieces of insight.") Then use the Student-Friendly Rubric to score the response.

- Ask students to continue working independently to revise their own open-ended responses and use what they learned in revising the class piece to make their own answers better.

- Have students work in partnerships and coach one another, following the same procedures. ALL students must continue to revise their pieces until the teacher gives them a score of 4 (the highest score for the actual state test). Kathy's students finished their revising at home.

Wednesday

Kathy wanted to emphasize insightful thinking in the open-ended responses, so she showed students several examples of classmates' open-ended responses that included insightful thinking. She expected students to apply that knowledge in a new narrative reading test. In addition, Kathy asked students to set a goal for themselves—something they needed to remember to do in order to get a better score. Finally, she reviewed time-management strategies for a 30-minute reading test and then timed students while administering another narrative reading test.

- Demonstrate how some students used insight in their open-ended responses. Discuss why each example showed higher-order thinking that extended the meaning of the text. Show Minds on Fire Thinking strategies (see page 70).

- Ask students to think about ways to revise their demand test's open-ended response to add more insight and use Minds on Fire Thinking strategies.

- Discuss time-management strategies for taking a 30-minute reading test (Figure 8.5).

- Administer the second narrative reading test to students, and time them using the same parameters as the state test.

Thursday

Kathy's students needed hands-on practice with revising a fellow student's open-ended response. Some of her students still were not including insightful thinking. Kathy received permission from a student to copy his response from the previous day's practice test. Kathy and the class revised until it included insight, and then she asked the class to continue to revise the student's response in partnerships. Afterward, students worked independently to revise their own responses.

■ Get permission from one student to copy his/her open-ended response. Copy that response for all partnerships in the class.

■ Begin revising the focused student's response together by adding clear thinking and insight, and then ask partners to color-code parts of the response that need more revising. Partners write suggestions on the back of the focused student's response for how to revise it.

■ Partnerships share their ideas on revising the focused student's open-ended response with the class.

■ Encourage students to work independently to revise their own open-ended response from the previous day's test.

■ Work in small groups with students who need more support and coaching while other students are working independently revising the previous day's open-ended answer.

Friday

Kathy used the Minds on Fire game (pages 70–73) to strengthen insightful thinking in open-ended responses, using questions she developed based on her current read-aloud.

■ Play Minds on Fire with students, using questions based on your current read-aloud.

  Tips on how to develop open-ended questions that relate to your read-aloud:
  ● Look for places to stop in the read-aloud that lend themselves to open-ended questions.
  ● Use a sample open-ended question from your state test as a model for your questions until you feel comfortable making them up on the spot.

■ Ask students how the Minds on Fire game helped them make their open-ended responses more powerful.

■ Ask students to revise their last open-ended responses from the practice test to make them better.

■ While your class is revising their responses, confer with students and meet in small groups with those who need more support.

Food for Thought

PLANNING YOUR READING TEST PREP UNIT CAN BE A VERY STRESSFUL EXPERIENCE. WHY NOT MAKE YOUR LIFE EASIER BY USING THIS CHAPTER AS A MODEL THAT YOU COULD MODIFY WHEN YOU PLAN YOUR UNIT?

- What will you use for a demand test that you administer at the beginning of your test prep? You can visit the Web site links suggested on page 24, if you need a sample test. You can study my test sample on pages 89–94.

- How can you and your colleagues use the Students' Study Sheets to help you design your own study sheets for your students?

- As you examine the list of possible lessons and the accompanying figures in this chapter that I used with teachers and students, which ones could you adapt to help your students?

- How can you adapt Kathy Doyle's reading test-prep schedule in Read How It Worked to fit your students' needs?

CHAPTER 9

Craft a Test-Prep Unit in Writing Workshop That Matches Your State Test

Highlights

- Help students get the jitters out before the test.

- Design test prep for narrative, explanatory/descriptive, and persuasive tests.

- Examine a revision activity that you can do with all aspects of writing test prep.

- Develop time-management suggestions for your state writing test.

- Plan practical lessons and a workable schedule for the state writing test.

T he state writing test is rapidly approaching, and you worry if your students will use all the writing strategies you have taught them. You are not sure how they will perform when they must construct a writing piece in the middle of a time-pressured situation. You want your students to feel ready and organized, so that they keep the different parts of the writing test straight, feel calmer about taking the test, and show what they know. This chapter will offer you an assortment of tools and testing strategies that you can modify and share with your students to help them comfortably and confidently take the state writing test.

Help Students Get the Jitters Out

Arnold Almaguer and Christie Mortara have several techniques that they use to calm their students before the state test: For starters, "Set up your room so it sounds like the test and looks like the test. When you give directions, try to use similar language as that in the real test. In addition, have students configure the room in the same way that the state requires. For example, have students clear their desks, or move their chairs the way the state mandates on test day.

"During our test test-prep lessons, we talked to our students about viewing practice tests like a 'scrimmage' or a 'dress rehearsal.' So when we administered a timed practice test, we coached the students into thinking that today will be our scrimmage or dress rehearsal. We saw that students became more at ease and approached test prep with a smile because we connected it to something with which they were familiar (sports and drama)." Arnold and Christie's students identified with the terms *scrimmage* and *dress rehearsal*, since they loved sports and drama. Select a term that your class identifies with. Lucy Calkins and her colleagues see the benefits of this type of a dress rehearsal, since it enables students to envision how their regular daily routines dramatically change on the day of the test (Calkins et al., 1998).

WHICH WRITING GENRES APPEAR ON STATE WRITING TESTS?

Narrative writing, persuasive writing, and explanatory (or expository) writing are the most common genres on state writing tests.

■ In a timed exam, students usually have a brief amount of time to write a composition in a genre that the state selects, and that composition is frequently based on a state prompt.

Integrating Test Prep into Reading & Writing Workshops © 2011 by Nancy Jennison • Scholastic Teaching Resources

■ Many states offer released samples of previous writing test prompts on the state Web site. (See Chapter 2, pages 42–43.) Most states also have their writing rubrics on their education department Web site, so we will know how their scorers grade the students' work. Depending on the state, some state writing tests include multiple-choice writing questions, like those highlighted in Chapter 2. (See page 42.)

■ If your state includes a composition as well as a multiple-choice writing test, you will want to consider including both in your test prep. By giving students demand tests in both areas, they know what to expect on test day, and this baseline assessment gives you information, so that you will know how to help them during the test-prep unit. (I am borrowing the term "demand" from work done at the Teachers College Reading and Writing Project.)

Plan Your Writing Test-prep Unit

Writing experts advise us to plan a test-prep unit that reflects the format of the writing test, and to think of it as just one of the units that we teach during the year. The test-prep unit occurs in the weeks right before the state test (Allan et al., 2009; Fuhrken, & Roser, 2010).

Here are a few suggestions for planning your writing test-prep unit:

✓ List the different sections of your state's writing test.

✓ Visit your state education department's Web site and locate the released samples and scoring rubrics.

   ● Some states offer samples of their writing tests for easy download on their Web sites. If your state does not release sample tests, you can consult Chapter 2, for a list of state Web sites that do offer samples. In addition, certain states have interesting resources for sale. For example, the State of New Jersey offers the *Criterion-Based Holistic Scoring: A Writing Handbook,* which presents samples of narrative and persuasive writing at different grade levels. It is available from the New Jersey Department of Education Publications and Distribution Office, PO Box 500, Trenton, NJ 08625-0500.

✓ Think about which tested writing genre you will focus on for the beginning of your study. Some teachers begin with a genre that students know well, or one that relates to a recent unit of study, because their students tend to feel more confident starting with familiar subject matter. On the other hand, some teachers save the easiest genre for last, so they can review it quickly.

Test Prep for Narrative Writing

ADMINISTER A DEMAND TEST

A demand writing test is a test that students take before they begin preparing for the state test. Reading and writing authorities Robert Calfee and Roxanne Miller state, "The most important assessment record is the one that serves the teacher in documenting student learning and steering instructional decision making" (2007, p. 271). Demand tests are vital tools for teachers as they make instructional judgments about what to teach in their test-prep unit. Demand tests show what students know and illustrate what they need to know. They last just as long, and have the same format and demands, as an actual state test. If your writing test gives students two pages for pre-writing and three pages for writing, be consistent with the demand test.

CHOOSE OR CREATE A DEMAND WRITING TEST

There are several options for selecting demand writing test resources:

- Choose a released state sample from your state's Web site, or download other states' released samples that are most like yours.

- Develop your own demand writing test in the genre that you decide to use to launch your writing test-prep study. Once you study several examples of the genre-writing prompts that your state uses, you can make your demand test sound and look state-like, in the test language, format, and time and space requirements.

USE THE DEMAND TEST TO ASSESS YOUR STUDENTS AND TO PLAN TEST-PREP INSTRUCTION

Janet Angelillo, teacher and writing expert, writes that assessment is the foundation of teachers' work with students (2005b). Administering the demand writing assessment on your first day of writing test prep offers you a clear baseline of your students' writing strengths and areas in need of support. I time the demand test, using exactly the same limits as the real test.

ASSESS STUDENTS' DEMAND TEST RESPONSES

- Use the same rubric that your state uses.

- Look for qualities of good writing that match your rubric.

- Check for strong narrative structure with proper pacing in the story.
    - Have students addressed the issues from the narrative prompt and stayed on topic?
    - Have students opened with a lead that interests the audience and closed with a powerful ending?

Integrating Test Prep into Reading & Writing Workshops © 2011 by Nancy Jennison • Scholastic Teaching Resources

- Have they developed the problem and clearly shown how it was resolved?

- Are their word choices and sentence structures effective?

- Do their quotes move the story along and show character development?

- Did they elaborate well with action, thoughts, setting, and/or dialogue?

- Is their writing well organized with effective transitions between sections?

- Are their conventions strong—spelling, punctuation, and grammar?

- Do they take compositional risks that your state scores higher? (Some states count beautiful images, realistic dialogue, humor, effective use of literary devices, voice, or amazing word choices as possible compositional risks.)

- Use sticky notes to jot down revision suggestions for students and attach them to their demand tests, as you score each piece based on your state rubric.

Writing researcher Charles MacArthur reported that students who need more support often have limited revision ideas and goals. He believes that we can help these students to make more effective revisions by giving them clear revision goals that match their writing pieces (2007). In other words, when you take the time to jot down revision suggestions for students in your test prep unit, you make revision more concrete and reachable for them. As you meet with students in conferences and small groups, you make positive results more realistic and achievable for them.

PLAN FOLLOW-UP INSTRUCTION AFTER YOU SCORE THE NARRATIVE DEMAND TEST

Janet Angelillo (2005a, 2005b) tells us to assess our students' writing and interpret what we see by using two different lenses: how well students have learned what we taught, and the evidence of our teaching that is present in their writing. When we think reflectively, we improve our teaching, because if we don't see evidence of our lessons in our students' work, we may need to reteach those lessons.

- Once you finish scoring the demand tests, do a mini-lesson on the quality of writing that students' responses indicated was most in need of reteaching. If your students had difficulty sticking to the topic of the prompt, for example, make focused writing the teaching point in your follow-up mini-lesson. Demonstrate for your students how to revise an unfocused response (with the consent of the writer, of course).

- Expect all students to revise and edit their demand writing pieces on their own and with partners. Coach students with similar writing needs in a small group and also later confer with others who need your help, individually or in partners. (See page 57 for suggestions.) If your state rubric is based on 5 points, by the end of the day, after revision work, all students must achieve a score of at least 4 out of 5. If needed, some may have to finish revising and editing at home. If you have students who cannot achieve the 4, look closely at their writing and plan to meet with them and coach them in a small group.

CREATE A GRAPHIC ORGANIZER TO KEEP TRACK OF THE HELP THAT YOUR STUDENTS NEED

After you score your state's genre writing demand test by using your state's writing rubric, create a graphic organizer and list the qualities of good writing that your state expects across the top, and the names of the students across the side. Place checks beside each area where students need more support.

- Use this organizer to plan other mini-lessons and small-group work.

- If your state test also includes a multiple-choice writing component, note which types of questions stumped your students. Add those categories to your organizer. Then address those issues during your test-prep by referring to writing mini-lessons from earlier in the year that are already familiar to your students. Reteach them in a different manner, if necessary.

- Design test-prep lessons that build on your earlier writing mini-lessons to foster your students' confidence. Remind students that they already know how to use certain writing skills and briefly mention the past lesson to jar their memories.

GET READY FOR YOUR TEST-PREP UNIT: CREATE STUDENT STUDY SHEETS

Study sheets calm students' nerves because they include proven writing and management strategies for all writing test components. I made these for every tested grade level in my school district, and the teachers stapled them together in study packets for each student. We all used them during our test-prep unit.

- There are study sheets for each of the genres that are part of the state test.

- This is a condensed way for students to see descriptions of all of the state test's writing components, as well as strategies and tips for a successful performance.

- We introduced each genre during test-prep instruction by using the study sheet, which also offered students a quick and easy one-page review on the days prior to the test.

- Figure 9.1 shows an example of a study sheet that describes a state narrative writing test. It includes the time element of the test that the state mandates, an example of a state-like prompt, getting-started management strategies for students, and a description of Airplane Writing.

Integrating Test Prep into Reading & Writing Workshops © 2011 by Nancy Jennison • Scholastic Teaching Resources

Figure 9.1

Test time: 30 minutes

Writing Task: Gives you the prompt. *Example:* "A young girl woke up one morning and happily planned for her visit to her grandmother's house. However, later that day, as she arrived at her grandmother's home, she was very upset that she had forgotten something that was very important. How could she solve her problem? Write a STORY about the girl, her problem, and how she solves her problem."

Strategies for Managing Your Time

Take only 5 minutes to do these:

First: Read the prompt very carefully. Be a detail detective and notice ideas that you can use in your story.

Second: Think about the two or three characters and the setting. Name them. Think of what your main character wants, and also think about the problem and the solution. Think of traits and dialogue that show what the characters are like.

Third: Write a few ideas on the pre-writing planning sheet in whatever way works for you. Suggestions include the following: a list—c, s, w, p, sol. (c = character, s = setting, w = wants, p = problem, sol. = solution) or a story map, a T-chart, Beg/Mid/End, or another way of planning that you like to use that you can do *quickly*!

Write your story on the lined writing sheet.
Use AIRPLANE WRITING, your best writing!

- Strong Lead That Gets the Audience's Attention
- Stay on the Topic That Relates to the Speculative Prompt
- Logical Progression of Ideas
- Specific Details and Vivid Description
- Dialogue That is Appropriate and Reveals What the Characters Are Like
- Effective Word Choice
- Simile, Alliteration, Onomatopoeia, Personification, or Metaphor
- Variety of Sentences and Different Beginnings of Sentences
- Transition Words
- Powerful Ending
- Edit for Spelling, Punctuation, and Grammar
- Remember to Write in Paragraphs

EXAMINE THE COMPONENTS OF AIRPLANE WRITING

Literacy researchers have confirmed the benefits of using mnemonic strategies, especially for writers who need more support and students with and without learning disabilities (Graham & Harris, 2005). *Airplane Writing* is a term that I coined to use with all students that matches the most important criteria on the state rubric.

- Airplane Writing explains the state rubric in student-friendly terms.

- It helps students differentiate between the writing they do in open-ended reading responses and on the genre-writing test. Airplane Writing matches the genre writing test. You could use this term and adapt your description of Airplane Writing on your students' study sheet to match your state test. See the descriptors under the airplane in Figure 9.1 that are a student-friendly version of the New Jersey rubric.

- Airplane Writing originated from a writing class that I conducted with fourth-grade students at Rolling Valley School in Fairfax County, Virginia. A student, Carlos, raised his hand and said, "Writing a paper is like taking a plane trip." He meant that a composition, like flying in an airplane, needs a powerful take-off (the lead), interesting details and examples from the captain and flight attendants (effective elaboration and word choice), a trip that stays on the right flight plan (a paper that stays on topic), and a smooth landing (a strong, smooth ending).

HELP STUDENTS GET ORGANIZED FOR NARRATIVE WRITING TEST PREP

Writing expert, Janet Angelillo warns us not to deprive students from practice in thinking about test prompts, or else their writing may be disappointing (2005b). The Narrative Writing Study Sheet (Figure 9.1) is a practical tool to help students get organized. It gives students strategies for closely analyzing the prompt in a step-by-step way. These strategies work in a time-pressured situation. Before I administer a new narrative prompt, first we use it as a tool to help students know how to begin. The text below in italics shows what I might say:

- **First:** *Read the prompt very carefully. Be a detail detective and notice ideas that you can use in your story.* Some students also need help with boxing and underlining key words in the prompt, as well as telling in their own words what the prompt expects them to do. (For a visual of boxing and underlining, see page 182.)

- **Second:** *Think about the two or three characters and the setting. Name them. Think of what your main character wants, and also the problem and the solution. Think of traits and dialogue that show what the characters are like.* These strategies help my students write better stories. If they have too many characters, they easily get off track. They think of what the main character wants and develop a stronger main character. When they think of the problem and solution, they relate it to what the main character wants.

Integrating Test Prep into Reading & Writing Workshops © 2011 by Nancy Jennison • Scholastic Teaching Resources

■ **Third:** *Write a few ideas on the pre-writing planning sheet in whatever way works for you. Suggestions include the following: a list—c, s, w, p, sol. (c = character, s = setting, w = wants, p = problem, sol. = solution) or a story map, T-chart, Beg/Mid/End, or another way of planning that you like to use that you can do quickly!* I encourage students to do whatever planning strategy works for them, since pre-planning leads to a more focused story with a stronger narrative structure.

RECOGNIZE THAT THE PROMPT SHOWS THE GENRE

A first step for students is to recognize the writing genre that test designers embed in the test question. It is important to teach students to look for key words that show the genre: *Tell a story* for narrative, *explain* for expository, *convince* for persuasive, and *describe* for descriptive (Kiester, 2000).

Strategies That Students Use on Their Own to Quickly Generate Ideas

Here are questions for students to ask themselves:

✓ Relate the prompt to yourself. In this case, what problem could I have if I went to my grandmother's and forgot something?

✓ Relate the prompt to fit a friend or to an experience. In this case, what problem could my friend who went to grandmother's and forgot something have? What have I ever seen or been part of that reminds me of this and gives me ideas for my story?

✓ How can I make my story interesting and exciting by adding dialogue, inner thinking, and actions?

Strategies That You Can Use to Generate Ideas With Your Students

✓ Do a class brainstorming session. List problems suggested by the students that match the prompt and vote on the most interesting and exciting one.

✓ Invite students to name two or three characters that go along with the prompt (c), name the setting (s), name what the main character wants (w), state the problem (p), and name the solution (sol.).

✓ Have students tell the story, beginning with a powerful lead, and teach them how to get to the problem very quickly.

✓ Dramatize parts of the story to see where more effective dialogue, inner thinking, or actions can be added for more effective details.

Help students generate ideas for their stories. Again, here is an example of a narrative prompt: *A young girl woke up one morning and happily planned for her visit to her grandmother's house. However, later that day, as she arrived at her grandmother's home, she was very upset that she had forgotten something that was very important. How could she solve her problem? Write a story about the girl, her problem, and how she solves her problem.*

EXPLAIN AIRPLANE WRITING TO STUDENTS

It is most strategic to explain Airplane Writing so students see examples of it in the context of a real piece of writing. When I conduct this lesson, students work with their writing partners. They study a copy of a well-written student's story that we use as a student exemplar from a previous year.

Student Writing Exemplars

Using student writing exemplars in teaching is a proven effective strategy, since it is so concrete (Allan et al., 2009). If I do not have a student sample handy, I create one of my own that is student-like but fits the criteria of Airplane Writing. As I review the parts of Airplane Writing on the students' Narrative Writing Study Sheet, I remind students what they already know from previous work earlier in the year about each of the components of Airplane Writing: "Do you see that another category of Airplane Writing is using specific details? Remember when we did our fiction unit of study? You learned about three different ways to elaborate and add details: through dialogue, inner thinking, and actions. Remember how we used *Journey* as our mentor text, and we saw how Patricia MacLachlan elaborated? You can use those same strategies to elaborate when you write a story for the state test."

Teaching Point: Say: "Test takers need powerful and successful strategies to write narrative stories. Notice how the Narrative Writing Study Sheet reveals the characteristics of Airplane Writing. It shows the qualities of writing that need to be in your stories for the state writing test. You can use this study sheet to help during test prep, and you can also remember and use the strategies for writing stories that you already learned earlier this year."

Student Work: (The teacher has already reviewed the characteristics of Airplane Writing, as well as what students have learned about effective writing from previous units.) Say: "Work in your partnerships or small groups and study your copy of last year's student's story. Read the story aloud and look for the characteristic of Airplane Writing that I assigned to your group. Discuss whether that quality is in the writing and then highlight it. Did the student do a good job? Practice what you will tell the class when we share."

Integrating Test Prep into Reading & Writing Workshops © 2011 by Nancy Jennison • Scholastic Teaching Resources

NOTICE STUDENTS' REACTIONS TO LEARNING ABOUT AIRPLANE WRITING

When students personalize images with mnemonics, they recall the information more readily. Daniel, a Tenafly, New Jersey, fifth-grader, stated, "The first lesson on Airplane Writing helped, because I imagined the airplane running on vivid words, like good words, for fuel."

Students also use Airplane Writing as a very effective revising tool. Paul added, "One lesson that I think helped me the most was Airplane Writing. It helped me because now I can craft my stories better. Earlier, my stories didn't have a smooth beginning and ending. And I'd get a terrible score. Now I know how to make the beginnings and ends better than before."

And as another student, Andrew, confirmed, "When we looked at Airplane Writing and looked at it over and over again, it got the elements in my head . . ." Once Andrew knew what the state expected, he kept those qualities in mind while writing stories and felt more confident.

USE PROVEN LESSONS THAT ENERGIZE STUDENTS IN THE MIDDLE OF NARRATIVE TEST PREP

Lesson 1: Co-model with a student and share that student's writing.

A lesson that always energizes students in any kind of genre test prep involves conducting a revising mini-lesson using a classmate's piece of writing. For example, Kathy Doyle noticed that Amber, one of her students, wrote a story that was a prime example of Airplane Writing but still needed more revision work. Amber agreed to share her story with her peers. Kathy, Amber, and the class brainstormed how to revise Amber's story according to the components of Airplane Writing. One student in Kathy's class commented weeks later, "Revising Amber's writing to show us what we needed to do with developing the setting, powerful lead, ending, and action was the best lesson in test prep."

I have found that the more I model revision explicitly when students and I co-revise a classmate's writing, the easier it is for them to remember to apply those teaching points when revising their own writing. My students also learn a great deal when they watch and help me revise my own writing.

Lesson 2: Play a game of Get That Story Moving to take pressure off students.

Play is important, even in the middle of test prep. It lightens up the mood. I created this game to help students gain confidence while they compose stories together in a timed situation. It fosters time-management and organizational skills. Modify it to fit your narrative test.

Teacher Kathy Doyle wanted to "balance the written practice during test-prep with game-like practice . . . I have to remind myself of the importance of play!" When her students played Get That Story Moving (see Figure 9.2) during narrative test prep, they not only had fun and learned tips for stories but also learned how to speed up their performance in a timed situation. But a problem surfaced in Kathy's class when one student rushed through a story so fast that it received a low score, even though his team had planned it well! This created a lasting memory in the students' minds of what not to do, as well as what they needed to do to be successful. This game definitely helped students plan comprehensively without taking too long. Speed practice is important, since some students spend too long on planning their pieces during the test, and then they have less time for the scored piece of writing (Angelillo, 2005b).

Figure 9.2

Get That Story Moving! A Game with Pizzazz

Prompt for the Game (Post so students can see it.)

Melissa likes to explore in her huge yard because she is interested in everything she finds that relates to nature and science. One place she likes to explore is a dark wooded area that no one ever uses. Write a story about Melissa and what happened the last time she explored that dark area in her yard.

Roles of 7 Students Needed for Game: Clock Watcher, Motivator, Solver, Planner, Problem Solver, Storyteller, and Tester

1. **Clock Watcher:** keeps students on task and times how long it takes for each student (except for the Storyteller) to complete each part of the game,

2. **Motivator:** says, "Get it moving! You can do it!" and sounds like a cheerleader to each student before he/she gives instructions about the task.

3. **Solver:** explains what the narrative prompt means in his/her own words.

4. **Planner:** writes a quick plan for the story and must include the following: **c**—the names of the **c**haracters (no more than 2 or 3); **s**—**s**etting; **w**—what the character **w**ants; **p**—**p**roblem; and **sol.**—**sol**ution.

Integrating Test Prep into Reading & Writing Workshops © 2011 by Nancy Jennison • Scholastic Teaching Resources

5. **Problem Solver:** tells at least two *possible ways* of introducing the problem *right away* in the story that make sense with the plans that the Planner made.

6. **Storyteller:** tells the story using the ideas from the Planner's notes and one of the problems suggested by the Problem Solver.

7. **Tester:** listens to the story carefully to evaluate if the Storyteller:

   ■ had a powerful lead

   ■ immediately introduced the characters and setting and detailed the problem

   ■ stretched out the scene that led to the solution

   ■ resolved the problem at the end, and ended by using a technique that the teacher taught for the ending.

   Tester scores the story based on the Students' Scoring Rubric for a Story About a Prompt (see page 213.)

Procedure:
What the teacher does before the activity begins:

Write the narrative prompt on the whiteboard or chalkboard so it is easy for students to see. Write c, s, w, p, sol. in a vertical line, with room between each. Select students for the above-listed roles.

Let the Game Begin!

   ■ The **Motivator** calls out to the Solver, "Get that story moving! You can do it!! Tell us what the prompt means."

   ■ The **Clock Watcher** says, "Go! Do your job and make it quick!" The Clock Watcher times how long it takes for the Solver to tell what the prompt means

   ■ The **Solver** tells what the prompt means in his/her own words.

   ■ The **Clock-Watcher** tells the Solver how long it took and either says, "You've got pizzazz!" (The Clock Watcher does a dance or pretends to be bored and sleeps.)

   ■ The **Motivator** calls out to the Planner, "Get that story moving! You can do it! As fast as your hand can go, jot down quick, abbreviated ideas for **c, s, w, p, sol.**"

a. "That means, **c**—name the characters, **s**—tell the setting, **w**—tell what the character wants, **p**—tell the problem, and **sol.**—tell the solution. Get that story moving! You can do it, I know you can!"

b. The **Planner** jots down quick, abbreviated, and specific notes for c, s, w, p, and sol.

c. The **Clock Watcher** tells the Planner how long it took and either says, "You've got pizzazz!" (Clock Watcher does a dance or pretends to be bored and sleeps.)

d. The **Motivator** says to the Problem Solver, "Get it moving! I KNOW you can do this, and it will be great! You must tell me at least two possible ways of introducing the problem RIGHT AWAY in the story that make sense with plans that the Planner made."

■ The **Problem Solver** quickly suggests two possible problems.

■ The **Clock Watcher** tells the **Problem Solver** how long it took and either says, "You've got pizzazz!" (Clock Watcher does a dance or pretends to be bored and sleeps.)

■ The **Motivator** says to the **Storyteller**. "You can do it, Storyteller! Tell us an amazing story using the plans and one of the problems. I am not timing you, so tell a detailed, complete story!"

■ The **Tester** listens to the story and makes sure that the story has Airplane Writing evidence, sees if the story relates to the prompt, and judges how amazing it is whether or not it:

a. had a powerful lead

b. immediately introduced the characters and setting and detailed the problem

c. stretched out the scene that led to the solution

d. resolved the problem at the end, and ended by using a craft technique that the teacher had taught.

The **Tester** uses the Students' Scoring Rubric for a Story About a Prompt to give feedback, then scores the story and tells how to make it better. Audience members also give feedback.

Integrating Test Prep into Reading & Writing Workshops © 2011 by Nancy Jennison • Scholastic Teaching Resources

Students' Scoring Rubric for a Story About a Prompt

Score	Reason
5: Wow!	Told or wrote an amazing story related to the prompt and included many parts of Airplane Writing
4: Very Good	Told or wrote a very good story related to the prompt and included a number of parts of Airplane Writing
3: OK	Told or wrote a pretty good story that was related to the prompt and included a few parts of Airplane Writing
2: Not Quite OK	Told or wrote an unclear story that was only slightly related to the prompt and left out many parts of Airplane Writing
1: Uh Oh	Told or wrote a weak story, or no story, that included little or no Airplane Writing

Debriefing: The teacher asks the students, "How did this game help you get ready for the Narrative Prompt Test? What did you learn?"

Test Prep for Explanatory or Descriptive Writing

Preparing for the explanatory or descriptive writing test is similar to preparing for the narrative writing test. The previous sections related to how to construct a demand test apply here. An excellent way to begin is to administer an explanatory/descriptive demand test on the first day of test prep. After this test, you design lessons that match what your students need, based on their scores from the demand test.

SOLVE A PROBLEM WITH LACKLUSTER COMPOSITIONS

Kathy Doyle evaluated her class's demand explanatory tests and found that all of her students remembered to answer all of the questions in the test prompt correctly, but unfortunately a large number of them forgot about Airplane Writing. Their compositions were lackluster, and Kathy was very concerned. Even after students revised the demand tests on their own, some of them still neglected to add the components of Airplane Writing. Kathy wondered how students who did so well on the narrative test prep now seemed to fall apart in the explanatory/descriptive test prep. She asked me to help.

CO-PLANNING A LESSON TO HELP WITH LACKLUSTER COMPOSITIONS

I suggested that Kathy model revising part of a student's piece with the class, using highlighters to identify parts of the piece that showed evidence of Airplane Writing. Kathy demonstrated how to make sentences stronger in several of those parts.

I also suggested that students work in small groups and continue to revise copies of the same student's piece. We both felt that this allowed all students to have a better grasp on revision.

One student, Michael, agreed to share his piece with the class. Kathy selected Michael's piece because it was already quite good but still needed some improvement. In other words, it was in the zone of proximal development of a high grade—but lacked a few things. Kathy felt that if the students could find what to add to this already strong piece, they could surely see how to improve their own. Details on how Kathy taught the lesson appear below.

Revise a Student's Explanatory/Descriptive Piece with Your Class to Make an Amazing Difference!

Kathy began by sharing the Explanatory Writing Study Sheet (see Figure 9.3) with the class. Her focus, based on an assessment of students' demand tests, was that students need to include the components of Airplane Writing for explanatory/descriptive writing. Kathy told her students that when they used Airplane Writing strategies in the explanatory writing test, those writing skills had many similarities to what students already knew from previous units in writing workshop.

Kathy co-modeled with her student Michael how to reread his explanatory piece, (Figure 9.4) look at the requirements of Explanatory/Descriptive Airplane Writing, and highlight parts in yellow that showed evidence of Airplane Writing.

Integrating Test Prep into Reading & Writing Workshops © 2011 by Nancy Jennison • Scholastic Teaching Resources

Figure 9.3

Test time: 30 minutes

Answer the *questions* in the *prompt* by writing a <u>composition</u> that describes or explains your thinking.

Strategies for Managing Your Time

Take only <u>5 minutes</u> to do these:

First: Read each question and underline or box KEY WORDS. Say to yourself, "That means that I am supposed to . . ."

Second: Number the questions you have to answer.

Third: On your pre-writing planning sheet, number the questions and jot down a key word or two for each question on the left.

Fourth: Jot down a couple of quick ideas on the right of your pre-writing planning sheet for how you will answer the questions.

Fifth: Check off each question and answer idea from your pre-writing planning sheet as you use them in your composition. That way, you will remember to answer all of the questions!

Write your composition on the lined sheet. REMEMBER to use AIRPLANE WRITING, your best writing!

- <u>Powerful</u> Lead to Hook the Reader
- Stay on the Topic of Answering the Questions
- Ideas That Fit Together From Beginning to End
- Effective Dialogue
- Specific Details and Vivid Description
- Rich Words
- Simile, Alliteration, Personification, Onomatopoeia, or Metaphor
- Variety of Sentences—Short, Medium-Length, and Long
- Different Beginnings of Sentences
- Transition Words
- <u>Powerful</u> Ending
- Be Clear! Remember Your Audience
- Edit for Spelling, Punctuation, and Grammar
- Remember to Write in Paragraphs

Figure 9.4

Explanatory Prompt Example and Michael's Explanatory Writing

Michael, a fifth grader, read the accompanying practice test prompt and wrote a response. His classmates gave him revision suggestions.

Explanatory Prompt:

Has there ever been something important to you that you could hardly wait to do? Write about it. Include the following: What was so important to you that you could hardly wait to do? Why was it important to you? Did you imagine yourself doing it before you did it? How did you get ready to do it? Did you do it alone, or were others with you? Did you enjoy it?

Michael's Response:

A smile started to spread itself across my face. I felt a surge of energy running threw my body. Taking the steps two at a time I began to imagine.

My mind raced as I thought of all the things we could do. I could see the images in my head like a TV. My smile reached for my ears. My teeth began to show.

As I heard the door being opened I rushed for under her arm and opened the car door. I jumped in the car. My seatbelt was in, in a flash. I could feel my body hopping up and down and if I was not wearing a seatbelt I would have hit my head on the car roof, and maybe even gone threw it.

As my mom started the car I could feel my body shaking. It has been so long since the last time I saw him. My Mom pulled out of the driveway and stepped on the accelerator. As the car accelerated, so did my mind.

Thoughts races threw my head as my Mom pulled up at a house. I opened the door to the car and walked to the back gate. I opened it.

I waved.

He looked at me and smiled. My best friend had a soccer ball at his feat. He kicked it but missed. As he ran over His smile grew. "This is going to be the best vacation ever."

Integrating Test Prep into Reading & Writing Workshops © 2011 by Nancy Jennison • Scholastic Teaching Resources

Kathy's purpose was to show Michael and others that even his strong piece of writing still needed revision. She modeled how to read Michael's piece and find places to insert more bits of details into what was there, rather than to replace what he had. Students helped Kathy and Michael in finding another place to strengthen.

Next, Kathy divided the class into partnerships and distributed yellow highlighters. Each group chose a different section of Michael's piece to revise, based on places that the class had marked together. Students highlighted where Michael had some evidence of Airplane Writing.

Then, small groups directly wrote suggestions on their copies of his writing. At the end of the lesson, students shared their ideas, and Michael received all students' suggestions on the copies of his writing. Kathy said, "My students drew on all that they learned about writing in the first eight months of school! I don't think it would have been possible to teach them how to do this without yearlong writing work." Here are some of the very specific suggestions that Kathy's students made:

- "Add more description in the first paragraph, after 'I felt a surge of energy running threw my body.'"

- Two students suggested that Michael add this next: "It was as if whole gallons of adrenaline were washed into my bloodstream."

- "Add more bits of setting in each paragraph."

- "Stretch out the section after 'I waved,' to show more of what Michael was doing. Was he standing there? Was he walking toward his friend?"

- "Add a bit of setting or action to the last line: Instead of saying, 'This is going to be the best vacation ever,' consider this ending:

The grass was wet, but the sun peeked through the clouds as we skidded across the grass, chasing each other and yelling 'The best vacation ever!' back and forth to each other."

Finally, the class used a student-friendly rubric to evaluate Michael's work after the class revised it together. See the information on Airplane Writing at the bottom of Figure 9.3 for a list of what the state expects. Later, students used similar strategies to revise their own writing.

STUDENTS' REFLECTIONS ON WHAT HELPED THE MOST IN EXPLANATORY WRITING TEST PREP

When students reflected on which lessons in test prep had helped them the most, this lesson was of monumental importance. Weeks after the state test was over, fifth-grade students commented on how integral the lesson on revising Michael's piece had been to their success.

- Gabriel said, "One lesson that helped me was when our class revised Michael's writing that he did. It helped me by teaching me to look back and revise. It taught me what Airplane Writing looks like. That helped me by teaching me that I should never be done revising."

- Tia explained, "Taking Michael's explanatory writing and revising it by adding Airplane Writing showed me what I could do to improve my writing on the test. Another reason is that on the test I used the strategies you taught us in that lesson. You showed us how to make our sentences more powerful."

 ## Read How It Worked

Rejuvenate your students' interest in revision during test prep by using an activity called Hit the Jackpot

Donna Klein designed an activity to generate more excitement about revision. "This activity energized my students, and it gave them confidence," she reported. "They realized how much they already knew about revision and felt more prepared for the state test."

Materials

- A state-released scored piece of student's writing (state anchor paper)
- A student-friendly rubric that mirrors your state rubric in student-friendly terms (Gain ideas and modify the Students' Scoring Rubric for a Story About a Prompt, page 213.)
- A demand writing test for your students that is similar to your state test
- Your students' demand writing responses
- Sticky notes for each student

Procedure

- Time students as they write a demand piece of writing that responds to a practice state prompt.
- Discuss a student-friendly rubric with students that matches the state holistic scoring rubric.
- Show students a state-released anchor paper (from the state Web site) with a similar prompt and ask, "What grade would you give it?" All students write a grade, along with specific and concrete reasons for the grade, on a sticky note.

- Tell students what score the state has given the writing and discuss the state scorers' comments. Students think about the state score and tell what they think the writer did well, as well as where the writer could improve.

- Return students' own writing pieces from the demand writing prompt and ask students to revise them.

- Tell students if they get a score of 5, they "hit the jackpot!" Donna selected a score of 5, since 5 was the highest possible score on her state's rubric. (Each teacher will determine the prize when students hit the jackpot. For example, Donna's students received a free homework pass for that evening.)

- Grade students' revised writing pieces and give reasons for the grades. Donna used the state rubric to score them. (If this part of the activity is too time-consuming, consider having writing partners use the student-friendly 5-point rubric to score each other's writing.)

- Select two students' pieces to share. Donna got the students' approval for her to share their writing. Ask the class, "What grade would you give it?" Donna's students all scored each piece on sticky notes and gave reasons for the score, using the same student-friendly 5-point rubric.

- Have students revise their pieces again. Donna's students showed strong improvement in their revisions.

Donna stated, "By inspecting anchor papers scored by the state, students had a renewed sense of what they needed to do for the state writing test. When I insisted that they take what they learned and use it to revise their own pieces, it helped give them a concrete example of how to improve. They felt more confident, and their attitudes toward revision were much more positive!"

Test Prep for Persuasive Writing

This section of test prep is easier for students if you have already taught a unit of study on persuasive writing earlier in the year. (See pages 96–108.) When beginning this test preparation section, I recommend doing the following:

- Study your state's persuasive essay or persuasive letter prompts and rubrics.

- Chapter 2, pages 42–43 contains suggestions for Web site connections for persuasive writing, if your state does not have released samples and rubrics. Either use a state-released sample or create your own to use as a demand test. (See the sections on page 202 to construct demand tests.) Administering a persuasive demand test on the first day of test prep is the first step.

- Based on the results of the test, note students' areas of strengths and areas where they need more support. For instance, a common problem that students exhibit in the persuasive essay is giving weak reasons to support their thesis. Design activities and lessons to match what your students need. If your students' reasons to support their theses are undeveloped or do not support their theses, the following skit-based activities may be just what you need.

Read How It Worked

Wishy-Washy or Powerful? Using Skits to Breathe Life Into Essays With Strong Supporting Details

Jennifer Angerson's fifth-grade students were in the middle of a writing unit on essays, but Jennifer felt that they were "uninspired and blocked." In particular, their supporting details needed work. "In order to breathe life back into the unit and get them writing again, I decided to have them work in partnerships and develop short skits. The objective was for Character A to try to convince Character B of something he or she wanted."

Guidelines:

Students work in partnerships. Partner 1 takes on the role of Character A. Partner 2 takes on the role of Character B.

Procedure:

- Character A thought of what she or he wanted, accompanied by three strong reasons and supporting details.

  Example: Character A is acting as herself, and her goal is to have a half-hour-later bedtime. Character B is the mother or father. Character A could jot on a sticky note the three reasons:

  1. I am older. **2.** I do chores. **3.** I am a wonderful student.

- Character A needs to state those three strong reasons along with supporting details persuasively in order to convince character B.

- Character B needs to have at least two valid reasons why Character A should or should not get what he or she wants.

- After Character A finishes the persuasive argument, Character B says either, "wishy-washy" for a less-powerful presentation, or "powerful" for a strong presentation. Character B must state the two reasons why the performance was either wishy-washy or powerful.

- The next step is for the partners to switch roles. Character B becomes Character A and does a different skit. Character A becomes Character B, and decides whether to give the new Character A what he or she wants.

Example:

"Mom, I deserve to stay up later because I am a whole year older, and I still am going to bed at the same time as last year. I know I won't be too tired, because I am usually awake for about one-half an hour in bed anyway after I turn off the lights . . . So this way, I could stay up later and read for one half hour.

"I also deserve to stay up later because I do chores every day for you and Dad. Every night I clear the table and wash the dishes, and it takes me about one-half an hour. So I need to get that one-half hour back by staying up later!

"Finally, I get good grades, and I always finish my homework. I think I ought to have a reward. I really, really want to stay up one half-hour later. A perfect way for you to show me you appreciate what a wonderful student I am is for you to let me to stay up one-half hour later each night. What do you think?"

Character B responds: *"That was powerful! You convinced me. I didn't know that you were awake each night anyway. That makes me feel better about your staying up for one-half hour each night. I don't have to worry that you will lose sleep. And I agree that you do deserve it. I am really proud of your grades, and I appreciate your helping me out each night in the kitchen."*

Jennifer concluded, "I found this activity to be very effective. As a class, we observed each skit and discussed each afterward. The students were able to clearly see the difference between a less-powerful reason and a strong one. They noted the necessity of supporting details for each reason. I was excited and felt it made a difference in their view of essay structure. I was impressed with the way that when I conferred with them about their own essays, I could ask them if their own reasons were wishy-washy or powerful. They knew exactly what I meant. Now they know how to write *powerful* supporting details."

SUGGESTIONS FOR PERSUASIVE WRITING TEST-PREP ACTIVITIES

MATCH YOUR FOLLOW-UP INSTRUCTION BASED ON STUDENTS' WRITING TO THE PROMPT ON YOUR PERSUASIVE DEMAND TEST

Introduce your follow-up instruction with the Persuasive Writing Study Sheet for students. (See Figure 9.5.) You can adapt this sample to match what your state expects students to be able to do. For example, the Georgia Department of Education posted this component as part of its rubric for persuasive writing for grade 3: "Writes a persuasive piece that states a clear position." So Georgia teachers could simply add this to the components of Airplane Writing: "Writes a persuasive piece that states a clear position." Just as I revised the Narrative and/or Explanatory Airplane Writing components in Figures 9.1 and 9.3 to match the genre of Persuasive Writing in Figure 9.5, you can modify Airplane Writing to fit any writing genre.

COACH STUDENTS TO MAKE ELABORATIONS MATCH THESIS STATEMENTS

If your students still are unsure of how to make their elaborations fit the thesis, consider some of these suggestions:

- Write a sample essay response with students, and then score it based on your rubric.

- Share state-released samples and have students score them.

- Use a Persuasive Essay Organizer (page 103) with a small group of students who have difficulty matching their elaborations to their thesis statements.

  Ask students to write the thesis in the box and a statement of each elaboration in each bullet. Make sure they get your approval of the logic of their ideas on the organizer before they begin their drafts.

USE PROVEN IDEAS TO RAISE TEST SCORES

The key in this part of the test prep is to have your students continually revise what they write, until their persuasive essay or persuasive letter receives a high score. Make your coaching more specific as you note what areas need work and confer and/or meet with students in small groups. Other tips include:

- Revising a student's piece with the class and then in small groups.

- Using writing partners to help students with revision.

- Using activities such as Wishy-Washy or Powerful. See pages 220–221.

- Sharing mentor persuasive texts that you or students have written as teaching models.

STUDENTS EVALUATE THEIR PERSUASIVE WRITING

The Persuasive Writing Student's Checklist (Figure 9.6) helps students evaluate their work. Students check yes or no to indicate whether or not their persuasive writing includes what is cited in the checklist. The rule of thumb is that students can check yes only if the writing is almost perfect; if they check no, they need to write themselves notes in the suggestion area for how to improve their writing.

Figure 9.5

GRADE 6 NJ ASK | Persuasive Writing
STUDY SHEET

Test time: 45 minutes

Writing Task: Gives you a prompt that will ask you to persuade your audience to think a certain way about something. You may be asked to use an essay structure or to write a letter. For example: Do you think it is a good idea to have a nutritious breakfast program at your school? Write a composition explaining your ideas. Use examples and other evidence to support your position.

Strategies for Managing Your Time

Take *only* <u>10 to 15 minutes</u> **to do these:**

First: Read the prompt very carefully. Box and underline key words. Be a detail detective and make sure that you understand what you are supposed to do.

Second: Plan your thesis statement for your position and your argument that you will use to convince your audience to agree with you. Include three clear and specific reasons to support your idea.

Third: Write a few ideas on the pre-writing planning sheet in whatever way works for you. For example: Draw a "persuasive organizer" listing your persuasive thesis, three supports, and a conclusion, or use another way of planning that you like to use that you can do *quickly*!

Write your story on the lined sheet.
Use AIRPLANE WRITING, your best writing!

- Strong Lead that States Your Opinion and Gets the Audience's Attention
- Stay on the Topic That Relates to the Persuasive Prompt
- Logical Progression of Ideas That Persuades the Audience
- Specific Details and Developed Supports
- Effective Word Choice
- Variety of Sentences and Different Beginnings of Sentences
- Transition Words
- Powerful and Clear Conclusion
- Edit for Spelling, Punctuation, and Grammar
- Remember to Write in Paragraphs

EVALUATE IMPORTANT MINI-LESSONS FOR PERSUASIVE WRITERS

Important mini-lessons that assist persuasive writers include: open with a lead that hooks the reader, develop the topic or thesis with details and logical arguments, use transition words to bridge one idea to the next, write clear and varied sentence structures, show a logical progression of ideas that persuades the audience, and end the piece convincingly. You probably taught most of these already in your persuasive writing unit. (See pages 96–108.) Based on your assessments, do you need to reteach any lesson during your persuasive writing test prep?

Figure 9.6

Persuasive Writing Student's Checklist

	Yes	No	Suggestions for making it better
❑ I used a clear, inviting lead that hooked the reader.			
❑ My topic was clear and well-developed.			
❑ I included specific details, explanations, and examples that were appropriate and convincing.			
❑ I used a logical organization that moved my reader from one part to the next and strengthened my argument.			
❑ Transitional words helped my reader connect paragraphs and ideas.			
❑ I used clear and varied sentences.			
❑ I used vivid words correctly and varied my word choices.			
❑ I capitalized, spelled, and punctuated correctly.			

Time-Management Suggestions for the State Writing Test

We need to prepare students for timed writing tests (Angelillo, 2005b) by teaching them time-management strategies. My strongest writers, as well as those who need more support, have difficulty finishing a 30-minute test. Often, they spend too long with the pre-writing section and run out of time with writing the rest of their stories.

Integrating Test Prep into Reading & Writing Workshops © 2011 by Nancy Jennison • Scholastic Teaching Resources

When I introduced time-management suggestions, my students felt more at ease. It gave them a plan and helped them feel more organized. I told my students that the five-minute time period to prewrite was a definite, as was as a five-minute revising time at the end. Although the rest of the times do look rather specific, I told students that the other times are approximate. As you observe your students and see where they need help, you can modify these suggestions to be an exact fit for your students.

30-Minute Narrative Writing Test Time-Management Plan

30 minutes: Students do their pre-writing.

25 minutes: Students start stories and begin to add the problem.

20 minutes: Students make sure they added the problem to the story, then work on the middle.

15 minutes: Students complete the middle and move toward the ending.

10 minutes: Students finish the ending.

5 minutes: Students reread their stories, then revise, and edit.

PERSUASIVE WRITING TIME-MANAGEMENT PLAN

Use the narrative time-management plan as a model and modify it to match the time of your state's writing test. For example, if the time limit for your persuasive writing test is 45 minutes, your students may need more time to prewrite their thesis and plan their logical and elaborated arguments. You may give your students 10 minutes for the pre-writing. A 45-minute persuasive writing time-management plan might look like this, but we need to modify it to meet students' needs:

45-Minute Persuasive Writing Test Time-Management Plan

45 minutes: Students plan thesis and logical arguments.

35 minutes: Students introduce the thesis and begin to add the first elaborated detail to support the thesis.

25 minutes: Students add the second elaborated detail to support the thesis.

15 minutes: Students add the third elaborated detail to support the thesis.

10 minutes: Students end the persuasive writing powerfully.

5 minutes: Students reread their writing to see if all details support their thesis, then revise, and edit.

Sample One-Week Test-Prep Sequence for a State Writing Test

MONDAY: Give students a timed demand test in one of the writing genres that appears on your state test. Do not offer the students any assistance; this test is for baseline assessment.

Follow-Up:

✓ Assess the responses using the state rubric and the Airplane Writing sheet. See Figures 9.1, 9.3, or 9.5.

✓ Look for qualities of good writing that match your rubric.

✓ Jot down suggestions for revisions on sticky notes and attach them to students' writing.

TUESDAY: Do a mini-lesson on the writing skill that students' responses indicated was most in need of reinforcement (for example: leads need work). Model your teaching point with the whole group using a current student's composition and revising it together, then in small groups. (See suggestions earlier in this chapter on page 214.) Expect all students to revise and edit their pieces on their own and with partners. Have them reread their pieces after your mini-lesson and write on sticky notes how they plan to revise their pieces. They will use the ideas you wrote on sticky notes on their pieces, as well as their own. The more concrete the students' revision suggestions are, the better their revisions will be.

Follow-Up:

✓ Confer with students.

✓ The expectation is that by the end of the day, all students must achieve the highest or second-highest score.

✓ If needed, ask students to finish revision and editing at home.

✓ Work in small groups with the students whose scores are not high enough.

WEDNESDAY: Do a brief mini-lesson on time-management, then time students as they take another practice writing test. See Time-Management section on pages 224–226. Or, if your students need more help with revision, play Make It to Hollywood, pages 173–175, Hit the Jackpot, pages 218–219, or Get That Story Moving, pages 209–213.

Follow-Up:

✓ Assess the students' responses with the state rubric and the Airplane Writing sheet. See Figures 9.1, 9.3, and 9.5.

✓ Look for qualities of good writing that match your rubric.

✓ Jot down suggestions to help students with revision on sticky notes and attach them to students' writing pieces.

THURSDAY: Do a mini-lesson on the writing skill that students' responses indicated was most in need of reinforcement. If needed, use a current student's composition as part of your mini-lesson so that all students can revise it together. Later, they will continue to revise it in small groups.

Follow-Up:

✓ Expect all students to revise and edit Wednesday's pieces, on their own and with partners.

✓ Ask writing partners to give each other suggestions for how to revise, and score each other's pieces after revisions have been made.

✓ Confer with students and/or with small groups. The goal for this piece of writing is for all students to achieve the highest or second-highest score.

✓ Have students finish revision and editing at home, if needed.

FRIDAY: Do a mini-lesson on the writing skill that students' responses indicated was most in need of reinforcement. Ask students to write on index cards what they think each needs to do better. What was a typical student's reaction to this activity? Gabriel stated, "The most important lesson was when we wrote on the card on what we needed to improve on, because after that, I made sure I included it."

On this last day of the test-prep format week, you may do another timed prompt, or you may still have students revising Wednesday's piece. It will vary, depending on what type of writers your students are.

Follow-Up:

✓ Note issues that still need work.

✓ Continue meeting with small groups to help students improve their scores or plan to address the writing problems in the next writing genre test prep. For example, if you noticed that your students' endings still needed more work, you could easily reteach endings in another mini-lesson in your next writing genre that you review for test-prep.

REVIEW WEEK SUMMARIZES ALL PARTS OF THE STATE WRITING TEST FOR STUDENTS

Review Week is the week before your state test. During this week, you sum up everything you taught in your test-prep unit and administer final practice tests.

- Plan to give students a timed writing prompt for each genre that is part of the test.

- Review the following with students before you administer the practice test: student's study sheet for the genre that you are testing, Airplane Writing, and the time-management suggestions.

- Give students additional writing strategies that will help them.

- Consider using the ideas in Cheerleading for Confidence below. Do your students need to relax more and feel empowered that they can do well on your state's writing tests? Cheerleading for Confidence made a huge difference in the attitudes of Kathy Doyle's students before the test.

CHEERLEADING FOR CONFIDENCE

Kathy knew her students needed a confidence-building activity that motivated them and calmed their nerves before the state test. The tension was palpable as they entered her classroom; she could feel how much they hoped to show what they knew on the narrative writing test.

Kathy created a quick team-building activity to relax them as part of their morning opening exercises. As the students entered her classroom, she gave each one an index card and asked that they write something on the front of the card "that you need to remember to do, in order to do well on the narrative writing test."

Kathy took the stress of the day away by asking students to pretend they were cheerleaders by doing the following activity: "We went around the room and they cheered out their ideas, like little cheerleaders, with enthusiasm and pizzazz! I modeled first for them, so they would feel the fire! It was a fun, yet a quick, stress-breaking, energizing review."

Food for Thought

PLANNING YOUR WRITING TEST PREP UNIT CAN BE A VERY CHALLENGING JOB ESPECIALLY IF YOU ARE PLANNING INSTRUCTION FOR MORE THAN ONE WRITING GENRE. WHY NOT TAKE SOME OF THE STRESS AWAY BY USING THIS CHAPTER AS A MODEL TO HELP YOU IN YOUR PLANNING?

- How can you use the Student Study Sheets to create your own materials to help students prepare for your state's writing genre tests?

- As you read over the activities cited in this chapter, which ones will you use?

- As you look at the components for Airplane Writing, which do your students need to be taught in mini-lessons?

- How can you adapt the time-management suggestions and the test-prep schedule to meet your students' needs?

Professional Literature Cited

Allan, K. K., McMackin, M.C., Dawes, E.T., & Spadorcia, S.A. (2009). *Learning to write with purpose: Effective instruction in grades 4–8.* New York: The Guilford Press.

Allington, R. L. (2002). You can't learn much from books you can't read. *Educational Leadership,* 60 (3), 16–19.

Allington, R. L. (2006). *What really matters for struggling readers: Designing research-based programs.* (2nd ed.). New York: Pearson Learning.

Allington, R. L. (2009). If they don't read much . . . thirty years later. In E.H. Hiebert (Ed.), *Reading more, reading better* (pp. 30–54). New York: The Guilford Press.

Angelillo, J. (2002). *A fresh approach to teaching punctuation: Helping young writers use conventions with precision and purpose.* New York: Scholastic.

Angelillo, J. (2005a). *Making revision matter: Strategies for guiding students to focus, organize, and strengthen their writing independently.* New York: Scholastic.

Angelillo, J. (2005b). *Writing to the prompt: When students don't have a choice.* Portsmouth, NH: Heinemann.

Atwell, N. (2002). *Lessons that change writers.* Portsmouth, NH: Heinemann.

Beck, I., McKeown, M.G., & Kucan, L. (2002). *Bringing words to life: Robust vocabulary instruction.* New York: The Guilford Press.

Beck, I., McKeown, M.G., & Kucan, L. (2008). *Creating robust vocabulary: Frequently asked questions & extended examples.* New York: The Guilford Press.

Beers, K. (2003). *When kids can't read: What teachers can do, a guide for teachers 6–12.* Portsmouth, NH: Heinemann.

Beers, K. (2007, March). *Developing fluency in older struggling readers.* Workshop presented at the 72nd Saturday Reunion of the Teachers College Reading and Writing Project, New York NY.

Calfee, R. C., & Miller R. G. (2007). Best practices in writing assessment. In S. Graham, C. A. MacArthur, & J. Fitzgerald (Eds.), *Best practices in writing instruction* (pp. 265–286). New York: The Guilford Press.

Calkins, L. (1994). *The art of teaching writing*. Portsmouth, NH: Heinemann.

Calkins, L. (2001). *The art of teaching reading*. New York: Longman.

Calkins, L., & Cruz, M. C. (2006). *Writing fiction: Big dreams, tall ambitions*. Portsmouth, NH: Firsthand Heinemann.

Calkins, L., & Kesler, T. (2006). *Raising the quality of narrative writing*. Portsmouth, NH: Firsthand Heinemann.

Calkins, L., & Martinelli, M. (2006). *Launching the writing workshop*. Portsmouth, NH: Firsthand Heinemann.

Calkins, L., Montgomery, K., & Santman, D. (1998). *A teacher's guide to standardized reading tests: Knowledge is power*. Portsmouth, NH: Heinemann.

Clay, M. M. (1979). *The early detection of reading difficulties*. Portsmouth, NH: Heinemann.

Coco, P. (2007). Fueling the future: People across the country are working to find newer and cleaner fuels and energy. In *Teaching text structures: A key to nonfiction reading success* (pp. 64–65). New York: Scholastic.

Coco, P. (2007). Warming Up. In *Teaching text structures: A key to nonfiction reading success* (pp. 183–185). New York: Scholastic.

Conrad, L. L., Matthews, M., Zimmerman, C., & Allen, P. A. (2008). *Put thinking to the test*. Portland, ME: Stenhouse.

Darling-Hammond, L. (1997). *The right to learn*. San Francisco: Jossey-Bass.

De La Paz, S. (2007). Best practices in teaching writing to students with special needs. In S. Graham, C. A. MacArthur, & J. Fitzgerald (Eds.), *Best practices in writing instruction* (pp. 308–328). New York: The Guilford Press.

Duke, N., & Martin, N. (2008). Comprehension instruction in action: The elementary classroom. In C. C. Block & S. R. Parris (Eds.), *Comprehension instruction research-based best practices –second edition* (pp. 241–257). New York: The Guilford Press.

Ehrenworth, M., & Vinton, V. (2005). *The power of grammar: Unconventional approaches to the conventions of language.* Portsmouth, NH: Heinemann.

Fisher, D., & Frey, N. (2009). Feed up, back, forward. *Educational Leadership, 67*(3), pp. 20–25.

Fisher, D., Frey, N., & Lapp, D. (2009). *In a reading state of mind: Brain research, teacher modeling, and comprehension instruction.* Newark, DE: International Reading Association.

Fletcher, R. (1993). *What a writer needs.* Portsmouth, NH: Heinemann.

Fletcher, R. (1999). *Live writing: Breathing life into your words.* New York, NY: Avon Books.

Fletcher, R., & Portalupi, J. (1998). *Craft lessons: Teaching writing K-8.* Portland, ME: Stenhouse.

Fuhrken, C. (2009). *What every elementary teacher needs to know about reading tests (From someone who has written them).* Portland, ME: Stenhouse Publishers.

Fuhrken, C. & Roser, N. (2010). Exploring high-stakes tests as a genre. In B. Moss, & D. Lapp (Eds.), *Teaching new literacies in grades 4–6: Resources for 21st century classrooms* (pp. 186–198). New York: The Guilford Press.

Gambrell, L. (2009). Creating opportunities to read more so that students read better. In E. H. Hiebert (Ed.), *Reading more, reading better* (pp. 251–266). New York: The Guilford Press.

Graham, S., & Harris, K. R. (2005). *Writing better: Effective strategies for teaching students with learning difficulties.* Baltimore: Brookes.

Graves, D. (2000, October). *Let characters help children to read and write.* Presented at Heinemann Workshop, Secaucus, NJ.

Greene, A., & Melton, G. (2007). *Test talk: Integrating test preparation into reading workshop*. Portland, ME: Stenhouse Publishers.

Greenwood, S.C. (2004). *Words count: Effective vocabulary instruction in action*. Portsmouth, NH: Heinemann.

Griffith, L. W., & Rasinski, T. V. (2004). A focus on fluency: How one teacher incorporated fluency with her reading curriculum. *The Reading Teacher*, 58(2), 126–137.

Harvey, S., & Goudvis, A. (2000). *Strategies that work: Teaching comprehension to enhance understanding*. Portland, ME: Stenhouse.

Harvey, S., & Goudvis, A. (2005). *The comprehension toolkit: Language and lessons for active literacy*. Portsmouth, NH: Heinemann.

Heard, G. (1999). *Awakening the heart: Exploring poetry in elementary and middle school*. Portsmouth, NH: Heinemann.

Heard, G. (2002). *The revision toolbox: Teaching techniques that work*. Portsmouth, NH: Heinemann.

Janeczko, P. (2003). *Writing winning reports and essays*. New York: Scholastic.

Keene, E. (2008). *Assessing comprehension thinking strategies*. Huntington Beach, CA: Shell Education.

Keene, E. O., & Zimmerman, S. (1997). *Mosaic of thought*. Portsmouth, NH: Heinemann.

Keene, E. O., & Zimmerman, S. (2007). *Mosaic of thought* (2nd ed.). Portsmouth, NH: Heinemann.

Kiester, J. B. (2000). *Blowing away the state writing tests: Four steps for teachers of all levels*. New York: Maupin House.

Kohn, A. (2000). *The case against standardized testing: Raising the scores, ruining the schools*. Portsmouth, NH: Heinemann.

Lane, B. (1999). *Reviser's toolbox*. Shoreham, VT: Discover Writing Press.

Lane, B. (2003, February). Writing fiction workshop presented at Teaching Revision Strategies workshop, Saddlebrook, NJ.

Lane, B., & Bernabei, G. (2001). *Why we must run with scissors: Voice lessons in persuasive writing 3–12*. Shoreham, VT: Discover Writing Press.

Lukens, R. J. (1999). *A critical handbook of children's literature* (6th ed.). New York: Longman.

MacArthur, C. A. (2007). Best practices in teaching evaluation and revision. In S. Graham, C. A. MacArthur, & J. Fitzgerald (Eds.), *Best practices in writing instruction* (pp. 141–162). New York: The Guilford Press.

Moskal, M. K., & Blachowicz, C. (2006). *Partnering for fluency*. New York: The Guilford Press.

Murray, D. (1985). *A writer teaches writing* (2nd ed.). Boston: Houghton Mifflin.

Murray, D. (1998). *The craft of revision* (3rd ed.). New York: Harcourt Brace.

Rasinski, T. V. (2003). *The fluent reader: Oral reading strategies for building word recognition, fluency, and comprehension*. New York: Scholastic.

Schmoker, M. (2006). *Results NOW: How We Can Achieve Unprecedented Improvements in Teaching and Learning*. Alexandria, VA: Association for Supervision and Curriculum Development.

Schmoker, M. (2009). Measuring what matters. *Educational Leadership, 66*(4), 70–74.

Scott, J., Skobel, B., & Wells, J. (2008). *The word-conscious classroom: Building the vocabulary readers and writers need*. New York: Scholastic.

State of Delaware Department of Education. (2008). *Delaware Rubric for Stand-Alone Writing*.

TAKS Texas Assessment of Knowledge and Skills Information Booklet, Writing, Grade 4, Revised, 2004, (pages 1–32). Texas: Texas Education Agency.

The Teachers College Reading and Writing Project. (2009–2010). Reading Curricular Calendar, Grades 3–5. NY: Teachers College Reading and Writing Project.

Tolan, K. (2004). Annual July Institute on the Teaching of Reading, NY: Teachers College Reading and Writing Project.

Tolan, K. (2004, July). *Engaging our disengaged readers: Creating classrooms where children want to read*. Keynote address presented at the annual July Institute on the Teaching of Reading, New York, NY.

Tovani, C. (2000). *I read it, but I don't get it: Comprehension strategies for adolescent readers*. Portland, ME: Stenhouse Publishers.

Yancey, K. (2009). *Writing in the 21st century: A report from the National Council of Teachers of English*. 1–9. Urbana, IL: National Council of Teachers of English.

Young, C. & Rasinski, T. (2009). Implementing readers theatre as an approach to classroom fluency instruction. *The Reading Teacher,* 63(1), 4–13.

Zinsser, W. (1998). *On writing well*. New York: HarperCollins Publishers.

Children's Literature Cited

Appelt, K. (2008). *The underneath*. New York: Atheneum Books for Young Writers.

Applegate, K. (2007). *The buffalo storm*. New York: Clarion Books.

Bauer, M. D. (1987). *On my honor*. New York: Random House.

Brinckloe, J. (1986). *Fireflies!* New York: Simon & Schuster Children's Publishing.

Buss, F. L. (2002). *Journey of the sparrows*. New York: Penguin Group.

Campbell, S. C. (2008). *Wolfsnail: A backyard predator.* Honesdale, PA: Boyds Mill Press.

Curtis, C. P. (1997). *The Watsons go to Birmingham—1963*. New York: Random House Children's Books.

DiCamillo, K. (2000). *Because of Winn-Dixie*. New York: Scholastic.

DiCamillo, K. (2001). *The tiger rising*. Somerville, MA: Candlewick Press.

DiCamillo, K. (2006). *The miraculous journey of Edward Tulane*. Cambridge, MA: Candlewick Press.

Estes, E. (1973). *The hundred dresses*. New York: Scholastic.

Fenner, C. (1997). *Yolanda's genius*. New York: Simon & Schuster Children's Publishing.

Fletcher, R. (1995). *Fig pudding*. New York: Bantam Doubleday Dell.

Fletcher. R. (1997). *Spider boy*. New York: Bantam Doubleday Dell.

Fletcher, R. (1997). *Twilight comes twice*. New York: Clarion Books.

Grimes, N. (2008). *Barack Obama: Son of promise, child of hope*. New York: Simon & Schuster.

Guiberson, B. Z. (1996). *Into the sea*. New York: Henry Holt and Company.

Hannigan, K. (2004). *Ida B . . . and her plans to maximize fun, avoid disaster, and (possibly) save the world*. New York: Greenwillow Books.

Hesse, K. (1993). *Lavender*. New York: Scholastic.

Hesse, K. (1999). *Come on, rain!* New York: Scholastic.

Jenkins, M. (1999). *The emperor's egg*. Somerville, MA: Candlewick Press.

Jenkins, S. (1998). *Hottest coldest highest deepest*. New York: Houghton Mifflin.

Jenkins, S., & Page, R. (2008). *Sisters & brothers: Sibling relationships in the animal world*. Boston: Houghton Mifflin Company.

Krull. K. (2000). *Wilma unlimited*. New York: Houghton Mifflin Harcourt.

London, J. (1998). *Dream weaver*. New York: Harcourt, Inc.

MacLachlan, P. (1987). *Sarah, plain and tall*. New York: HarperCollins Publishers.

MacLachlan, P. (1991). *Journey*. New York: Yearling.

MacLachlan, P. (1998). *What you know first*. New York: HarperCollins Publishers.

Markle, S. (1999). *Down, down, down in the ocean*. New York: Scholastic.

Marsden, C. (2002). *The gold-threaded dress*. Somerville, MA: Candlewick Press.

McCully, E.A. (2007). *The escape of Oney Judge: Martha Washington's slave finds freedom*. New York: Farrar Straus Giroux.

Mezger, G. (1997). *The Jesse Owens story*. Logan, IA: Perfection Learning Corporation.

Mortenson, G. & Relin, D. O. (2009). *Three cups of tea: One man's journey to change the world . . . one child at a time*. New York: Puffin.

Patent, D. H. (2008). *When the wolves returned: Restoring nature's balance in Yellowstone*. New York: Walker & Company.

Paterson, K. (1987). *Bridge to Terabithia*. New York: HarperCollins Publishers.

Paulsen, G. (1987). *Hatchet*. New York: Aladdin.

Pennypacker, S. (2006). *Clementine*. New York: Hyperion Books.

Ride, S. & O'Shaughnessy, T. (2009). *Mission save the planet: Things you can do to help fight global warming*. New York: Roaring Brook Press.

Ryan, P. M. (2000). *Esperanza rising*. New York: Scholastic.

Rylant. C. (1985). *Every living thing*. New York: Aladdin Paperbacks.

Rylant, C. (1991). *Night in the country*. New York: Simon & Schuster.

Sachar, L. (1998). *Holes*. New York: Farrar, Straus, & Giroux.

Schulman, J. (2008). *Pale Male: Citizen hawk of New York City*. New York: Alfred A. Knopf.

Shange, N. (2009). *Coretta Scott*. New York: HarperCollins.

Simon, S. (2001). *Animals nobody loves*. New York: SeaStar Books.

Smith, D.B. (1988). *A taste of blackberries*. New York: HarperCollins.

Smith, N. (2010). America the beautiful: Scenic coins honor U.S. parks and other sites, In *Scholastic News Edition 4* (p. 6). Jefferson City, MO: Scholastic, Inc.

Soto, G. (1990). "The bike." In *The summer life* (pp. 19–21). NY: Bantam Doubleday Dell Publishing Group.

Integrating Test Prep into Reading & Writing Workshops © 2011 by Nancy Jennison • Scholastic Teaching Resources

Spinneli, J. (1998). *Wringer*. New York: HarperCollins Publishers.

Walters, N. M. (2010). Marine invaders: Lionfish are taking over the Florida Keys, In *Scholastic News Edition 5/6* (p.6). Jefferson City, MO: Scholastic, Inc.

White, E. B. (1974). *Charlotte's web*. New York: HarperCollins Publishers.

Wiles, D. (2005). *Freedom summer*. New York: Simon and Schuster Children's Publishing.

Yolen, J. (1987). *Owl moon*. New York: Penguin Group.

Acknowledgments

Thanks to my amazing colleagues, who have worked with me on this book for the last two years and who have generously given their time, energy, and incredible talents: Donna Klein, Jen Angerson, Arnold Almaguer, and Christie Mortara of Mackay School in Tenafly, New Jersey, Melissa Erickson and Stephanie Tesorero of Richer Elementary School in Marlborough, Massachusetts, and Amy Fabrikant-Eagan of Solomon Schechter Day School in Milford, New Jersey. Special thanks to Kathy Doyle of Smith School in Tenafly, New Jersey, for her brilliant work, suggestions, and support. Because of each of you, readers will hear teachers' voices threaded through each chapter.

I also want to acknowledge and thank these dedicated teachers whose wonderful ideas appear in the book: Reina Pattner of Maugham Elementary, Alice Rassam, Joan Shayne and Judi Feinberg of Smith Elementary, and Stacey Bailey of Stillman Elementary in Tenafly, New Jersey. Thank you also to Tenafly school administrators.

Special thanks go to Mary Beth Allen, a professor at East Stroudsburg University in Pennsylvania, a lifelong friend and also colleague as a national presenter, who spent many hours offering me feedback and encouragement. I also sincerely appreciate my staff developer colleagues from Tenafly, New Jersey, who offered backup support when I needed it: Carine St. John, Terri Eisenberg, Julie Di Giacomo, and Meredith Alvaro.

While I worked in Tenafly, New Jersey, for ten years as the literacy staff developer, I had the honor of attending training at the Teachers College Reading and Writing Project at Columbia University. I am profoundly grateful to Lucy Calkins, Kathleen Tolan, and Melanie Brown. You helped me grow professionally in ways that I treasure.

I appreciate Mary Dill and the students formerly from Rolling Valley School in Fairfax County, Virginia, where I began my test-preparation work as the school's reading specialist. And, thanks to the students in Tenafly, New Jersey, and Marlborough, Massachusetts, whose work is featured in this book. You helped me grow as a teacher.

I sincerely am grateful for the support from Scholastic from my expert editors, Joanna Davis-Swing, Sarah Glasscock, copy editor David Klein, and from the editor in chief, Virginia Dooley, who counseled me that "less is more." Special thanks go to the former editor in chief of Scholastic, Terry Cooper, for believing in the three books I co-wrote or wrote.

Thanks to my real editor in chief, my husband, Chris. Your ideas are golden.

Integrating Test Prep into Reading & Writing Workshops © 2011 by Nancy Jennison • Scholastic Teaching Resources